Contents

Rodinsky's Room

RACHEL LICHTENSTEIN
and
IAIN SINCLAIR

Granta Books
London

Granta Publications, 2/3 Hanover Yard, London N1 8BE

First published in Great Britain by Granta Books 1999
This edition published by Granta Books 2000

A CIP catalogue record for this book is available from the British Library.

5 7 9 10 8 6

Typeset in Minion by M Rules
Printed and bound in Great Britain by
Mackays of Chatham plc

For David

List of illustrations

RACHEL LICHTENSTEIN
IN PLACE

Iain Sinclair

Did you see the black coat? A zaddik.

They can make themselves invisible I've heard.

David Hartnett, *Black Milk*

A young Englishwoman, heavily pregnant, is admitted to the office suite of a New York literary agent. She endures all the usual status games with an amused sense of being in an over-rehearsed play: the long wait in the outer chamber, the low chair that leaves her staring across a shimmering meadow of carpet at the big desk, the gilded blitz of family photographs. 'So, you got twenty minutes. A *frummer* in the attic, he disappears. Who should care? Where's the story?' She laughs, delivers her pitch. She's told it before, often, but it always has the same effect. Rachel becomes the thing she is talking about. He listens. (In the film version you could freeze-frame the cigar smoke.) It's a performance and it's true. Rachel Lichtenstein *is* the story, a mad quest to discover all that is to be known about a synagogue caretaker, a Talmudic scholar, a holy fool; a man who invented himself through his disappearance. A simpleton who achieved competence in half a dozen languages, alive and dead. A sink-school dropout who made translations from the cuneiform texts of the Fertile Delta. A penniless haunter of cafés. A city wanderer who assembled a library that filled more than fifty cases. Rodinsky was a shape whose only definition was its shapelessness, the lack of a firm outline. The more documentation Rachel could file, the more artefacts she could photograph and label, the more elusive this fiction, David Rodinsky, became. She improvised with all the required roles: private detective, archaeologist, curator, ghost-writer, ventriloquial deliverer of Rodinsky's voice and art. She realized, with a proper sense of dread, that the business of her life, this stretch of it, was to complete whatever it was that Rodinsky had begun: to pass beyond ego, and all the dusty particulars of place and time, into a parallel state. Disincarnate. Unbodied. Eternally present.

There was something mesmeric, possessed, in the way Rachel told her tale. Agents, editors, patrons were instantly persuaded by the passion in that calm, reasonable, Esturine voice. They were dazzled by the wide-set, almond-shaped eyes. Fixed, burning. The young woman with the careful *maquillage* had arrived for this meeting, unflustered, at the very last moment. What she is describing is happening *now*, on the instant. The past is adapted, absorbed. She seems to have witnessed events that occurred long before her birth. Like the best detective stories, her narrative is broken into not-quite-resolved episodes. Hooks, cliff-hangers. Telephone calls from the officially dead. Recently found evidence that contradicts all that has gone before. There are no comfortable assumptions to be made. They *had* to know how it turned out, this tale that began with a sealed room in a deactivated Spitalfields synagogue, and moved out to the eastern borders of Poland and the Ukraine, to New York, Israel, Toronto. The factual and the fabulous met in riotous conjunction. Shallow-breathed whispers from ancient relatives. Internet connections. Death certificates. Numerous fragments that composed an unreliable biography. The man became intimately associated with the place, the dissolution of the Jewish ghetto. There was even, if you wanted to find it, a conspiracy of sorts. Vested interests who preferred to keep the wretched caretaker buried in the files. Files that had long since been lost or destroyed. Rodinsky's life was pressed into legend. It belonged at the end of an era, before memories became memorial plaques. An abandoned room contained all that was left of a man's life and Rachel Lichtenstein understood that it was her task, nobody else could do it, to live that life again, and to complete it. Find some resolution or lose herself forever in the attempt. That was her joy. That was her burden. That was what terrified and excited the men to whom she made her pitch.

Go there today, to Princelet Street, Whitechapel. Number 19, the Heritage Centre. The building releases no light, the windows are shuttered, blind. A weaver's bobbin that hangs from the wall looks like a prayer scroll, a holy relic. I thought of an object I'd seen in the Witney Museum in New York, the legendary Teletype roll on which Jack Kerouac had beaten out *On the Road*. The thin paper was frayed at the edges, but the text was endlessly flowing, without paragraphs, lurid with real names for real people, uncensored, unrevised. First thought, best thought. The whole delirious, Benzedrine-fuelled narrative spurting onward through digression, *faux-naïf* hesitation, self-doubt, confession, rhapsody and strategic lyrical thefts from the overwhelming rush of the ordinary. This Spitalfields bobbin became, to my prejudiced eye, the spindle from which just such a roll had been stripped. A memento for a missing text. A text that had been worn away by indifference, the exigencies of the everyday. A text that could only be reassembled by sympathetic magic, some peculiar marriage of scholarship and obsession.

The casual visitor needing visual evidence, the confirmation that such a man once lived in such a place, crosses to the south side of Princelet Street in order to bring Rodinsky's attic, the old silk weaver's gallery, into sight-line. Failure is the inevitable consequence of any attempt to conjure a face, some slight movement, at the darkened window. There is nothing. A TV aerial hangs from the building at your back, doubling with the Heritage Centre's bobbin. What is this heritage? Doors as brown as coffee essence or bottled blood. A stern exterior that gives nothing away. A structure in abeyance. One of those classic Spitalfields views, the frenzy of Brick Lane behind you and the rescued elegance of Wilkes Street ahead. As if this drift in time were an option: Georgian, Victorian, post-war squalor,

Thatcherite make-over, pick a card. Houses become sets. Fashionable tailors service the City, squatting in apartments that have not yet been de-restored to their Huguenot inheritance. Dirt and cobwebs and rat turds, ash in the grate. Entropy as a cultural value. We scrape off the compacted layers of wallpaper to reveal some signifier of a past life. Developers as psychics. The planchette of original wood panelling. Blue plaques induce guilt, forcing us to remember those who might prefer to be forgotten. But we can't allow it. We want to hold them here, in place, to give meaning to our own temporary residence. Number 17 Princelet Street: 'Miriam Moses, the first woman mayor of Stepney. 1931–1932.' But there is no plaque, as yet, for David Rodinsky. *Meshuganer*, cabbalist, spook. Inspirer of fictions. Retro-golem. He's unwritten, unexplained and therefore free.

There is no cult for Princelet Street to rival the Anne Frank house. A house that has become a name, an industry, the spectral representation of a person whose brief autobiography must stand for all the other extinguished, but unauthored, lives. The queues form early on the Prinsengracht canal in Amsterdam. From a distance you can see the shuffle of tourists, backpackers, schoolchildren with their set books: to a site that has become, according to Fodor's guidebook, 'one of the most frequently visited places in the world'. The story of a secret life, a young girl's diary, a house within a house, has become painfully public. I watched the steady procession from the street. I thought there was a possible connection that I should investigate with the still-occulted Rodinsky myth, the diaries I had seen in his attic; the scribblings, quotations, scraps of verse, the stumbling translations. But this was altogether too exposed. A crisp February afternoon, low sun on the water, and still the crowds came, formed, knotted, edged towards the exposed building. Looking for the confirmation of what they knew, the evidence that would release visions that had already formed from a story they understood too well.

Spitalfields has been floated. It's delousing itself in readiness for a stock market quotation. One of nature's quislings, the area has always been prepared to trim its cloth to the fashion of the moment. The 'catacombs' beneath the old Fruit Exchange of Spitalfields

Market are now used as storage space for craft hawkers, peddlers of organic vegetables, sentimental tat, ethnic pillagings and food so fast you're hungry again before it hits your stomach. There's nothing wrong with this. It won't last. It's a stage the territory has to pass through before it is totally colonized by the land greed of the City. But there's a loss of undertext. Everything is suddenly explained, overemphasized, brochured. Photographs of deserted streets must imply uncatalogued crimes. Mark Holborn, in a tribute to the Czech photographer Markéta Luskačova (with her obsessive interest in Brick Lane's Sunday market), asserts a direct line of descent from Eugene Atget by way of Bill Brandt, who saw examples of Atget's work in Man Ray's Paris studio in 1929. It's a swift transit from an empty metropolis to an underground city peopled by sleepers (Brandt's wartime Hasids in the crypt of Nicholas Hawksmoor's Christ Church). Atget's archive, Holborn says, 'entered the canon of surrealism'. Lucid dreaming. Prows of buildings so stark and threatening that they demand a compensatory act of displacement on the part of the viewer. A theatre of shadows and obscure hints. Emotive emptiness against the captured hustle of Sunday morning at the top end of Brick Lane; the alchemy of light that Luskačova's lovingly pirated subtractions worked on Whitechapel's street markets. By her listing of particulars, she makes an overloud somewhere into an estranged and marvellous nowhere. She detaches the fertile chaos of Cheshire Street from the rest of London. Her animal traders under the railway arches are fictionalized through documentation. The album of images becomes a self-portrait. Emblems for a puppet play that can only be 'read' by some future scholar. Romanies, Jewish *shmatter* merchants, Bangladeshi girls asleep, animals hidden under coats and, everywhere, solitary musicians. An orchestra for the last days. Scrapings and flutings that remain unheard. Anthems from impossible instruments.

Just to the north of the old Spitalfields Market, walking through the zone where vagrants and winos, at dusk, used to cook up vegetable refuse (a scene captured, in snowfall, by Luskačova), are the finest examples of restored Georgian housing: the remnant of Spital

Square, Folgate Street and Elder Street (blue plaque for Mark
Gertler). These streets announce, in their height, their austerity, the
shimmer of highly polished windows and freshly painted shutters,
that they are too good for us, too good for the period in which they
find themselves beached. Here, in Folgate Street, the casual ped-
estrian notices the flicker of gaslight. A house, number 18, that
clearly intends to draw attention to itself by dressing down and past-
ing its motto, AUT VISUM AUT NON ('You either see it: or you don't'), in
the window. As with the Princelet Street synagogue, there's a
weaver's bobbin (but this one has been imported). Number 18 is the
home, the 'private residence', of Dennis Severs, a Southern
Californian who has taken it on himself, over the past twenty-odd
years, to conduct a personal interrogation of the past. He sees the
house as a set, a sequence of still-life conversation pieces, tableaux,
in which (and with which) no backchat is permitted. Severs is an
aether broker, a man dedicated to creating 'atmosphere', sculpting
rococo fantasies out of his own ectoplasm.

Responding (with measured lethargy) to a loud knock, one of the
acolytes takes the cash at the door, and lets visitors know how they
are expected to behave. Go into the 'wrong' room in the wrong order
and Severs himself, the smiling director, will realign you with a violent 'Shush!' It's a strange experience: to sustain the required tiptoe
mood and to pantomime an improper relish for the bells and smells,
the brimming chamber-pots and half-digested cakes. The audience
are the ghosts, expected to pick up, at least subliminally, on the quotations: the kitchen table laid out like an illustration from Beatrix
Potter's *Tailor of Gloucester*, the attic with its Dickensian horrors.
The house is a parallel reality through which you are ordered to
float, observing, appreciating, silent. In privileged reverie. Through
rooms that never were, moved by false histories (heavily documented) of families that never existed.

How close is this to the experience of the Princelet Street Heritage
Centre? It's like the far side of a distorting mirror. The brown doors
of the old synagogue are never open, but the building harbours
vague ambitions of turning itself into a museum of immigration

and false memory. The structure of the building, seen in cross-section, is hierarchic: from the eighteenth-century kitchens, the subterranea of the cellars and stone-flagged dreaming spaces, through the synagogue to the rabbi's living quarters, and Rodinsky's garret. But it is cold, unwelcoming, independent in spirit. The custodian, working away at his own project, desk heaped with papers, is reluctant to grant access to outsiders. He hovers, eager to shepherd them out, to let the empty chambers return to their own quiet pulse. Every invasion, he implies, destroys the understanding he is beginning to acquire, fractures the slow meditation.

Everywhere in the Severs house there are watchers, lurkers, nondescripts doing very little, unconvincingly. Part of the cast. Resting actors. A chorus of extras with carefully ironed faces, bright with cultist excitement. Antiquarian amateurs in fetching bohemian disguise. The studied nonchalance with which they poke the fire, or stand at a dirty window, contrasts with the sombre procession of paying guests. Who are too well-dressed. They don't know how they are expected to behave. They want to signal their appreciation, that *they* understand, but they've been forbidden speech. They nod in dumb show at Severs. They realize, of course they do, that the arrangement on the table, the punch-bowl, the clay pipes, the tumbled chair, mirrors the painting on the wall, the Hogarthian scene of riot. This is a polite riot, a riot that has frozen, spilled over, neutralized its venom. Become part of the Folgate Street play, the theatre in which the dominant element is the set. Severs, as visible director/author, is pleased with himself, with the house (his programme notes spell out the message); he's Brecht in a baggy sweater. Resins smoke. Candles flicker. Recordings of church bells peal out from every curtained corner. It's a ceremony, a High Church ritual. The notion is that the house has become a theatre of ghosts. It's passed beyond reconstruction and authenticity, these are the spectres of people who never drew breath. The imagery on Severs's prompt sheets is almost sexual: 'candle-lit chambers from which, apparently, their 18th and 19th century inhabitants have only just withdrawn'. You can smell them, see the rumpled sheets, the congealing food. You can read the instructions to the servants. 'Leave ash be,' says a warning note pinned to the side of the fireplace. 'It's about what you have just missed.' A house of mirrors, reflections, ancestral portraits of elective families. (Only the yellow bicycle hanging from a wall in the yard gives the game away. Or perhaps that too is another Brechtian jolt.)

The ascent through the Severs house, with its staged manifestations, its vanished presences, runs in parallel (split-screen) to the trudge up the broken stairs of the Princelet Street synagogue. The synagogue's minder will be at your heels, telling you nothing, wishing you away. Severs sweeps you on, playing the illusionist, enforcing a mild mysticism: 'It is what we cannot see that makes sense of what we can.' Severs has conjured a family of 'six poor souls', the Jervises, for his garret. Weavers huddled around a phantom loom. He works hard to maintain the cobwebs, the wool, the Victorian squalor. 'Go on,' he whispers, 'experience it all.' Pain and hunger have climbed like tired smoke. Under the roof beams, you will notice pigeon droppings instead of the chirrups of caged birds. (The real birds were picked off by the hawks of Christ Church.) Will we at last stumble over skeletons in rags, the wretched poor whose plight was canted by the Victorian philanthropists, the Quaker brewmasters? Will there be a moment when the assault on our senses, the raree-show, will be transcended? No chance: 'You will discover the rooms empty of their inhabitants who have departed to walk to the River.'

A space as empty as Rodinsky's attic. Or as replete with stopped time. Severs's stage management insists upon respect for what was, echoes from the past, privileged and paid for. The presences, withdrawn from these rooms (which become the separate acts of a costume drama), are those of the special effects boffins, the assistants who pose as visitors. The stinks and the tapes condition you. They tell you how you are supposed to read the scene. It's very different in Princelet Street. Nothing is known about Rodinsky, much is rumoured. There is nobody to explain the story. One day a man who lived alone in a dead building, in a forgotten part of the town, walked out, disappeared. But it was not a true disappearance, because nobody noticed it. It was a trick without an audience. A retrospective vanishing. That was its power. The room, closed up, sealed with its books, clothes, calendars, was the sole entrance to the narrative. Visitors on the point of departure from the Severs house hear a child's voice: 'Mother – who are these people?' The theatre has been staged to assert its own immortality, that the cunningly crafted rooms in a surviving Georgian house exist in the abstraction of eternal time. Timeless. Mimicking decay. A warm dust breath. And we, passing rapidly across the stage, are the spooks of the future. Without purchase on life, encouraged to look and admire but forbidden to touch or taste, forbidden to discover that the books in their casual heap are no more than odd volumes of the Waverley novels scavenged from the caves of Cheshire Street.

Chaos is also a condition of Rodinsky's room. But it is a casual chaos. A chaos to which no one is expected to return. The room dominates the temporary trespasser. Rodinsky thrives on what can never be known. He auditions the archetypes. And that is the hook for the unwary. His play is unwritten. There is too much evidence. It will take a fine recklessness to complete the story that this stifled writer began: a room that was so purposefully disarranged, stacked with hints and echoes. Open the wardrobe. Sample the diary. Begin anywhere and you will find more material, tributaries branching from tributaries, than any one life can hope to unravel.

THE PRINCELET STREET SYNAGOGUE

Rachel Lichtenstein

A story: a man went to Cracow and on his return tells his friend, 'The Jews of Cracow are remarkable people. I saw a Jew who spends all his nights dreaming and all his days planning the revolution. I saw a Jew who spends all his time studying Talmud. I saw a Jew who chases every skirt he sees and I saw a Jew who wants nothing to do with women. I saw a Jew who is full of plans to get rich quick!'

The other man says, 'I don't know why you are astonished. Cracow is a big city and there are many Jews, all sorts of people.'

'No,' says the first, 'it was the same Jew.'

Rafael Felek Scharf

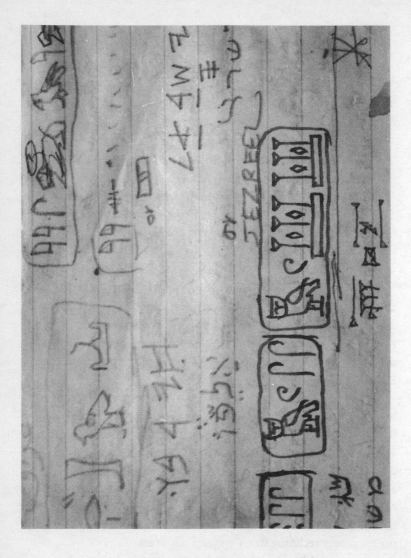

My father's parents, Gedaliah and Malka Lichtenstein, escaped from Poland in the early Thirties and settled in East London. After the war they moved, with their three sons, to Westcliff in Essex. As my father and his brothers became successful businessmen they decided to anglicize their surname. I was born, in April 1969, Rachel Laurence.

Malka died of leukaemia when I was twelve years old. I remember her, head thrown back in laughter, revealing a mouth full of gold teeth that I would beg to be shown. I remember her bright auburn wig, which my sister and I would watch slowly sliding off her head during her afternoon nap. Through the crack of the door we would admire her majestic figure, wrapped in a red velvet cloak, draped over her pink *chaise longue*. I would stare in awe at the photograph that rested on the mantelpiece, showing her as a young woman, provocatively reclining in a V-necked silk dress.

In contrast, I have a memory of an anxious woman pacing outside the gate on our arrival, crying uncontrollably if we were five minutes late. 'My darlings, I thought you wouldn't come, I thought I'd never see you.' But most of the time she would be in the kitchen,

cooking endless amounts of delicious food. My sister and I would sit at the table as our plates were piled up with fried chicken, gefilte fish and heaps of other delicacies. 'Eat, eat, think of all the starving children in Africa, eat and be well.' Guilt-ridden, knowing that as a girl she'd never had enough to fill her small belly, we would try to please her, stretching our skinny frames to bursting point.

I remember the way my grandfather always ate. He would lower his head nearly into his food, wrap his right arm protectively around his plate and, using the other hand, shovel his meal with alarming speed, barely stopping for breath. He never lost this habit, always aware of potential hungry siblings. My grandparents were colourful characters in my childhood; they both fascinated and terrified me. They were different from the other people around me, louder, bigger somehow.

When I was seventeen my grandfather died. He was over eighty and everyone agreed he'd had a good long life. After the funeral I remember entering his study, which was lined floor to ceiling with books. They were written in many different languages, none of which I could understand. I found a velvet bag in his bedside table, embroidered with Hebrew letters I could not read. Inside was a large piece of woven blue-and-white cloth and a small leather box with long leather ties. I did not know what they were for, but kept them anyway. I rescued his suitcase, full of old clock parts, certificates, photographs. In my room I examined them for hours.

When he died I panicked, realizing that with him was buried the key to my heritage. I became determined not to let it die with him. A week after his death I took the first step towards a reconnection between my past and my present and reclaimed by deed poll the surname Lichtenstein. That same summer, I left my parents' home to complete a degree in Fine Art, specializing in sculpture, at Sheffield University.

My desire to go to art school had been greatly influenced by my grandfather. When I was about eight years old, I asked him who had drawn the ink sketch of an old man that hung in a heavy gold frame in the hall of their house. He told me this story:

It was me. As a young man I was very talented, although I did not dream too much about becoming an artist. I was poor, from a small village. I was not allowed to have such ambitions. But I had an uncle who lived in Łódź. He was very influential and grand, involved in politics I think. Well, one summer, he came to stay with us. My uncle saw my drawings and was greatly impressed. He had some influence at the art school and managed to secure a place for me there. After much persuading my mother let me go. My uncle was to pay the fee and I would live with him. I could not believe my good fortune and left the following week. The journey to Łódź was long and difficult then. We travelled by horse and cart and it took us nearly three days. The next morning I was to begin my studies. I cannot even describe to you my excitement that night. I could not eat or sleep. Eventually I must have drifted off, because I shall never forget what happened next. I awoke in a blind panic. The moon

was still high in the sky but there was no possibility of me
sleeping again that night. I had experienced the most terrifying
and vivid dream and before even discussing the matter with my
uncle I began to pack my bags to return home. I had dreamt
that my brother was dying. The image and sensations were so
real I had to check if he was all right. We did not have
telephones in those days. The only way to know for sure would
be to return to the village. By the time dawn had broken I was
ready to leave. My uncle was understandably shocked and
disappointed, but I would not change my mind. He arranged for
my travel back and I began the long journey home, dreading my
arrival with each mile that took us closer. Eventually we reached
the outskirts of the village, and I ran home not stopping to greet
anyone and found the house ominously empty. I stepped
outside into the street to see my younger sister in floods of tears.
She had just come from the cemetery where they were burying
my brother. He had fallen into a fever the night I left and died
the following day of cholera. I never returned to Łódż, but
instead stayed and looked after the family, being now the eldest
son. Soon after, things became difficult for us and the family left
for England. I have not drawn anything since.

I took the opportunity my grandfather never had, and during
my three years at art school nearly all my sculptural work was based
on his life story. In my final year, against the advice of my tutors, I
decided to write my thesis about Jewish immigration from Eastern
Europe to the East End of London, and the process of assimilation
and integration in the new country. I travelled to London to conduct
the necessary research, spending a week at the Museum of the Jewish
East End, situated in Finchley. While there I befriended an elderly
volunteer who suggested I take a visit to the Heritage Centre in East
London, a former synagogue that was, he told me, now a museum of
immigration. I caught the tube to Whitechapel. The name, Princelet
Street, sounded vaguely familiar, but at the time I could not place it.

After travelling for about an hour I arrived at Aldgate East station.

I took a left up Brick Lane and found the turn-off for Princelet Street. Number 19 seemed a most unlikely museum, with no plaque outside, and apparently derelict. I rang the bell anyway but there was no response. Gently, I pushed against the large wooden doors and, finding them open, stepped inside. The temperature change was extreme. I began to shiver and I put on the jacket that had been unnecessary in the heat of the summer day.

A single bulb was attempting to light up the dark-green wood-panelled corridor in which I found myself. When my eyes adjusted to the dim light I could make out a large red metal safe to my left, and behind it a locked door. To the right, worn stone steps led up to another floor. Stacked in the corner behind the entrance doors were boxes of empty beer bottles, their staleness adding to the odour of dampness and dust. I could hear muffled voices ahead, and a light seeped under the door at the end of the corridor. I moved to call out, but the words stuck in my throat. The atmosphere still retained the oppressiveness of a religious space; it seemed natural to speak in whispers. I felt my way along the corridor and opened the door at the end. The peeling paintwork of the synagogue was lit by warm yellow candlelight. The faded purple cushions on the *bimah* were covered in tattered prayer shawls that looked as if they had been sitting there for decades. The wrought iron balcony was thick with dust and cobwebs. Various artefacts from the attic were strewn around the floor. I cried. I had spent the previous three summers in Poland, travelling around the country with a guidebook attempting to locate former Jewish sites. During these trips I had visited numerous similar buildings, and it appeared to me now as if the Princelet Street synagogue had been transported direct from Eastern Europe. In fact, I later learned, this was almost exactly what had occurred. The ark had been hand carved in Poland and brought over, along with the brass chandeliers and other religious items, by Polish and Russian refugees intent on resurrecting their community in London.

The synagogue was full of people running around, shouting at each other. They were students from the National Film School, halfway through a production called *The Golem of Princelet Street*. The cobwebs had been sprayed on for cinematic effect. The plot of the film was loosely based on the story of a cabbalistic scholar and his friendship with a local Muslim boy. I was told by one of the film students that an orthodox scholar called David Rodinsky used to live in the attic rooms above the synagogue. One day in the late Sixties he disappeared and his locked room had not been disturbed for over a decade. It was opened for the first time in the Eighties, with everything in place just as he had left it. This was the first time I had heard of Rodinsky. A bored lighting technician followed me around the building, feeding me tales of Rodinsky's room. 'I heard that when they first opened the room, a mummified cat was found sleeping in his bed. There were hundreds of books up there, containing mystical formulas, and it is believed he managed to transport himself out of the room without ever leaving.' The lighting man leaned closer. 'His boots were still there, standing in the corner, filled to the brim with dust.'

The moment I entered 19 Princelet Street I knew I was meant to be there. When I spoke with my father about the building later that night, he told me my grandparents had their first marital home and ran a watchmaking shop at 32 Princelet Street. He supposed they had been married in the synagogue. These revelations only fuelled my desire to spend time in the building. After numerous telephone calls I managed to track down Donald Chesworth, the chairman of the project. We met, a week after my first visit; by then I had an over-ambitious proposal to become artist-in-residence at Princelet Street. This would involve running guided tours of the area and the building; conducting educational events with just about every section of the community imaginable; archiving and cataloguing the entire museum collection; organizing and curating historical and artistic exhibitions; and, in my spare time, producing my own art work. Mr Chesworth was very supportive of my plan and presented the proposal to the Heritage Centre committee. It was accepted. I was to become the unpaid artist-in-residence. On completing my degree that summer I moved to London and found a flat in Brady Street, Whitechapel. I took up my new post, beginning with an exhibition of my own work.

Entitled 'Forever Green', the work was shown in the building's basement. It was a culmination of the Polish trips and the sculptures I had made about my grandfather. Images of documents retrieved from the Jewish Historical Institute in Warsaw, boys innocently

smiling into the camera in the early years of the Łódź ghetto. Menorah and spice boxes on the concrete steps of the old market in Kraków. A tower of books wrapped in blue velvet. Objects from my grandfather's watchmaking shop permanently sealed in resin with heavy frames of steel.

Each day I would open up and wait in the damp basement for the bell to ring. About ten visitors a day came in the first few weeks, mainly elderly people who used to live in the area, many of whom used to worship in the synagogue. I spent many fascinating hours talking with these people, hungry to hear their stories, which they were only too happy to tell. I wanted to learn all I could about Whitechapel and began to walk there every day, jotting down sites of Jewish interest. It was during this time that I met Professor Bill Fishman. I had been using his book *The Streets of East London* to learn about the area. I had no idea he was connected to the building. One day, while in the basement, I heard a key turn in the lock and the sound of many feet making their way into the synagogue. I went upstairs and listened as Bill Fishman gave his talk on the Princelet Street synagogue to a group of young history students. Bill's knowledge of the history of the Jewish East End is unrivalled. He knows his material so well that when he speaks it sounds as if he is quoting directly from one of the many books he has written. This is what I remember he said that day in the synagogue:

Between 1870 and 1914, East London experienced the greatest influx of 'strangers' ever. Over 120,000 mainly Russian and Polish Jews came to seek asylum here. By 1850 the ghetto was firmly established around the focal point of Petticoat Lane with some offshoots extending beyond the narrow alleyways around Brick Lane, such as Princelet Street. For those that had just arrived or were impervious to change and circumstance, the synagogue sustained their ambiguous response to their new environment. There were at least fifty synagogues scattered around these few streets, but this one is very special. It is the third-oldest purpose-built synagogue still standing in England today. The synagogue is not the oldest part of the building. It was built by Russian and Polish refugees in 1870 in the back garden of this house, which was originally used by Huguenot silk weavers and built in 1718 by Samuel Worrall, the master carpenter for the architect Nicholas Hawksmoor.

I want to read to you an excerpt from the great East London writer Israel Zangwill, who was born only a few streets away from here. This description vividly portrays what this building would have been like in its heyday:

'The *stiebel* consisted of two large rooms, knocked into one, and the rear partitioned off for the use of bewigged, heavy-jawed women, who might not sit with the men lest they should fascinate their thoughts away from things spiritual. Its furniture was bare benches, a raised platform with reading desk in the centre, and a wooden curtained ark at each end containing parchment scrolls of the law, each with a silver pointer and silver bells and pomegranates. The room was badly ventilated, and what little air there was was generally sucked up by a greedy company of wax candles, big and little, stuck in brass holders.

'Here the worshippers came, two and three times a day. They dropped in, mostly in their workday grime, and rumbled and roared and chorused with prayers that shook the windowpanes. This synagogue was their salon and their lecture hall. It supplied them not only with their religion, but their art and letters, their politics and their public amusements. It was their home as well as the Almighty's. They enjoyed themselves in this *shul* of theirs; they shouted and skipped and sang, they wailed and moaned; they clenched their fists and thumped their breasts, and they were not least happy when they were crying.'

This synagogue is special in many ways. Apart from being one of the oldest synagogues in London it also has a remarkable story connected to it. Many years ago, when the synagogue was still functioning, there was a caretaker who lived in the attic rooms above the building. He was a Polish Jew called David

Rodinsky and a brilliant scholar; he spoke many different languages. I remember, when I was a boy in the Thirties, walking past and seeing him in the attic, bent over his books by candlelight. He looked very old to me. He was a lovely man, a real *tzaddick*, meaning a righteous individual. I saw him walking around the streets here with pockets full of change giving out money to beggars. It makes me sad to think about him. One day, in the Sixties, he just disappeared – nobody knows what happened to him. His room was left locked up for a long time. We can't go up there now, the stairs are too dangerous, this building is incredibly fragile. So please, have a look around the synagogue and then we'll move on to our next stop.'

While Bill's students were admiring the building I introduced myself. He recognized my name immediately. 'I heard about you from the committee, they let me use this building for my tours.' He was extremely charming and enthusiastic about my residency and took all his students down to the basement to see my exhibition. I asked him if he knew any more about David Rodinsky, and he suggested I visit Bishopsgate library and talk to the local historian there. He had directed my first step on a quest that would take me years.

I soon abandoned my desire to make sculpture in the synagogue as the building left me in a state of artistic paralysis. Its aesthetic richness and history were overwhelming, there was little I could do to compete with it. I sat alone in silent admiration on the empty wooden benches, visually saturated by the scene before me: twisted brass chandeliers against a backdrop of golden hand-painted Hebrew names, sepia-stained plaster walls framed by dusty velvet drapes, lit with a soft pink hue from the stained-glass roof.

Once a month or so the building would be hired out to film crews eager to take advantage of the unique setting. A major part of my time in residence was spent arguing with these crews. I would skulk around in the shadows of the women's balcony, watching their every move below, shouting out furiously as I spotted a set designer about to paint the ark a different colour so he could get the right shot, wincing inside as I heard the shattering of the glass lamps on the *bimah* as a cameraman carelessly backed into them. I took over what I thought of as Rodinsky's role, becoming the unpaid caretaker of the Princelet Street synagogue, fiercely defending its fragile construction.

Unable to produce my own work I became increasingly drawn to Rodinsky's room. It no longer existed in its original state, as an abandoned tomb. The room had been dismantled, the contents boxed up by the Museum of London, then taken to storage rooms to dry out in stable conditions before being returned to the synagogue. When I first saw the room, Rodinsky's belongings were neatly piled away in archival boxes lining the walls in large stacks. At first, outside the boxes, the room seemed to contain little evidence of Rodinsky's long time in residence. But gradually I began to uncover the clues. I found his old gramophone records lying under the bed, and a large collection of dust-covered empty beer bottles in a cupboard in the corner. Stiffened pyjamas and fossilized blankets still remained in his wardrobe. While fondling his piano one day, I lifted the lid to discover faint traces of pencil on the ivory keys: strange indecipherable symbols, written in his own hand. In the centre of the wooden ceiling was a rusty gas lamp, surrounded by a charcoal halo from constant use. The peeling wallpaper behind the door had also been marked, with faint traces of handwriting hidden beneath the sodden edges. The floorboards were bent and cracked next to the enamel sink where I presumed he had washed every day.

His table stood in the centre of the room, covered in a green baize cloth, and it was here that I would perform my daily ritual of excavating his remains. Wearing protective cotton gloves, I would slowly remove his belongings from their archival boxes, gently unveiling them from their acid-free wrappings, before photographing each one and attempting to define and catalogue it.

At first this seemingly arbitrary archaeology revealed little, the objects appearing mute with the loss of their originator's voice to explain them. I spent countless hours in his room. Heaps of inac-

cessible, rotting material piled up around me. Most of the languages
in which he wrote I could not read. A large amount of Rodinsky's
clothes, saucepans, shoes and other personal items were thrown
away. I arrived one day to find them bagged up on the street, and
sneaked them back upstairs.

More often than not the cold, or the overwhelming sensation of
being watched, would drive me out of the room, with the hairs on
the back of my neck prickling. But every day I would be back at the
table, fascination overcoming fear. Gradually, over time, through
careful examination of his vast collection, a faint image of a man
began to emerge: a scholar harbouring secrets, a meticulous anno-
tator of texts, a comedian, an enigma.

I discovered handwritten notebooks revealing his knowledge of
languages – Sumerian, Arabic, Japanese, Hebrew, Yiddish, Greek
and Russian – and of Egyptian hieroglyphics. I found an old rent
book that dated back to 1936. There were foreign travel books,
though I doubted somehow that Rodinsky ever visited these places.
I found one notebook full of Irish drinking songs written in thick
red capital letters, and I discovered a crumpled cabbalistic diagram
stashed behind his wardrobe.

There were other scraps of evidence suggesting he had been
orthodox in his beliefs: the kosher food packets, the religious books,
the battery-operated razor, the shopping list for Shabbat: 'two chal-
lahs, candles, meat, six eggs, *kiddush* wine'. I unwrapped hundreds of
artefacts, thousands of small scraps of paper covered in coded messages, in different languages, by his own hand. On the backs of
chocolate wrappers, inserted inside his diaries and books, were
hand-drawn maps, indications of journeys around London, from
Hainault to Chigwell, Clapton to Hendon, with no clues as to who
he was seeing or what the visits were about. At first I was convinced
he lived alone, but bits of evidence kept cropping up suggesting he
had shared the room with other family members. I found an envelope addressed to a Mrs C. Rodinsky, his mother maybe, postmarked
'Essex January 1961'. And another, sad letter from St Clement's
Hospital social services department concerning the death of his

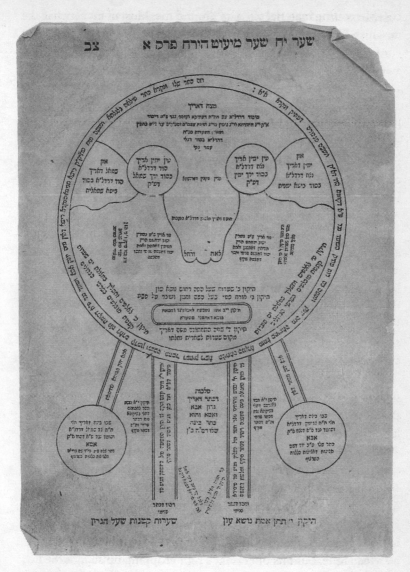

sister, Bessie Rodinsky. It required him to come and collect her possessions, 'one pair of gold earrings'. He had scrawled over the type in red ink the words 'diabolical concentration camp'.

I decided to take Bill Fishman's advice to visit the local history

department of the Bishopsgate library. I wanted to know what the
room had looked like when it was first opened up. Bill had told me to
ask for David Webb, the chief librarian, which I did on my arrival. A
small, greasy-haired bespectacled man appeared behind the tall
mahogany desk. I asked if he had any information on the Princelet
Street synagogue. He told me he often had people coming to the
library with that request, furious that they were unable to gain access
to the building. He knew of a number of demonic attempts over the
years to enter the abandoned room, with people banging on the door
for hours and journalists throwing bricks through the window. A few
years ago, he thought, the whole story had reached a level of hysteria,
when there were claims that the first person into the room tripped
over a mummified cat. He thought that in another fifty years the
story would become as misrepresented an urban myth as Dirty Dick.
'It'll be on the stop of every tour guide, with tales of ever-increasing
exaggeration.' He scurried off into the back, returning with a large
blue folder full of newspaper clippings. I settled myself into a secluded
corner of the room and devoured the information before me.

There were a number of articles concerning Rodinsky's room.
The *East London Advertiser* described one visit under the headline:
SECRET OF THE LOST ROOM:

> Workmen refurbishing one of Spitalfields' historic buildings
> have revealed a twenty-year-old secret. They have uncovered a
> lost room in the weaver's attic on Princelet Street. The room was
> the home of a reclusive Polish Jew called Michael Rodinsky. He
> was a self-taught language fanatic who spent lonely days
> studying ancient dialects. His huge collection of dictionaries has
> been found in his room. So have his spectacles and a weighing
> machine ticket that he used as a bookmark. But suddenly in
> 1969 he disappeared. Rodinsky's room has remained untouched
> ever since, changed only by a thick covering of dust. To this day
> no one knows what became of him.

I found various other articles, all more or less telling the same story: a David or Michael Rodinsky, of Polish or Russian origin, mysteriously disappeared from his attic room in 19 Princelet Street some time in the late Sixties. There were other articles about the street in the file, grisly stories of vicious attacks and dilapidated buildings, written about the same time as Rodinsky's room was discovered in 1980.

CASTRATION HORROR

A man was savagely and deliberately castrated in a horrific attack by a knife wielding maniac as he walked alone down a dark alley off Princelet Street. One theory is that the cruel knifing may have been the work of a woman who bore a grudge against her victim.

Other articles of that time described the horrendous slum conditions of the area.

A housing co-operative has given hope to Spitalfields tenants living in a street of crumbling houses reputed to be the worst slum in London. The co-operative is seeking government money to buy the decaying properties in Princelet Street and renovate them. The three-storey brick houses have been neglected for years, but many are packed with tenants who cannot find alternative accommodation in the area. One tenant likely to benefit from the renovations is a 71 year old widow who has lived in Princelet Street for 41 years. Mrs Daren lives on the first floor of a squalid house that smells of rats' droppings. Giant cracks in the back wall let in the light, damp in other walls has stained the peeling paper. Mrs Daren has an outside toilet, no hot water and faulty wiring. A council inspector declared the house unfit for human habitation. The development officer says her home is not the worst in the street, and some of the Bengali households are deplorably overcrowded.

And then I found what I had been longing to set eyes on: photo-

graphs of Rodinsky's room when it was first opened. They were fantastically seductive, beautifully lit and composed, fulfilling every
element of my romantic fantasy of what the room must have looked
like. There was an image by Danny Gralton, in a newspaper article,
that particularly excited me. It showed Rodinsky's table in exactly
the same situation as it still stood, covered in the same green baize
cloth I had been working on only hours before. The table was piled
high with books and papers, giving the room the appearance of the
scholar's garret that I imagined it to have been. Behind his table I
could see his wardrobe, full of clothes, and I spotted an enamel wash
bowl resting on the sideboard. It looked like the same bowl I had
managed to rescue from the street when someone had tried to throw
some of Rodinsky's belongings into the skip. There was another
beautiful photograph in the book *The Saving of Spitalfields*. The
caption read: 'Rodinsky's room as revealed when the Trust opened
the door for the first time since his mysterious disappearance twenty
years earlier, photograph by Danny Gralton.' The image was serene,
carefully composed like a Vermeer painting, with a tactile quality
that made the viewer want to reach out and touch the wallpaper so
seductively dripping off the walls, that made the viewer gaze in
wonder at the headline on a newspaper on the table, ISRAEL REBORN,
perfectly positioned in the foreground. The light from the weaver's
windows falling on the book-laden table added to the feeling that
one was looking at an old Dutch masterpiece. It was easy to see why
the story, backed up with these perfect pictures, had attracted so
much curiosity back in the early Eighties. I was drawn further into
the Rodinsky web.

The last article I came across revealed a more sceptical point of
view. It was a piece in the *Guardian*, by Iain Sinclair, entitled 'The
Man Who Became a Room'.

Patrick Wright alerted me to a fable that is acquiring great
potency in the amoebic principality of Spitalfields – the myth of
the disappearance of David Rodinsky. Rodinsky, a Polish Jew
from Piotsk or Lublin or wherever, was the caretaker and

resident poltergeist of the Princelet Street synagogue: an
indistinguishable *chevra* without the funds to keep a scholar-in-
residence. He perched under the eaves, a crow, unremarked and
unremarkable – until that day in the early Sixties when he
achieved the great work and became invisible. It is uncertain
how many weeks or years passed before anyone noticed his
absence. He had evaporated, and would remain as dust, his
name unspoken, to be resurrected only as a feature, a necessary
selling point, to put alongside Nicholas Hawksmoor in the
occult fabulation of the zone that the Eighties demanded to
justify a vertiginous inflation in property values.

The legend had escaped and the street doors were padlocked
behind it; the windows were sealed in plasterboard, painted
versions of themselves. Rodinsky's room was left as he
abandoned it: books on the table, rug flung from the bed, cheap
calendar with the reproduction of Millet's *Angelus* fixed forever
at January 1963.

The newcomers, salivating over an excavated *fricassée* of
chicken, followed by smoked collops and green flummery, had
discovered a quaint little myth of their own, without blood and
entrails, a Vanishing Jew. They fell upon it, like a wood-panelled
stairwell or a weaver's bobbin. The synagogue, complete with
dark secret, passed rapidly into the hands of the Spitalfields
Heritage Centre – where it is now possible, with the aid of a
good torch, to climb the damaged staircase and by confronting
the room, discover the man.

On August 2 1957, Rodinsky weighed 12 stone 12 pounds: he
preserved the weighing machine ticket as a bookmark. His
height, to judge from the jackets hanging in the wardrobe,
would be about 5 foot 9 inches – which put the ceiling less than
a foot above his head. He wore spectacles: the empty cases are
inscribed with his name. And though his clothing was drab he
favoured exuberant Kenneth More-style paisley cravats or even
a glittering gold-painted tie: soberly putting on the Ritz.
Perhaps not too soberly – the chest of drawers is decorated

with enough empty Wincarnis bottles to support an all-night session of Harold Wilson's kitchen cabinet. The inner man found solace at the piano or the gramophone, with a collection of 78s that ranged from D'une Prison to Ol' Man River. Newspapers were trusted friends, never to be turned out: DUKE'S GUARDED THE HONEYMOON, 1923; 72 YEAR OLD WOMAN TIED TO A CHAIR, 1932. The headlines never change. All stars are swallowed by the Sun.

But if Rodinsky did not simply walk out, fade into another social identity, or fall victim to some arbitrary cancellation by violence, then the search for his secret would begin with the books and diaries. The obsession with language as code: dictionaries and primers in Hebrew, Russian, French, Ancient Middle Eastern texts. As the room itself had been converted from a refuge to a shrine so Rodinsky translated a Letts Schoolgirl's diary to his own system of universal time and language – moving through Julian, Georgian and Armenian versions, breaking from Indian to Latin to Sumerian markings. The work ceases only with his disappearance. 'KI-BI-MA . . . SPEAK!' 'by he she/aren't so not take' is the final entry.

The irrelevant details pile up and the man begins to fade. He does not go away, that was unnecessary. There is still so much of him here that he no longer needs to be present in any other form. The room, as he left it, has gone and will never return: Rodinsky is what remains, a museum of ephemera and dust-breath. A trap. He converted himself into these shards, tempting to carry them off, so that his work is continued. The ruin is immortal.

Sinclair's article had a big effect on me. He was right, the room was a trap, and I felt that he was sending me some sort of prophetic warning. But I was too entrenched in the room to be easily warned away. Too connected to the building by my own history to give up yet. I wanted to meet Iain Sinclair, to interview him. He was the first person I had come across so far who had witnessed Rodinsky's room in its original state.

I did not know how to contact Iain Sinclair so I focused on Bill Fishman, the one person I had met so far who had actually seen David Rodinsky. Bill and I became friends, and he took it upon himself to pass on his knowledge of the area, helping me to become a tour guide of the Jewish East End. During our many walks around Whitechapel, he pointed out the buildings that had been previously used by the Jewish community, such as the communist meeting hall where Lenin once spoke and the mission where Jews were paid six-pence for listening to Christian ministers. We walked to the former sites of old department stores, jewellers, Jewish dairies, the Russian vapour baths. In reality there was little left to see. But viewed through Bill's eyes the Jewish East End was still alive. The only place where it was possible still to witness it was the Kosher Luncheon Club in Greatorex Street, just to the east of Brick Lane. My first visit was with Bill in the summer of 1991.

Paul Levine, the owner, greeted us warmly at the door. Bill told me that all customers, regular and new, received this kind of welcome, whether stopping for a chat and a glass of lemon tea, or staying to eat a three-course feast of barley soup, herring and gefilte fish. On the back of the menu was a description of the Kosher Luncheon Club and its history:

> During the eighteenth century eating houses started up all over
> the East End. They were at first little more than soup kitchens
> but as the community prospered, so the variety of the menus
> improved, reflecting the regional dishes brought over by the
> refugees. The downfall of these eating houses was in fact due to
> the business success of the refugees they so faithfully served.
> The community moved on to better areas and the eating houses
> closed down. This is the last of its kind to survive in London.

For what remained of the community it was a meeting place. Somewhere to share memories and show off photographs of new grandchildren.

The luncheon club became my ace card when conducting my own tours of the area in subsequent years. By then there was little left of the Jewish East End: crumbling buildings, derelict sites, rapidly fading signs. 'This used to be —— now it is a car park.' ... 'If you look really hard you can just make out the mark of a *mezuzah* here.' After traipsing around the streets of Spitalfields, the crowds of tourists invariably were despondent by the end of the tour. Then I would take them to the Kosher Luncheon Club. That was alive and kicking. Crisp white tablecloths, the clink of glasses and the slurp of soup to a backdrop of Yiddish and laughter. It retained the warmth I've so often heard people talking about when they describe the Jewish world of East London.

In 1994 the luncheon club stopped trading, another victim in the story of the disappearing Jewish East End. Bloom's restaurant was to close less than a year later, and then Marks Deli in Wentworth Street. The luncheon club had certainly not had an easy time of it in recent years, and nearly closed down in 1992 after suffering a racist arson attack. The arsonists heaped up prayer-books from the synagogue next door before dousing them with white spirit and setting them on fire, causing ten thousand pounds' worth of damage. The attack came only nine months after vandals had broken into the club and daubed the walls with Nazi slogans and symbols. The fire started on the holiday of *Shavuot*, at the same time of year that I returned to the club in 1997, three years after it had closed down. I had been invited to an art event, organized by a gallery in Spitalfields Market that was being run from the former site of the old luncheon club. I was too curious not to take a last look, and walked from Whitechapel in the dank drizzle to Greatorex Street.

The once spotless blue-and-white hall now resembled a seedy nightclub. The tiles had been ripped from the floor and painted black. The old wooden table at the front of the hall that once housed an ancient till was littered with beer bottles and fag butts. The tables had disappeared and in their place stood black-clad artists shifting about uncomfortably. I moved through the crowd in a state of shock, reaching the end of the room, where a long trestle table covered in black velvet faced me. On the table were strewn flowers and open books. On closer inspection I realized the books were religious volumes belonging to the synagogue.

I passed the table and moved with the herd into the adjacent room. In all the times I had visited the luncheon club I had never been into the Great Garden Street synagogue before, even though I had known it was situated next door. A magnificent building: beautifully carved wooden *bimah* standing proudly in the centre, the pews still in place, with seat numbers carefully painted in white on their backs. The ark was surrounded with marble tablets commemorating various stages in the life of the synagogue and its members. All this was hard to focus on. I felt as if someone had dropped a tab of acid into my beer and I was not having a good trip. I moved slowly through the dark, smoky room, stopping behind the *bimah* to gain my balance. It was Friday night, Shabbat. Where the rabbi and cantor would have stood, a long-haired DJ with baseball cap secured by giant headphones was busily spinning nightmarish techno tunes while struggling to light a disintegrating cigarette protruding from his mouth.

Each corner of the *bimah* had a flame-throwing gas torch fixed to it, adding to the image of hell. Spaced-out ravers, with Technicolor trousers and dreadlocks, frantically waved their arms about in the pews. Others sat about, stubbing out cigarettes on the carpet. The ark had been shut off by a string of cheap flashing fairy lights, and from the women's gallery a smoke machine billowed obnoxious air to the revellers below.

My head began to spin, and, as I turned, attempting to make sense of the scene before me, I lost my footing and fell. The bouncer eyed me suspiciously: another raver who had popped one too many. Friends picked me up and ushered me out, suggesting we go and look at the art. In a daze, I re-entered the hall of the former luncheon club and moved towards the door where a gaggle had gathered to witness an 'art performance'. On a raised stage two women sat dressed in baby pink vinyl, garish make-up smeared on their blank faces. They sat behind a large desk piled knee-deep in old books arranged in a most aesthetic and appealing way. I pushed to the front of the zombified crowd. The young ladies were stamping the books with large rubber implements and then elegantly ripping pages out of them and tossing them on to the floor.

I approached the table and began to scrutinize the books. Ancient prayer-books were strewn around, broken spines balancing on top of old receipt books, registers and other archive material dating back to the beginning of the century. My hand rested on a large faded album. I picked up the book and flicked through: C10113, BURIAL SOCIETY OF THE FEDERATION OF SYNAGOGUES, 1 March 1933, Chaya Jablonsky, age 92 years, Hackney Hospital, Homerton . . . exquisite handwriting filled every page with painstaking additional notes on each deceased person, their occupation described in detail, financial situation, next of kin, place of birth, Hebrew name, presence of watcher over each corpse.

'What the fuck do you think you're doing, this is a performance?' one of the pink plastic babes screeched.

'Excuse me, what exactly are you doing?' I howled back.

'We have been told to stamp these books and rip them up. You are in the way, put that fucking book down.'

A row ensued, and friends looked on in horror as I became part of the event; the crowd drawled greedily. In a quasi-hypnotic state I heaped books up in my arms and began walking towards the door. The pink girls screamed abuse and continued maniacally stamping and ripping books to shreds.

My friend Michelle managed to restrain me for a few moments and suggested it might be more constructive to try to locate the organizers of the show. Eventually, Marco from the Commercial Gallery arrived. I spoke quickly and urgently for ten minutes, pointing out that the performance was offensive and suggesting that maybe they might consider that the books were historically significant and would be better placed in a museum. At the end of that time the two men were apologizing profusely. 'We had no idea what they were, terribly sorry,' etcetera etcetera. The performance was stopped. The young women sulked on their chairs, then joined their friends in the synagogue. I told Marco that I would contact the appropriate parties and try to get the books housed or buried. He was willing to help, and then told me about all the other material that had been found in the synagogue: *tefillin*, prayer shawls, all manner of religious books. Thank God, they had had the sensitivity to store some of this material away. I also told Marco that I was taking the book I had picked up, the Register of Deaths. He did not argue with me.

I had seen insensitive events like this happen before on a number of occasions at the Princelet Street synagogue. Film crews would repaint the ark to create the right mood, artists would hang offensive work in the synagogue, and the stench of stale cigarettes and beer would often greet me when entering the building on a Monday morning. I accepted that buildings become abandoned, that synagogues are deconsecrated, and that new owners have every right to adapt them to suit their new purposes. But to destroy the books? Scenes of Nazi Germany came to mind. These books had not been ripped from the homes and synagogues of terrified Jews, they had been abandoned by the Federation of Synagogues, left scattered on the pews for new occupiers to play with.

The following Monday morning I telephoned the Tower Hamlets Local History Library and talked to a quietly spoken librarian there. I explained the situation and asked if they would be interested in rescuing the material for their archives.

'Oh, we would of course, yes but Greathorex Street is not in Tower Hamlets, out of our jurisdiction you see, so I am afraid we are unable to help you.'

'No, no, Greatorex Street is most definitely in Tower Hamlets.'

'Greathorex Street is not in Tower Hamlets, we cannot help, goodb——'

'*Please*, Greatorex Street is absolutely in Tower Hamlets, just off Brick Lane, next to . .'

'Listen, *I know* there is no Greathorex Street in Tower Hamlets, why don't you try the. .'

'Greatorex Street is absolutely without doubt in Tower Hamlets, off Whitechapel High Street and Brick Lane, G-R-E-A-T-O-R-E-X Street.'

'Oh ... Greatorex Street ... hmm, yes, we would be interested ... do you have the number of the present owners of the building?'

'Yes, yes.'

Numbers were exchanged and the librarian diplomatically suggested he would speak to the owners personally. 'It might appear a little less hysterical, shall we say, coming from me?' I agreed and put down the phone in relief. I turned to the shelf where the register I had taken from the performance had been sitting unopened since Friday night. I sat on the sofa for the next few hours, reading the book.

C10337, Mr Milner, son of Samuel Milner, deceased, one son only, a tailor, now he is in slack. One son living in Paris, he is paralysed. They say the synagogue kept the old man who used to spend all his days there, in fact the synagogue paid him 6/ for a room in the lane. His son is not in a position to pay, but does not want charity, said will endeavour to get £3 and will pay off whatever else will be required of him in time. Mr Gaber said the old man was most respectable he knows the son as well, decision subject to revision, WATCHER Mr Nathan Tuesday 10.30 am Mrs Lipman Tuesday 5.30 pm ... C10338, Benjamin Rabinovitch, 50 years, died heart failure 19.3.33, deceased was an attendant of the picture palace, eldest son musician, no regular work. Father of deceased has grocery shop in Cable Street, a member of Warsaw Lodge synagogue. I asked the minimum, the father bargained, burial responsibility of society. NO WATCHER ... C10339, Milly Rosen, age 32 years, died 8 Alan 5693, miscarriage, husband is a fish fryer, employee, pays rent, has two brothers in same occupation, other brother, Harry Mason the fighter, the father told me he went bankrupt, not fighting any more. I asked for the minimum, they bargained, offered £12, subject to revision, NO WATCHER ... C10340, Bella Abrahams, C10341 Hyman Jankovitch, C10342 Solomon Ginskey,

10343 Esther Bodinsky, handwriting unclear, could be Rodinsky.
Esther Rodinsky, 5 Weaver Street, female 41 years, date of death
8.6.33 Thursday 10 am, Hebrew date 14 Sivan 5693, cause of
death, suicide, nearest relative of deceased Hyman Rodinsky,
relationship: brother.

I scrutinized the faded handwriting again and again, unable to
believe my eyes. I had stumbled across a lost relative of David
Rodinsky.

I tried to track down Esther Rodinsky but I was unsuccessful. I gave
up on her and desperately tried to find traces of David. I made
posters and distributed them in the window of the bagel shop on
Brick Lane, in the Jewish old people's home in Stepney, in Toynbee
Hall (where there are still weekly Yiddish poetry meetings for the
remaining Jewish community) and in local cafés and businesses.

DID YOU KNOW DAVID RODINSKY?

HE LIVED ABOVE THE SYNAGOGUE IN PRINCELET STREET

OFF BRICK LANE, LONDON E1

I WOULD LIKE TO SPEAK TO ANY FORMER MEMBERS OF

THE PRINCELET STREET SYNAGOGUE

OR

ANYONE WHO LIVED IN PRINCELET STREET

WHO MIGHT HAVE KNOWN HIM

If you think you can help, please contact:

RACHEL LICHTENSTEIN on 0171 690 8412

Many thanks for your time!

For weeks I heard nothing and then I had a phone call from a man
who said his name was Charlie. I had placed a poster in the window
of the Market Café in Fournier Street. Charlie lives in Wilkes Street,
which runs along the top of Fournier and Princelet streets, and from
his house there is an excellent view of the synagogue. When I met
him I realized I had seen him many times before in passing, in the

street, cafés and markets. This is just how he remembered David Rodinsky, walking around Whitechapel in the late Sixties. They had never spoken but he had noticed him coming and going to the synagogue with large bundles of books. He described him as appearing 'very shy. Quite tall and scholarly. Very much keeping himself to himself.' Charlie could not tell me much more than this, but I had found my second witness (the first being Bill Fishman) and I knew there must be others in the area.

I started to frequent a different pub or café each lunchtime, asking in each one if anyone remembered David Rodinsky. The answer was the same for months – nobody knew who I was talking about. Eventually I got lucky in Rossi's Café in Hanbury Street with the owner of the place, a friendly Italian man who has been running the business with his wife from the same premises since 1947. When I asked him about Rodinsky, his face creased into a broad smile. 'Of course I remember him, he was a regular visitor here, a very entertaining man. He never had any money but he would come and sit in that corner and play the spoons. Very good at it he was too. The customers would love it and buy him a cup of tea and slice of bread for his efforts.' I kept asking him if he was sure this was the same David Rodinsky from 19 Princelet Street. He assured me it was, he claimed to have known him well, he was a 'real regular at Rossi's'.

This information seemed to contradict the other scraps of evidence about Rodinsky I had managed to collect. Bill Fishman remembered him 'with pockets full of change giving out money to the poor', hardly a man who could not even afford a slice of bread, and Charlie described him as very shy, not the type of character you would expect to find amusing a café full of people. The café owner's description also clashed with the romantic image of him that I favoured, inspired by Bill Fishman's description of him: 'an orthodox man, bent over his books by candlelight in his attic'.

I spoke with a man from a local taxi firm in Brick Lane, who like Charlie recalled seeing David Rodinsky in the Sixties, 'scuttling around the streets in a long dirty coat and great white beard. His head was always bent down, don't remember his face. He looked like a Fagin-type character. He'd never stop to say hello, just kept going.' Although I was now greatly confused as to the true identity of David Rodinsky, the new information fuelled my desire to find out more. I was completely hooked. I tried desperately, walking the area and asking questions every day, but I learned nothing new. Maybe there were more answers back in the room.

As I carefully studied the photographs I had found at the Bishopsgate library, I realized that many artefacts were now missing from the room. I needed to speak to someone who had seen the room in its original state. I tracked down Rosemary Weinstein, a member of the original committee, who was now working at the Museum of London. She was the person who had co-ordinated the packing up of the room back in the early Eighties. A tall, slim, blonde woman arrived at the doorstep of 19 Princelet Street, which surprised me as I suppose I expected her to look more 'Jewish'. Rosemary's background turned out to be Huguenot; she was married to a Jewish man. She had not been connected to the building for a number of years, but she remembered a great deal of information about the synagogue and about the state of Rodinsky's room when the building was first opened up.

She told me there were definitely people who could help me, particularly a woman called Feona Hamilton, who had done her M.Phil. on Jewish immigration. She had done a considerable amount of research into her own family history – Rosemary remembered being shown wonderful photographs of Feona's family in Poland, going back four generations. Feona had been extremely interested in Rodinsky's notebooks and diaries, and had been one of the first people to gain access to them. I was anxious to try to contact her as soon as possible, and wrote to her at the address Rosemary had given me. The letter was returned to sender a few weeks later.

Rosemary had told me that Rodinsky's room was left in its original state for nearly a decade. The windows in the room were broken, the roof leaked, and rain was coming in. This proved extremely hazardous to the Rodinsky material and was why Rosemary had offered to look after the artefacts at the Museum of London while the building was being repaired. The boxed artefacts were returned around 1989, about the same time I first entered the room.

When Rosemary had arrived at the synagogue Rodinsky's room had only been opened a short time and everything was still in place. She showed me photographs taken by a Museum of London photographer to document the strange time capsule. She suspected that even before the photographer got in, the room might have been tampered with as it was a total shambles, with poles from the scaffolding outside coming through the windows.

There were so many notebooks, so many loose pages all over the floor. We did our best to gather it all up, lots had come adrift, nothing was thrown away, but the builders were due in and the room had been exposed to the elements for many years, things just blew away. Everything was documented but so many people had been in, things were moved about and so nothing was necessarily in its original place anyway, the clothes were in the

wardrobe but the old records and things were moved around
and picked up as people wanted to look at them. I mean I could
not guarantee that anything was original or in its rightful
location. It was such heaps of stuff and the way in which the
volumes had come adrift shows that people had been carelessly
rifling through the stuff, I don't think Rodinsky himself would
have done it. There was a burglary as well, when the scaffolding
was up, and his old gramophone had been stolen from the
room.

Rosemary thought the material in the room was fascinating, but
she believed it was a mistake to think of Rodinsky as a great scholar.
In her opinion he was interested in a great variety of fields, and his
notebooks, although curious, were filled with copied passages in
ancient languages with taped-in cuttings, and there was nothing
brilliant about them. To her the most interesting things in the room
were 'the vestiges from the pre-revolutionary days in Russia; there
were lots of roubles in his wallet and things like that. I remember the
wallet, it was very spooky when we found it, left in his jacket still
hanging in the wardrobe, full of personal artefacts, bits of paper
with hand-drawn maps on them, cigarette packets covered in
strange diagrams. Historically speaking, the most interesting thing
for me was his bar mitzvah certificate.' I knew I had been through
every single box of artefacts from the room and had never come
across that certificate. As she continued to talk, I realized how much
material had gone missing over the years. All sorts of people had
heard about the room when it was first opened and were given free
access. I doubted whether it would be possible ever now to get a full
picture of the Rodinsky story.

Rosemary was upset that some of the contents of the room had
been lost. 'We made such an effort to save everything. I can remember picking the stuff up from the floor, it was sopping wet, it had just
been abandoned there.' I asked Rosemary if she knew who had been
the first person to open up the room. She believed it was either
Douglas Blane, a trustee of the Spitalfields Building Trust, or David

Jacobs, a local historian. The addresses she gave me proved to be many years out of date. I had no success in finding either of them.

I realized that Rosemary would also have seen the synagogue in close to its original state. I asked her to describe it to me. 'It was amazing when we entered, Torah mantles just lying there, dripping on the seats where the rain had come through. It was very evocative to go into the synagogue and sense that atmosphere. It was very special, as though the spirits of the past congregation never quite

left.'

I asked Rosemary if she had ever found a photograph of David Rodinsky, explaining I was desperate for an image of the man, 'No, never, not a single one, although I was aware of a black-and-white photograph of his sister.' So that's who it was. I had come across this picture and been curious about it, a faint image of a sad face, framed by a large hood, making it difficult to distinguish whether the person was male or female. I had photographed the photograph myself, just as I had documented every artefact in the Rodinsky archive. When the reel of film returned from the developers I found that an accidental double exposure had occurred with just that one image, which I now know to be of David Rodinsky's sister Bessie. Her face had superimposed itself on top of one of the many language dictionaries in the room. This book must have been one of the first English-to-Hebrew dictionaries published after the new state of Israel was formed: the title of the book was *Evrit Hadasha*. These words had appeared over the top of Bessie's lips: The New Hebrew Language. This photograph none the less became my own portrait

of Rodinsky.

Every day I would open up the synagogue building and immediately go upstairs to Rodinsky's room to look through his artefacts, to catalogue and photograph them. Often, the atmosphere up there was so thick with dust and tension I would find it impossible to continue working and I'd make my way downstairs to the more neutral environment of the synagogue office. This was situated right at the front of the building: the window faced directly on to Princelet Street, allowing me a view of the world outside the time warp of the old synagogue. The most common sight was of muscular Bangladeshi men, struggling past with bloodstained white aprons, precariously balancing skinned dead sheep on their shoulders, on their way to the Indian restaurants on Brick Lane. There were always plenty of young boys running up and down the street with bundles of cloth and cardboard patterns, in a hurry to deliver them to one of the many workshops in the former Huguenot silk weavers' lofts above the old Georgian houses on the street. Occasionally I would wave at Bill Fishman passing by with an eager crowd on a tour of the Jewish East End, and every now and then the scene would be brightened as dark-haired women in brightly coloured silk saris drifted by.

It must have been mid-November when I saw him for the first time. It was far too cold to go up to the attic and I was spending all my time in the downstairs office, huddled in front of a small electric heater, wearing at least four layers of clothes. I was reading some terrible book on the Holocaust (research for an exhibition I was putting together for Rabbi Hugo Gryn at West London Synagogue) when I glimpsed his dark silhouette out of the corner of my eye. I only saw him for a fleeting second, as he scuttled rapidly past the window, but that glimpse made enough of an impression for me to run to the corridor, quickly open the heavy wooden doors and search the street for sight of him. I was just in time to see his tall, hunched figure, wrapped in a long dark coat, turn into Brick Lane. He was pushing a large trolley full of cardboard boxes, and as he crossed the road I caught a quick look at his face. He looked ancient, his skin was so pale and transparent it gave off a bluish hue, and hanging majestically underneath his nose was a long trailing white beard. His coat and large black hat were tattered and worn but unmistakably the costume of a Hasidic Jew, an unusual sight in the 1990s in Whitechapel. I was beside myself with excitement and fear. Convinced I had just sighted David Rodinsky, I ran out into the street after him. By the time I reached the corner I had seen him turn into only moments before, he had disappeared.

I was wild with frustration. I asked everyone locally about the mysterious figure I had seen but no one knew who I was talking about. I became convinced I had seen an apparition. My sleep was

fitful and full of nightmarish visitations. I began to feel nervous
about my quest to find Rodinsky. I found the synagogue, and particularly Rodinsky's room, a harder place to work in, and this had
little to do with the freezing winter temperature inside it.

A few weeks later, when I had convinced myself I had imagined the
whole episode, I saw him again. It happened just as before. I was
reading in the front office when his silhouette sped past the window.
This time I was ready, I leaped out of my chair and out on to the
street. He was pushing the same trolley heaped high with cardboard
boxes and wearing the exact same outfit I had seen him in previously,
but this time the ice on the pavement was slowing his progress. I
caught up with him easily and, with my heart racing, I followed him,
from a safe distance, into Brick Lane. He did not go far, stopping outside a small shop opposite the mosque and fumbling for some keys in
his coat pocket. After locating them he turned a key in the lock and
pushed the trolley inside. I stood on the corner watching. Eventually
I summoned up the courage to walk by, casually glancing into the
window of the shop he had just entered. I read the shop sign from the
other side of the street: 'C.H.N. Katz, String and Paper Bags'. The
shop window was thick with dust and unlit; lying inside it, on an old
piece of tea-stained paper, sat three large balls of brown string and a
couple of rolls of sticky tape. Behind the window, inside the shop, I
could see a long wooden counter and, on the floor, many large packages and cardboard boxes. At the end of the counter was a doorway
and sitting inside it, next to a desk piled high with papers, I could see
my Hasid, reading from a thick red book. I was desperate to go in and
speak to him, but my nerves got the better of me and I passed by and
turned back up Princelet Street.

For weeks, each day on my way to the synagogue I would pass by
the shop and look in to see if he was there. Most of the time the shop
was empty. I only saw him once again, but never mustered the
courage to go inside.

Then I received a telephone call from the Whitechapel Art
Gallery. The gallery was commissioning a few local artists to create
public art works for part of the Whitechapel Open Exhibition, and

the caller asked if I might be interested in participating. I was delighted to be asked. They told me they wanted to show the installations in shop windows in Brick Lane, and thought my work would be most suitably placed in the only remaining Jewish shop in the street, C.H.N. Katz. I could not believe it. They had approached the owner of the shop, and he had laughed them out of the door, saying he had no interest in contemporary art and to leave him alone. The Whitechapel Art Gallery was aware of my work and contacts in the area and thought if I approached the man personally he might be swayed. With my heart in my mouth I asked them for his name. Mr Katz. The moment I saw him enter the shop I had doubted whether he was David Rodinsky, but I realized now that Mr Katz would be an

excellent person to interview. He might have known Rodinsky and
I was sure he would have interesting tales to tell of the area. I was
aware that a man as orthodox as he appeared to be might not even
be able to have me in the shop alone with him, never mind be interviewed by me. But I was going to try anyway, the very next day.

A bell rang loudly as I opened the door, but it was some minutes
before Mr Katz appeared from his office. His face was even more
wondrous close up and he asked me, in a voice that sounded just like
my grandfather's, how he could help. I introduced myself, telling
him I was working at the old synagogue in Princelet Street. He told
me he knew it well and used to worship there himself for many
years. I asked if he lived in Princelet Street as I had seen him there a
number of times now, but he lived in Stamford Hill and had some
storage space in Princelet Street. I asked him if he had known David
Rodinsky. 'Of course, the *shames* at the synagogue, I knew him well.
We would speak together in Yiddish, I thought he was very clever.'
He told me he knew his daughter, a Mrs Lipman who used to visit
Mr Katz once a year on the way to light a *Yahrzeit* candle for her
father at the Princelet Street synagogue. He described her as old and
frail. He couldn't give me any other details but promised to get her
address the next time he saw her. She would be my best lead yet – I
pressed him for more information, asking thousands of questions:
what did he look like? what happened to him? did you ever meet his
father? I had discovered from Rosemary Weinstein and through
looking through the artefacts that David Rodinsky had shared his
attic room with his sister Bessie and his mother for at least some of
the time he lived there. But I could find no information about his
father apart from one creased sepia photograph with the Hebrew
word *Abba*, 'father', written across the top in black ink.

Mr Katz knew nothing of the father and became irritable at my
questioning. I had learnt, from the many interviews I had conducted
with elderly people in the area, not to push too much at the first
meeting, so I held back, realizing I had asked too much too soon.
Instead, I let Mr Katz do the talking. He was very curious as to why
a young woman like me would want to work in a disused syna-

gogue. I told him my story. When he heard the names of my grandparents, he became very animated. He remembered them and their
watchmaking shop in Princelet Street. This more than made up for
him not being the elusive David Rodinsky: I loved to hear stories of
my grandparents.

That first visit must have lasted at least an hour. I was about to
leave when I remembered the original purpose of my visit.
Fortunately Mr Katz had already inquired what I did for a living,
'apart from haunting old synagogues', he had said with a smile. He
was very interested in my work and had a thorough look through my
portfolio. I think he was the first person ever to whom I did not need
to explain a single piece of my work. He understood very clearly
what I was trying to do. I showed him the work the Whitechapel Art
Gallery wanted me to place in his shop window: objects from my

grandfather's watchmaking shop, sealed in resin and steel. Mr Katz had tears in his eyes when he saw them and he agreed to let me show my work in his window, which filled me with joy.

I installed the work with his generous help the following week. By the time I finished I could happily say we were firm friends. I would go into the shop for a chat whenever I was passing and he was there. About two weeks after the work had been installed I was walking past one day when he waved me inside. He told me there was a message for me, and returned from the back room with a flash postcard from a film company based in Brixton. The director was interested in filming my work for a documentary about Spitalfields. I thanked Mr Katz and arranged to meet the director at the synagogue in Princelet Street the following week. On the designated day, the doorbell of the synagogue rang sharply at ten o'clock. I opened up to see two smartly dressed men. The first introduced himself as Bob Bentley, the director. He then introduced the second man. 'I hope you don't mind, but I have brought along Iain Sinclair, the writer. He is also being involved in the film, talking about the area. I thought you two would be interested to meet one another and I know Iain has seen your work.'

Here was the man that had written the article 'The Man Who Became a Room', who I knew had been one of the first people to see Rodinsky's room. I had also recently read his book *Downriver* and was anxious to ask him about the Rodinsky research he had already conducted. I was aware we might have much in common, as we were both working around similar themes and in the same area. I remembered going cold as I read Sinclair's novel *White Chapell Scarlet Tracings*, and the vivid descriptions of the Jewish cemetery in Brady Street behind which I had lived since I moved to London many years ago. I told Iain about this and asked him about Rodinsky's room. We were soon ignoring the director who had introduced us. Iain expressed real interest in my work and invited me to meet him the following week to discuss it. We met in the back room of the Seven Stars pub on Brick Lane. Iain asked me to bring my portfolio and we talked late into the night about my work, his projects, Rodinsky's room, and Whitechapel. Iain told me he was writing a new book about London and wanted to include some artists in it. He was interested in writing about the work I was showing in Katz's window.

A few weeks after my meeting with Iain I became very ill. My asthma got out of control and I could barely move. Eventually I was diagnosed as having pneumonia. I spent six weeks lying on the sofa trying to breathe. The smoggy air of East London was suffocating me and I knew that returning to the dusty synagogue would not help. Moreover, being there was stifling me creatively. I needed to step back for a while, to take a studio somewhere neutral and to let my weakened lungs recover. A friend passed on details about an arts project in Arad, Israel, close to Masada and the Dead Sea. It seemed perfect: a six-month residency that would allow me the time and space to create my own work in a peaceful desert setting, thousands of miles away from the lure of Rodinsky's room. Arad is also world-famous as an asthma centre, boasting the purest air on earth. It stands on a mountaintop above the shimmering salt fields of the Dead Sea. I applied for the residency and was accepted.

While recovering in the sleepy desert town, I received a letter from Iain Sinclair. He wished me well and asked if I would be interested in making some work based on David Rodinsky for an exhibition that he was setting up to launch his new book, *Lights Out for the Territory*. The book included the piece he had written about me after our talk in the Seven Stars. He sent me a copy of the text:

> Lichtenstein was obsessive, ritualistic in her procedures. The quest for an identity, for a family that would confirm her essence and existence, took her on a series of journeys: to Poland, to New York, to Israel – and inevitably, to Whitechapel. Each exploration – interviews, recordings, buildings and contents listed and photographed – brought her closer to the point of origin. When it was all gathered (like the manic accumulations of holy junk in David Rodinsky's Princelet Street attic), she would cancel herself out. She would be free to travel in other dimensions. The

moment she confronted the existential terror of loss came when, as a teenager, she set herself to photograph a wall of photographs, Holocaust victims, children. She couldn't look at what she was capturing. She convinced herself that she had identified a provisional account of her own face. Her 1993 installation *Shoah*, at West London Synagogue, was, amongst other things, an attempt to appease this double (in an earlier rehearsal, at art school in Sheffield, she had covered all the mirrors in the college with printed sheets – faint impressions of the fated portraits. The gesture was unpopular. Lichtenstein replaced the white hoods as soon as they were torn down). For *Shoah*, Lichtenstein once again used photographs from the eradicated Polish ghettos, printed on to torn strips of linen. She embraced difficulty, the stitching and sewing, the long hours that became a protracted meditation on the impossibility of her project.

She would let nothing go, not an envelope, not a lock of hair. There was a quiet ferocity which was not to be found, or looked for, in Whiteread's *House*. *House* was a concept, the human elements were the flaws: it was the husk of an idea, extinguished in execution. The sooner it was disposed of the better: only then could it work on memory, displace its own volume. Lichtenstein would have filled albums from corners of curtain, cabinets of splinters. She had grown up among antique dealers, shuffling through boxes of depersonalized stuff, optional histories, invented pedigrees. Pawnbrokers, jewellers, gold merchants: these are the true custodians of heritage, knowing both the price *and* the value of everything. Lichtenstein's art was inspired by a love of these indestructibles, residual whispers. From the temperature that remained in found objects, she constructed new ceremonies.

It felt strange to read about myself as a character in one of Sinclair's books. I felt uneasy, but was impressed by his ability to tap into my work and life. I wrote back to him, agreeing to make a work about Rodinsky, hoping I would be back in Britain to attend the exhibition personally.

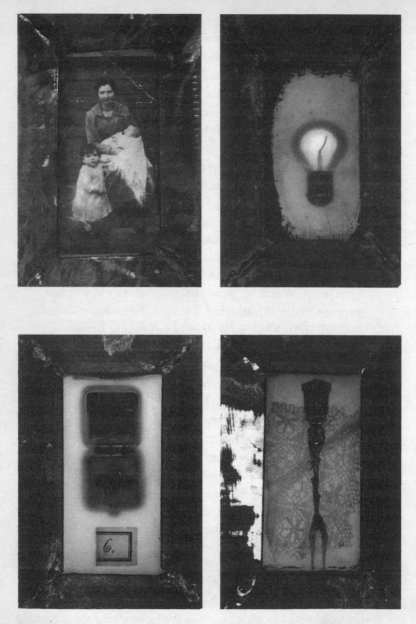

'Ner Htamid' – artwork by Rachel Lichtenstein shown in Katz's window.

WITNESSING RODINSKY

Iain Sinclair

ASTON: Where were you born?
DAVIES (*darkly*): What do you mean?
ASTON: Where were you born?

Harold Pinter, *The Caretaker*

I was thirsty for stories of the area, a good listener. A sponge. I checked out evidence, walking through accounts of notorious crimes (they contradicted each other). I eavesdropped on retired villains, challenged maps. Pedantically, I tried to fit this landscape to the visionary riffs of Blake and De Quincey. I pillaged legends, stole names (Swedenborg Gardens) back from their well-earned obscurity. Understood how men became places. How they could be recalled from the great dream, where proper humans with birth certificates mingle with immortal fictions, with Sherlock Holmes, Fu Manchu, Dr Jekyll, Dr Mabuse and the Golem of Prague.

To be recalled was to be betrayed. I cut the grass around the Hawksmoor churches and cleared shards of broken sherry bottles from beneath benches of sleeping vagrants. I was a stalker of rumours, a nark, an unsalaried spy. I actively searched out the labouring jobs that would feed my obsession with mythical geography, with potential energies locked in blighted ghettos, transitional end zones. The ullage cellar of Truman's Brewery in Brick Lane was the ultimate resource, a living metaphor I had been waiting for years to invade.

I'd worked my way in from the container-loading sheds of
Stratford East, through the never-ending white lines of Hackney
Marshes, to the scrawny grasslands of Limehouse, Poplar and
Canning Town; and now, with the brewery, to the heart of
Whitechapel. The source, the well-spring, of all the mysteries.

It wasn't easy. You had to be vetted, even for casual work; examined, checked for needle tracks. But the rooms where these
interviews took place were panelled, collegiate. There was a sense of
initiation. From the windows, as the official read out his long list of
questions, I could see heavy, horse-drawn carts jolting across the
cobbled yard. The brewery bells marked the passage of time, let the
plumbers (whom I started with, carrying tools, passing spanners)
know when to quit their hammocks (slung between hot-water
pipes), pop down to the betting shop to catch the last race, before
signing on for overtime. It couldn't last.

Speculators moved in, the days of benevolent paternalism were
drawing to a close. The brewery was no longer a labyrinth to be
explored, a reservoir of memories, fabulous and documented, but a
land value; an element in a chain of dereliction that stretched to the
Pedley Street railway bridge. I had only the vaguest sense of this, the
physical experience of the place, but the opportunity it gave me to
explore the neighbourhood was overwhelming. The Jewish ghetto
was a memory trace and Bangladeshi immigration was still a trickle.
There was one corner shop in Sheba Street, a dingy, cat-smelling
cave with lurid boiled sweets in bottles, damp fag packets, fossilized
Mars bars, pre-war newspapers. I dropped in most afternoons;
somewhere on the circuit between the Seven Stars and the Nazrul,
on the looping walk that followed its inevitable bias towards the
Minories and the river, the nether reaches of Mile End Road and the
sealed Jewish burial ground off Brady Street. Condemned tenements. Anarchist alleys. Waste lots with a sudden uplift of open
ground that looked back towards the City, jagged sunsets under
furious clouds.

The pavement outside the shop is frosted with broken glass. Black
smoke. Later there was a headline in the local press that lodged in

my mind as a chanted chorus, the title of a film that would never be made: PETROL BOMB IN SHEBA STREET. The first racist attack. Approved by elements in the brewery, some self-appointed Kray foot soldiers. The ones who spent their afternoons polishing their leather-interior Rovers. But, equally, the incident was an affront to a number of the older men, the storytellers. They remembered nights of fire-watching, the bomb that landed in the Jewish burial ground, depositing shattered corpses on the roof of the gravediggers' shelter. They remembered everything about the war. There was a Ripper specialist who photographed, with a plate camera, all the relevant sites. There were Cable Street marchers, pro and anti Mosley. There were geezers who had made up the numbers with veteran gang boss Jack Spot, and honoured him for his raids on the blackshirts. There were glassy-eyed alcoholics, a quart of stout from a pewter jug for breakfast to steady the shakes, who had been there when the Twins went toe-to-toe with the Watney Street mob. There were closet antiquarians who could give you the word on Spring-Heel'd Jack and Jack Sheppard. Men who had seen albino crocodiles in the ullage tanks. But in all of this, the hours of overtime, the nights in the cold store clustered around the lager tap, the formless afternoons in the complimentary bar, I heard no mention of David Rodinsky. Not one word about the vanishing caretaker of Princelet Street and his *Mary Celeste* chamber. This was an unrequired story. My feeling now is that the routines I listened to were the ones I solicited. I was looking for confirmations and extensions of what I already knew. Rodinsky was an empty space, a lacuna; that which was not to be uncovered, something sealed and forgotten. This was the period, the Seventies, between his disappearance and the breaking open of the attic room. He wasn't visible or invisible. He had neither presence nor absence. His story hadn't been formulated. It was too early to fit it into the Spitalfields canon. It belonged to an era that had not yet been rediscovered, or reinterpreted. Like the ghetto itself, the floating zone between the City and the covert world of the East End, the myth was on ice. In limbo. Unactivated. With the reimagining of the area that the developers, the energy pirates, of the Eighties would enforce –

the need to ground their presumptuous brochures in a neverworld of Huguenots, dancing Hasids, and blandly sinister Masonic serial killers – Rodinsky, his curious history and his spontaneous combustion, would be dragged into the light. Composed. Contrived. Authenticated. Grant us a ghost in the attic, a broken weaver's loom, and we will do you a dozen kosher Georgian units, at 200K a throw, for the Far Eastern catalogue. Hong Kong bankers were buying up Heneage Street apartments, site unseen, before Chris Patten had got his dogs out of quarantine.

In October 1987 David Rodinsky blinked into public consciousness when Patrick Wright published an essay, in the *London Review of Books*, linking the Princelet Street story ('a post-hoc fable of the gentrifying immigrant quarter') with a perceptive account of the current state of play – New Georgians, fogies, heritage sharks – in an area that had just woken up to its revised identity as 'Spitalfields'. (Banglatown was not yet a banner slung across Brick Lane.) Wright's characteristically thorough piece (as much lecture or performance as text) was entitled 'Rodinsky's Place'. The notion of this disappearance, the manipulation of its meaning, was foregrounded as the metaphor from which any understanding of the 'zone of transition' would begin. There had been, for years, an imaginary ha-ha (the hyperbolic Shoreditch) filled with dead dogs, broken bottles, chicken's feet and yellow vomit, between the City and its eastern neighbour. Whitechapel, according to Wright, had been 'red-lined' by banks and building societies. Without credit, the area was being starved, forced back on compensatory images from an heroic past. The City was happy that it should drink itself into oblivion. A healthy geography is defined by its liquidity. Exploiters were delighted that their near neighbour, once and forever a service territory (prostitution, lunchtime boozing sessions, strippers, curries), should become a desert. Let it crumble. Let it parch. So that the jackals could move in, colonize the future. The City was a nest of visionaries. They saw what is now visible to the rest of us: mustard-coloured offices, investment opportunities, canalside cubicles in place of the rag warehouses, the vendors of single shoes. *They* were the romantics, not the bemused Jewish writers, such as Emanuel Litvinoff or Willy Goldman, who returned to find traces of their childhood among the spectral survivors. Litvinoff savours 'the same broken tiles in the passage, the same rickety stairs, the pervasive smell of cats'. But it is not the same place. It can only be the same if he becomes what he was, unburdened of what he now knows. Nobody else sees him, understands what he is, his status. He's as invisible as Rodinsky. The streets, he believes, owe more to Warsaw and Kishinev than to the rest of London. The street market is immortal. The introductions to the reissues of accounts by these sober returnees (Litvinoff's *Journey through a Small Planet*, Goldman's *East End My Cradle*) are melancholy things. 'Compulsive forays', Goldman calls his excursions. The 'here' they remember is no longer to be found. They are looking for themselves. Goldman locates an eloquent absence: 'the demolished White Chapel that gave its name to the area is now a patch of grass; former synagogues in Brick Lane are mosques . . . I am for ever a prisoner in this not too tender trap. I can never escape from it and I would never want to.' Litvinoff recalls a failed scholarship that might have altered the trajectory of his life. 'Outside it was raining. I sat on the window ledge and carved my initials in the wood. When I looked they were still there, jagged and irregular, "E.L." So his memory had not let him down. There had once been such a person. His fingers traced the heat left in the indentations, the hard evidence.

I met Patrick Wright. He was passing through Hackney: a book for each address (*On Living in an Old Country* for Stoke Newington, *A Journey through Ruins* for Dalston – with his exploration of Dorset tank tracks, screwball fascist gentry, cloaked visionaries on every hilltop, reserved for his retreat to a Cambridge satellite). There was a lot of drift on the wrong side of Queensbridge Road. The incredulous in search of temporary credibility: embryo New Labour gentrifying Victorian husks. Wright, in St Philip's Road, was amused to see his near neighbour, the all-purposes culture pundit Waldemar Januszczak, doing his best to get to grips with the area's market

gardening tradition by pruning a lime tree with a pair of pliers.
Tony and Cherie Blair had bought into Mapledene Road, where
they could gaze across the great divide – hurtling traffic out of
bandit country, future exiles heading for Lea Bridge Road and the
M11 – at the spectral tower blocks of Holly Street, the nightmare
estate with the pit-bull lifts, darkened hundred-yard-long corridors,
and boarded-up windows waiting for the glaziers after the latest
jumper had made an unscheduled flight from the nightmare. This,
Wright considered, was the defining image of the era: the rusticated
cottage banged up against an apocalyptic skyscape. This is where
Blair developed his political skills, outmanoeuvring the Labour hard
left of the Queensbridge ward.

I visited Wright and was shown two of his most valued relics: a
red Letts Schoolgirl's diary that had once belonged to David
Rodinsky, and a silver fork engraved with the initials *T.F.B.* This
sanctified implement had passed down from an ancestor of
Wright, Thomas Fowell Buxton, a Quaker brewmaster who, in
October 1816, made a speech at the Mansion House appealing to
the City merchants for charitable aid for the destitute of
Whitechapel. There was, it struck me, a nice conjunction between
the twin fetishes, the diary and the fork. The diary had been 'rescued' from Rodinsky's attic (it would later be passed on to Rachel
Lichtenstein) as inspiration for the essay Wright was composing.
Things were vanishing so fast from Princelet Street that the social
historian felt obliged to preserve this significant document, a
jumble of translations and gnomic self-promptings. The fork
could just as easily have been fished out from the clutter on
Rodinsky's table, or been arranged on a suitably greasy plate in one
of Severs's tableaux in Folgate Street.

Wright explained how he had come across the Rodinsky story. He
had heard it from the architectural historian Dan Cruickshank.
Cruickshank was an enthusiastic New Georgian, a serious truffler in
the byways of Spitalfields. The disappearance of the synagogue caretaker, with his presumed cabbalistic practices, was a story fitted to its
time. Those with a vested interest in defining Spitalfields as a zone of

peculiar and privileged resonance needed a mythology to under-write the property values. Rodinsky, one erased life, one blank biography among so many, was elected. Essentially the trick of the thing was to strip him of his history and to translate him directly into the substance of the room that had housed him. I'd heard no mention of the tale in the Seventies – because it hadn't been formu-lated. Spitalfields was still an antiquarian conceit. The area, when I spoke of it, was Whitechapel. Friends referred to 'Brick Lane' or 'Cheshire Street'. 'The market'. 'The bagel shop'. 'The back room of the Seven Stars'.

Wright, following up on Cruickshank's hint, saw Rodinsky as the focus for an essay, a chapter of his *Journey through Ruins*. And, as much the vampire, I was hot to audition the Vanishing Jew for the cast of my novel *Downriver*. Wright had already been pressed into service in the character of Fredrik Hanbury, and we charged south down Queensbridge Road, over the humped bridge, into the terri-tory; in alliance, competitive, eager to see what could be made of this lost scholar. My sense, at that time, climbing the rickety stairs, poking about the shuttered chamber, was the sense I still have: a man who had become a room.

We are sucked, by a vortex of expectation, into the synagogue, and up the unlit stairs: we are returning, approaching something that has always been there. The movement is inevitable. But we also sensed immediately that we were trespassing on a space that could soon be neutralized as a 'Museum of Immigration': as if immigration could be anything other than an active response to untenable circumstances – a brave, mad, greedy charge at some vision of the future; a thrusting forward of the unborn into a region they could neither claim nor desire. Immigration is a blowtorch held against an anthill. It can always be sentimentalized, but never re-created. It is as persistent and irreversible as the passage of glaciers and cannot – without diminishing its courage – be codified, and trapped in cases of nostalgia. But we ourselves were ethical Luddites, forcibly entering the reality of David Rodinsky's territorial self: the apparent squalor and the imposed mystery.

There was no mystery, except the one we manufactured in our quest for the unknowable: shocking ourselves into a sense of our own human vulnerability. We were a future race of barbarians, too tall for the room in which we were standing. We fell gratefully upon the accumulation of detail: debased agents, resurrectionists with cheap Japanese cameras.

There was nothing astonishing in the disappearance of this man. He could not be more available. It was all still here: the wrappings, the culture, the work he had attempted, his breath on the glass – and even, if we carried it away, his story. We could provide the missing element, fiction, using only the clues that Rodinsky had blatantly planted. Fredrik's fateful choice in picking up the diary made it certain that the unfinished work of this chamber would be taken to its inevitable, though still unresolved, conclusion.

The man remains, *it is the room itself that vanishes*. You are looking into a facsimile, a cunning fake, as unreal as the mock-up of Thomas Hardy's study in Dorchester Museum. But the fake was crafted by none other than the apparent victim! The room's original has shifted to another place, achieved another level of reality. You would have to share Rodinsky's fate to find it . . .

The room emerges as a deconstructed shrine, sucking in the unwary, tying them by their hair to the weighted furniture. No one who crosses the threshold is unmarked. These psychic tourists escape with modest relics, souvenirs that breed and multiply in their pockets like pieces of the true cross. They propagate a dangerous heresy. They are scorched by shadows that do not belong to any three-dimensional object. Rodinsky is assembled, like a golem, in the heat of their attention. He is present in all the curious and seductive fragments left in this cell. And whatever was ferreted away behind all this stimulating rubbish has completely evaporated.

The assistant editors of the LRB had flagged Wright's Rodinsky piece, in red caps across the top of the front page, as SPITALFIELDS MAGIC. Beneath the teasing headline was a dim, inadequately reproduced cover photo (credited to Danny Gralton). The image is curated as 'coming from the Heritage Centre', with Rodinsky glossed as the caretaker of 'a Huguenot silk-weaver's loft'. The matrix of grey dots, floating and re-forming, offers a heavy, late-Victorian wardrobe as a device to hold down the speculative vortices of Wright's prose. The Gralton photograph is a paperweight. (Wright is much taken with the story, the afterlife, of this wardrobe – which he describes as 'classic 1890s repro'. What became of it? Was is sold off? Chopped up? Institutionalized? I was able to put his mind at rest. The ugly piece, after disappearing for years, is now safely wedged in the small storeroom at the back of Rodinsky's garret.) The wardrobe was an avatar of Rodinsky, a lugubrious displacement, a vertical tomb or conjuror's box through which he had stepped into another dimension. Rags spilled from open drawers, gravitating towards the exploded library of papers on the floor. The mirrored back of one of the doors reflects an unmade bed. There is no other space. The decorated shoulders on top of the wardrobe sweep towards a low wooden ceiling. The heavy object enforces claustrophobia, dividing light into rectangular panels; steep shelves with saucers and obscure domestic instruments that may be pressed into service for ritual purposes.

This cumbersome item of furniture, part barrier, part entrance to a parallel dimension (the mirrored panels access the worlds-within-worlds aspect), takes its place in the mythology of the Holocaust. The secret space that becomes a room for refugees. A room that can only be entered through the panels of the wardrobe. A room in which time moves slowly. A room in which fugitives, stopping their breaths, are granted invisibility. They vanish into their clothes, as in a Magritte painting.

Just such a space features in *Black Milk*, a novel by David Hartnett. Hartnett depicts a fictional ghetto, an enclosed city, a community of prisoners, threatened by dissolution, eradication.

Cattle-truck transports from the 'Spur' decimate the dwindling population, carrying their passengers to an unknown destination in the
east. *Black Milk*, with its echoes of Paul Celan, is a novel of the last
days; dreams, memories and ancestral archetypes are overwhelmed by
a fierce *realpolitik* of hunger, pain and the need to survive.

Josef Rosenfeld, once a scholar writing a thesis on Jewish messianic movements, has become an administrator, a compiler of
death lists, a functionary in the Judenrat administration. But,
through his sponsorship of the ecstatic visionary, Mendel, and his
creation of a private chamber behind his filing cabinet (a chamber
in which a record of everything that happened in the ghetto could
be preserved), he manages to keep faith with a notion of otherness,
privileged consciousness, the eternal. 'He would slide the cabinet
gratingly aside and step again into his secret world. . . . A stark geometry of witness and lament. It was his core these days, his centre
of gravity. As Mystical Theology had been.' The unseen chamber
has a compensatory function. It makes the other life bearable.

In the desperation of the final clearance, Rosenfeld decides that
his wife and children must be hidden in a hollow behind the
wardrobe in their room. 'The back of the wardrobe had been
removed and leant against the wall. The trick had been performed.
Something or somebody had become invisible.' Wardrobes and
invisibility, hidden spaces. There are so many curious resonances; as
if in listing these things, putting them together, an alchemical
process is initiated. A formula written down. The weight of the
wardrobe – its massive domesticity, the intricacy of the drawers,
brass handles, mirrors, the smell of varnish scorched by candles,
hairballs trapped among the stiff bristles of a blackened brush –
plays against the interior light on the far side. The possibility of dis-
incarnation, weightlessness, flight.

One of those who will be sealed inside Rosenfeld's wardrobe is a
consumptive freedom fighter, a girl called Rachel. Rachel was first
glimpsed as a wraith at a high window ('Come away from the
window Rachel you'll catch your death'). The passion of this 'ado-
lescent underground activist' is gradually transmuted to something

febrile and dependent. Reluctantly, she agrees to enter the wardrobe. 'The person who had been made invisible was about to be magicked back into the world.'

Hartnett has contrived an effective switch: Rachel, an eidetic seizure, framed behind a window, has glided to the foreground of the narrative. She has moved from someone whose voice is unheard, the subject of dreamlike sexual imaginings, to the status of adopted daughter, inhabitant of the family room. When the final purge comes, she steps into the wardrobe – where, despite the discovery of this hiding place, she remains unseen.

Obviously, reading *Black Milk*, I noticed the coincidence of the name, Rachel, the activist who is drawn into a narrative from which she can never escape. The observer who becomes part of a building. And then of one room in that building. Then a wardrobe. Then nothing.

There is an image of Rodinsky's room by the Hackney-based photographer Marc Atkins. It was taken some years after the Danny Gralton sequence, the clutter of the newly-opened loft. The first excitement of the uncatalogued rubbish, books, rags, mattresses, newspapers, has been tempered. A different story is taking form. Everyone wanted to hold on to the earlier version until they had extracted the elements that would justify their own researches. Architectural historians, social reformers, poets, performance artists, makers of MTV promos, Gothic F/X specialists. Robert Hewison, a cultural magpie, hopping in the wake of Patrick Wright, used one of the Gralton series – from the same position that Atkins would later adopt – in his book *Future Tense (A New Art for the Nineties)*. Hewison doesn't mention Rodinsky, but speaks of a space 'little bigger than a Victorian billiard room' that is 'eloquently empty'. An assertion that Gralton's image loudly contradicts. His black-and-white print, taking a dole of natural light from the unshuttered window, offers a perfect representation of *fin de siècle* romanticism: the garret of the starving artist. Upright piano, bottle and books on table, framed reproduction of Millet's *Angelus*, the unmade bed, and the floor strewn with papers, abandoned drafts. Marc Atkins, when

he contrives his composition, allows the light to fuzz at the window. It must be late afternoon, the sun moving around the spire of Christ Church. The bed has vanished. The books are gone. Weavers' bobbins and reels of cotton have magically appeared on the shelves. The table is bare. Apart from the young woman who is balanced against its edge, glancing up from an open book. It is Rachel Lichtenstein in Rodinsky's place. Backlit, looking away, at the beginning of the performance. Learning how to interpret herself, how to work the compromise between detective, revealer of Rodinsky's history, and artist of the room. How will she articulate this 'unmanifest existence', this pulling and drifting between worlds? How will she transcribe a work whose essence is to remain unfinished, incomplete, abandoned?

The reason I had come across *Black Milk* was the cover photograph. Another Marc Atkins image. A young girl is posed against a wall, shadowed, eyes down, modest, contemplative, or obedient to the photographer's instructions. The mood is nicely managed, solemn. There is an understated melancholy (with the advantage of an exposed, but tightly cropped, bosom). This model is not, and cannot be, an impersonation of the Rachel in Hartnett's fiction. That Rachel is wasted, dying, lit by internal fires. She's a crow, possessed by the story in which she finds herself. This other Rachel, this performance of a Rachel on the cover of Hartnett's book, is quite different. She has switched everything off, turned her cheek to model the passage of light. She measures the constriction of the room to which she has been brought.

And this is where Atkins's design folds back into Hartnett's novel, where the true connection is forged: on the rear cover the image is repeated, in a reduced form, but less tightly cropped. Now a brick wall is revealed outside the window. Now this room belongs to the ghetto, doubles for the space behind Hartnett's vanishing wardrobe, and for Rodinsky's attic. Now the place where the photograph was taken comes into its own.

Atkins lived at this period in a flat above another deactivated synagogue, in Heneage Street, a tributary running off the east side of Brick Lane. And that is where he staged the *Black Milk* cover shot. That is where his model was asked to transform herself into the incarnate ghost of a fiction. You had to look hard to find the traces of this synagogue, the Poltava; once a study house and *Landsmannschaft*. An association formed against the indifference of an alien city; a place that sustained the people of one small district. The galleries of the synagogue could be seen in a Bangladeshi supermarket, heaped with sacks of rice, gaudy with spices and glittering tins. Atkins sublet a long narrow room on the first floor, once the rabbi's apartment. The room in which David Rodinsky was seen for the last time. (Or, at any rate, the last eyewitness report that I had of the man.)

I'd published, shortly after my first visit to Rodinsky's room, a brief account of the place and the rapidly accumulating mythology. And I'd received a letter from a Mr Ian Shames of Stamford Hill who wanted to correct my 'assumption'. Mr Shames was the son-in-law

of the Princelet Street rabbi and had met Rodinsky on several
occasions.

> It was in 1948, while working at the German Hospital in Dalston
> as a male nurse, I attended a bar mitzvah at the Heneage Street
> synagogue, & to my surprise I met David, he was there for the
> *Kiddush*!
> He recognized me immediately, in the few years of my
> absence he had grown taller, more manly, & very coherent. He
> still lived at No. 19 Princelet Street, & to my surprise he was
> quite fluent speaking Arabic. This came about when I told him
> of the many places I had visited, & could converse to him in
> Arabic, as I had seen service at the Suez Canal & Cairo. This was
> my last meeting with him, & this ends my story.

Atkins, by whatever accident, had found the perfect location in
which to photograph an absence. The wall, as I stared at it, absorbed
the shape of the young woman, swallowed this 'Rachel' imperson-
ator, revealed itself as a curtain of brick. A screen on which to project
any self-declared fantasy.

The early Sixties were a time of disappearances. Michelangelo
Antonioni's *L'Avventura*, despite the scorn of the *Cahiers du Cinéma*
critics, was a festival prizewinner that settled itself for long runs in
most of the European capitals. Lethargy, a bleached landscape;
dispiritedness. Not the kind of film Rodinsky would have walked to.
The Chelsea Classic was too fierce a yomp. Desiccated art movies
didn't belong on his list. But his battered copy of the *London A-Z* is
marked with numerous obscure journeys. Sometimes he made marginal annotations, sketched in the bits that the mappers had left
out. Antonioni's dead-soul-of-Europe pictorialism was not for
Rodinsky. But the abrupt vanishing of Lea Massari, the absorption
of her role at the centre of the narrative by Monica Vitti, became
part of the drift, the dream-weave of the period. A film that could be
represented by stills, reimagined from a set of unmoving images.

The Millet calendar in Rodinsky's room was fixed forever at January 1963. The diary that Patrick Wright carried away had its last entry on 'Tuesday 20 December 1961'. The mood of the time required a vanishing act (a few years earlier, those who had picked up on Samuel Beckett would have insisted on a non-appearance, an empty set 'borrowed' by cross-talking stooges).

There was a once a writer, based near Clapton Ponds, a London wanderer, who did keep pace with the culture. He was hot for it. His Hackney novel, written in the early Fifties, was not published until 1990. In *The Dwarfs* a group of young men jostle for position, test each other in midnight kitchens, debate bus routes, talk theatre and greasy-spoon philosophy. They're up for it, the tradition whereby each scholar has his partner; thesis and antithesis, come-on and put-down. Harold Pinter, by inheritance and training, was well prepared to write the 1960 play that could be seen as prophetically enacting the Rodinsky fable. *The Caretaker* was much more than a job description. It was the earliest and most obviously visible version of the gentrifiers' ghetto playlet.

The stage for the opening of *The Caretaker* – 'Under this mound an iron bed . . . On the gas stove a statue of Buddha . . . A couple of suitcases, a rolled carpet, a blow-lamp, a wooden chair on its side, boxes, a number of ornaments, a clothes horse, a few short planks of wood, a small electric fire and a very old electric toaster. Below this a pile of newspapers' – floats between the two Spitalfields sets, Rodinsky's attic and the Severs house. Rodinsky's newspapers and Severs's strategically overturned chair (to which he will direct the attention of the audience). Loquacious rubbish. Memory prompts. Props that provoke language, initiate bits of pre-ordained 'business'. (Rachel Lichtenstein began by cataloguing the theatre of the garret, listing everything. 'I have photographs of the room, the objects,' she told me. 'Do you have a photograph of Rodinsky?' I asked. 'No,' she said. She was still the assistant stage-manager, waiting for the arrival of the principal actor.)

It's a nice conceit to imagine that Rodinsky, fading from the Princelet Street try-out, reappears up West as the amnesiac Davies in

The Caretaker. 'You know,' says Mick, the sharp brother, the potential developer (forerunner of the Spitalfields sharks), 'believe it or not, you've got a funny kind of resemblance to a bloke I once knew in Shoreditch. Actually he lived in Aldgate . . .'

Pinter, Michael Billington reveals in *The Life and Work of Harold Pinter*, was not, as had been frequently supposed in the past, descended from a Portuguese Sephardic family; his Ashkenazic grandparents came from Poland and Odessa. Billington asserts that Pinter made more use of the particulars of place and family than the critics of the time acknowledged. A garden overlooking a laundry. Mare Street library. Springfield Park and the River Lea. Instead of attending classes at RADA, he wandered the town, rehearsing litanies of street names, geographical arcana, that he would later exploit. When he became an actor he took the stage name David Baron, after his paternal grandmother. Baron is also the surname of the autobiographical character Mark (in *The Dwarfs*), and it echoes another former pupil of Hackney Downs school, another compulsive walker, Alexander Baron, author of *The Lowlife*. Returning, damaged from the war, Baron spent a number of years staying in his mother's Hackney house while he tried to fade into the narrative of the streets.

One of Pinter's uncles, Judah, took the role of the family mystery man, the urban drifter. He may or may not have been a boxer. He lived for a time in Whitechapel, rather than aspirational Hackney. Something went wrong. He came home. And then, one day, he vanished. 'He didn't die in a raid or anything. He simply moved out of his room, he'd gone. . . . He didn't say goodbye or anything. He didn't explain himself,' Pinter recalls. 'I've been looking for him all my life and I've never found him.'

Davies is not Judah. Davies is nothing but himself, and barely that. He exists only under the special and peculiar circumstances of the play. The lights come on, he enters the set. They are killed and he is gone. He has no identity, no name, no papers: 'I changed my name! Years ago. I been going around under an assumed name!' His consciousness stretches as far as the limits of the metropolitan imagination, to the outer edge of Rodinsky's *London A-Z*. Hospitals, asylums, monasteries that might or might not give away shoes, these are his border zones; travel beyond them and his fragile identity would disappear altogether. The scattered circumference of buildings in which urban nightmares are earthed makes life within the limits of a single room possible. Rodinsky campaigned for years, letter after letter, to have his disturbed sister released from her confinement in Clayberry mental home. Mr Shames remembered her in his letter: 'from my deduction she may be there still'. Davies feeds on these scraps, anecdotes of lost lives. He sustains himself with his vision of a pilgrim's progress to Sidcup, the shining suburb on the hill. What Rodinsky, the other caretaker, leaves behind when he drifts out of temporal reality is the detritus, the set where Pinter's play can begin. The room without its other occupants (Rodinsky's mother and sister, the two brothers who give Davies shelter) is intolerable. Without conflict there is no theatre. The voices that worry Davies are a form of schizophrenic possession. He clings doggedly to his memories of a past that never happened, that is happening still. He makes 'noises' in the night. He's suspicious of the 'family of Indians' who live next door. *The Caretaker* is a performance piece in which a 'father' is expelled by his 'sons'. Rodinsky has no father. He's in a ghost play that can only be written by a self-elected daughter, a young woman who can do justice to the testimonies of the mute mother and the troubled sister. Rodinsky's disappearance, interpreted by the cultural markers of the period, begins to look like an act of selfless heroism. A stepping out into the blizzard. A necessary sacrifice made to clear the set. Rooms, Pinter has said, 'change shape at their own will'. The Princelet Street room, its shifts and moods, its objects and furniture, is all we have. The story begins and ends there.

The splinter in your eye is the best magnifying glass.

Barnet Litvinoff (quoting Adorno)

Rachel Lichtenstein's sense of the streets around Brick Lane, the tributaries with their resonant names (Buxton Street, Woodseer, Hanbury, Princelet, Fournier, Fashion), was a privileged one. Ownership: without title deeds or rent book. Ownership, in the high Blakean style, by assertion; by incorporating the everyday particular into a mythological structure. Title by possession. By love. By painstakingly recovered memory. She'd escaped, many times, to Israel, Poland, New York, but she always returned. There was unfinished business. She harried parties of harmless sentimentalists around sites that might still hold a brick or an inscription from which the story of Jewish settlement could be extracted. Her trump card, on these walking tours, was the Kosher Luncheon Club in Greatorex Street. This was a functioning survivor; step down, exhausted, from the street and enter a world of noise, communality, good food. 'Barley soup, herring, gefilte fish and chips,' as Rachel recalls. A menu that read like the programme for an Arnold Wesker revival. The luncheon club was a bustling, modestly priced, loud, quarrelsome place that had not yet been found out. The photographer Sharon Chazan, with her project (logging life in the orthodox community), caught it just before it disappeared.

Such generous refuges were no longer viable. There was no community to support them. The dining room and the synagogue to which it was attached drifted into limbo, dusty, closed-off, prey to parasites and art guerrillas. The standard pre-development scenario. A building so shamed, so occulted, that it tried to camouflage itself; to hypnotize passers-by into believing that it wasn't there. But these are the very buildings that untenured artists sniff out. Modesty is seen as a provocation. They have to find some way to dishonour the slumbering absence before their secret patrons, the developers, assert their *droit de seigneur*.

Lichtenstein, alerted to one of these 'live art' manifestations, returned to the synagogue alongside the luncheon club to witness a performance piece in which two young women systematically destroyed books of record of the vanished community. Her reaction was on a moneychangers-in-the-temple scale. She snatched back the relics, thereby becoming part of the show. Righteous anger against inappropriate and inconsequential rituals. Against the abandonment of this place by the charitable boards, the protectors of tradition. Against time. Her fury, publicly enacted, compensated for quieter events where she had to keep herself in check; events such as the retrievals from Rodinsky's room presented at the Slaughterhouse Gallery in Smithfield. The exorcism came with a ceremony in the spoiled synagogue, in which she played slides of Rodinsky's room against the walls. Recordings. A marginal, virtually unnoticed seance, transporting the weavers' attic across Whitechapel, as it would later be carried with her on her journey into Poland. The room was detached from its physical and temporal base and turned into a cabinet of curiosities. And Rachel had become its keeper. She was the caretaker *in absentia*. Her task was to tell the story in which she now had the central part. To uncover the mystery of David Rodinsky by laying bare her own obsession with his life and work.

Liam Gallagher, according to a short sketch on Hatton Garden in the *Independent*, picked Patsy Kensit's engagement ring from the 'exclusive window' of Anthony Gray. 'It cost me an arm and a leg – more

than you earn in a year,' Gallagher is supposed to have 'growled' at
reporters. Mr Gray, the proprietor of this discreet establishment,
knows his rocks. He spent years on the road as a shrewd and successful antique dealer before going to ground in EC1. His business is
in London and his private home is on the coast in Essex. Anthony
Gray is Rachel Lichtenstein's father. Rachel changed her surname,
reverted to the older family name, in 1988. This was not a gesture of
revolt, a breaking away, but the signalling of her quest to discover the
story of her heritage. Who she belonged to and where she came
from. The future journey would not discount Hatton Garden,
Rachel had a visionary sense of that place: modest shop-floors, grey
carpets, precision mirrors, small cubicles of trinkets, with cellars
beneath. Caverns of unimaginable wealth. An underground river of
gold and jewels that ran in parallel to the submerged Fleet.

The glitter of Anthony Gray's shop was the inevitable extension of
the modest premises that Rachel's grandparents had occupied in
New Road, Whitechapel. (And before that in Princelet Street.)
Rachel was haunted by the detritus of the abandoned premises
opposite the London Hospital: bits of clocks, hair rings, tickets,
labels, unredeemed curiosities. The shop (now a kebab house) had
been built where the great Whitechapel Mound once stood, a pic-
turesque earthwork illustrated in the Batsford book on the London
Hospital, and glossed as 'a place for outings and sightseeing'.

The New Road shop became a sort of rehearsal for Rodinsky's
room. Lichtenstein curated the salvaged mementoes, framed them
in steel, and exhibited the result among the bales of twine in Mr
Katz's string shop in Brick Lane. She was practising her own brand
of cultural diffusionism, letting memory swim across time. She
nudged the map, realigning objects, re-examining photographs,
teasing out a new narrative. New Road was a marker, a fixed point
on which she could set her compass, to draw out the circumference
of her obsessions. It was to the kebab house she sent me, when I
invited her to stick a pin anywhere in the map of London, for a
walk I wanted to do as part of an exhibition at the Jago Gallery,
Shoreditch.

Rachel was not alone in this return to Whitechapel, in giving herself up to a process of re-immigration; 'excavating,' as she said, 'her
family heritage, collecting fragments of evidence and reassembling
them'. I have always thought that Sharon Chazan's brief and tragic
quest, the making of a documentary record of Hasidic life, was the
most extreme manifestation of this process. A young woman, restless and driven, turns from the achieved comfort of an assimilated
life back to the unknown, the dream of the ghetto. And in this
process she finds her subject; which, in Chazan's case, proves to be a
fatal choice.

Rachel repudiates the analogy. She wrote, when I outlined the
themes I would like to touch on in my introduction, that she was
'unsure about the addition of Sharon Chazan's story'. It was, she
felt, 'too close to the bone'. She couldn't see the connection. But,
although I respect her unease, the conjunction seems to me to be so
painfully obvious that it had to be explored.

'The shadow,' Lichtenstein wrote in a catalogue entry for a travelling exhibition, 'becomes the connection in time.' She conjured
up an artist/observer forced to form a relationship with the 'distant
figures' that he or she has created. Discovery mutates into obsession. Curated objects meld to form the narrative body of the
missing, the ardently desired other. Photographs, freezing the
instant, curl in the heat of the artist's attention. Time warps.
Inevitably a state is achieved where the thing that is pursued
becomes itself the pursuer. This territory is volatile. Rachel, pulling
away from her Princelet Street investigations, worked in Israel, in
an artists' community, on the edge of the desert. In a letter from
there, she wrote:

I spend my days a little like Rodinsky now, studying a strange
language & ancient texts. . . . When I was in London I spent 3
days in Rodinsky's room re-photographing some of his stuff. . . .
It's very strange to see it on the wall of my studio here – I think
he'd be amused, as Rabbis, Hebrew teachers & cabbalist scholars
try & make sense of it!

Shadows cast by a harsher sun fall across the fading prints. 'Connections in time.'

Sharon Chazan graduated from Newport School of Art at the period when Lichtenstein was reclaiming, by deed poll, her family name. Chazan was described as 'forceful' or 'fearless'. For a young woman, starting out on a career in a competitive field where she could expect no favours, she was evidently formidable. Talented, as so many others are talented, but driven in a way that few could understand. Her parents had separated. Her father was a medical man, a consultant in diabetes. Her mother operated a vegetarian restaurant in Cambridge. The family had lived for a time in Israel. Chazan, having travelled widely, and some thought recklessly, in remote places, returned to England with an essay entitled 'Following strange men home'.

This text, transcribed in an 'old, lined lesson book' (the kind that Rodinsky favoured for his translations), was as curious as its title. *Following strange men home.* There have been other such exercises in urban paranoia, material that operates like the shorthand summary of a Paul Auster novel. Projected mysteries that become actual. The nominating of the randomly accosted stranger as the protagonist of your story. 'It was,' wrote Caroline Moorhead in an essay entitled 'Last Testament', 'as if she wanted all these experiences.'

Of course she did. Wanted, needed, feared. That was the nature of her art. A hot diary from the edge, the moment when the story you are writing refuses to conform to the trajectory you have set for it. When fiction plagiarizes metafiction; when documentary truth becomes critical, turns in on itself, moves faster than its apparent author can transcribe. There is always a sense, in photography, that the artist is merely colluding with a subject that makes itself interesting as a kind of trap. Even with the perfectly realized, aesthetically balanced revelation of the Cartier-Bresson instant, those faces offer themselves, just once in the cycle of eternity, in order to seduce him. To force his finger down on the shutter release. The subject, far from having its soul stolen, has taken possession of the soul of the photographer. There are people, potential photographs (paintings or

stories), waiting for the unwary. They need the services of a technician to bring them into life. They will pull any stunt to achieve it:
picaresque derelicts busking in the gutter, Saturday-night victims
with their faces blown away, pre-fictional rooms with seductive
expressionist shadows.

Rachel Lichtenstein, in pursuit of the mystery of David Rodinsky,
the haunting properties of the Princelet Street attic, kept breaking
away, withdrawing, resuming other projects. But it was no good.
Rodinsky, *the idea of Rodinsky*, had become a *dybbuk*. The soul of a
dead person who enters the body of a living human and directs
their conduct. Rachel, alive, aware, was forced to take on the great
task of reactivating the unfinished work of a man whose death was
not yet established. Rodinsky hovered in the parentheses between
Welfare State poverty fable and Dostoevskian myth. His absence
was his potential. Lichtenstein, in the early days of the quest, had
hundreds of photographs of the objects from the room, Rodinsky's
books and belongings, but no image of the man himself. He existed
in contradictory accounts. He was auditioning his would-be biogra-
phers. Was he a scholar or a fool? A street comedian, a joker, or an
embittered solitary? A self-taught cabbalist or a deluded inadequate?

The themes that Sharon Chazan pursued reminded me of the
visionary film-maker Stan Brakhage's attempt to stratify the city
(police night patrol, open-heart surgery, the morgue). Chazan's early
portfolio covered the mortuary, circumcision rituals, drug addicts,
gypsies, Hell's Angels. Returned to London, she moved into a ware-
house flat in Wapping and began the task of photographing the
residue of orthodox Jewish life. Attending a symposium in Oxford,
she met Moshe Drukash, an East Londoner from Cable Street.
Drukash was a cabinet maker and a 'collector of antiquities'. He told
Chazan that he had been a Polish freedom fighter, 'involved with the
Jewish resistance, the Hagannah, during the British mandate of
Palestine'.

There is a portrait of Drukash in his Cable Street room taken by
Chazan. Pausing briefly in his monologue, he looks up at her; large
hands working away at a marquetry panel, a European synagogue.

The walls with their loud geometric paper are busy with other, similar objects, ovals and rectangles, ancestors, landscapes, framed
collections of watch faces in surreal alignments. Drukash was an
unacknowledged artist, a furious autodidact, a man determined to
make himself into his own museum. He fixated on Chazan. He gave
her presents that were like talismanic curses: red silk roses macerated
in aftershave, chocolates as dark as clinker, a photograph of his
mother and his sister, singed around its edges (as if it had been
raked back from the fire). He revealed that his mother and his sister
had been raped by Nazi soldiers. He was a solitary. This painful
account of the past was all he could offer. And it was overwhelming.
His phone calls plagued Chazan. He was the narrative other who
wouldn't go away. She had become the heart of his scenario of
redemption: a role that she never sought, didn't require, but was
unable to relinquish. The pressure of the past, remade and re-
visioned memories, was terrible. Drukash's letters, more and more
frenzied, desperately inarticulate, left her numb. 'You fail me and
silence. No mercy, the worst of my life . . . I'm innocence.'

Chazan agreed to meet him in the Artichoke, a pub that was
round the corner from Drukash's flat. She wanted to return the photograph of the mother and sister, and a watch that he had sent,
another of his excessive gifts. Nobody in the Artichoke remembers
seeing the couple that night. Chazan didn't come home. Valerie, her
mother, rang the police; and, just after midnight, they broke down
the door of the Cable Street flat. 'Two untouched glasses of cherry
brandy and a wrapped box of chocolates' stood on the table with its
decorated cloth. Chazan had been killed, shot through the temple
and the throat. Drukash had arranged his mother's silver necklace
around her neck, lain beside her, and then put the gun to his own
head.

There are places where stories overwhelm stories. Street names that
can't break free from the heritage album. Sidney Street, to the east of
the Royal London Hospital, will always be police helmets, rain capes,
soldiers lying full-length on the cobbles. Bobbies with shotguns

tucked under their elbows, like a fancy-dress shooting party. Bowler-hatted officials. A flat-capped mob, held back, waiting under a hissing gas standard. Smoke from the burning house. A hierarchy of hats. Winston Churchill, on a rare visit to the East End, dominated the frame by wearing a topper; assuring himself of his immortality by becoming an unforgettable image. The director of operations is also the director of the film of memory. He controls the weather, the disposition of the crowd, the lighting. This was a black-and-white event; good and evil manipulated in a class-war pantomime. An army summoned to crush a knot of dangerous aliens, bohemians, part-time artists – anarchists. To crush that word, eliminate it from the script. Churchill, in an account published in *The Times*, picked another term (straight out of yellowback fiction) to describe the men. He called them 'desperadoes'.

Drukash's room in Cable Street is too individual a tragedy, too private, hidden away. The pictures that accompany his story are striking, but they belong to an artist with her own clear sense of how truth should be documented and revealed. Cable Street will always be the battle between Mosley's blackshirts and those who erected barricades to stop his march. The famous image of the crowd rushing from the overturned lorry, the advancing police, doubles as a perpetual advertisement for S. GRONOFSKY. K. LIGHTNING. SUITS TO MEASURE. Reputations which lasted for generations were forged by that photograph. The post-war gang boss, Jack Spot (a.k.a. Comer), mythologized his involvement as a street-fighting anti-fascist; a Jewish warrior defending his people, razoring bigots in spielers. From these beginnings, he built a small empire of protection rackets, clubs and off-course betting scams (preparing the ground for the part-Romany, part-Jewish Krays). To be there, in the photograph, or just outside the frame, was to be part of history. Validated. Surrealist poets and Mass Observers, as David Gascoyne recalls, attended the event; thereby acquiring some sense of an unknown London.

Rachel Lichtenstein, drawn back to the streets from which her grandparents had made their living, nominated the story of David Rodinsky as a way of discovering (or creating) her own past. The vanished caretaker had orchestrated the elements of the classic 'locked room' mystery: a closed set, notebooks written in code, unreliable witnesses who seemed to be describing a series of totally different men. There was the stain of madness, forgotten or undisclosed crimes, and the black spider of the Holocaust, an event beyond language which haunted everything that Rachel undertook.

Once the task was begun, the lazy prohibitions of earlier exploiters of the Rodinsky fable were swept aside. We had discovered nothing because we didn't want to know, didn't want to destroy the comforting mystifications, our gothic anthology pieces: golems and cobwebs and chambers that were outside time. The true Rodinsky biography, its weight and its significance, was waiting for the true biographer, Rachel Lichtenstein. The first person who needed revelation rather than confirmation (that Spitalfields was a zone of privileged imagination). Very soon, Rachel knew more than she could absorb. Facts rushed at her wherever she put out her hand. She had only to enter a library or record office for the Rodinsky files to scorch her fingers. She was guided. She raced across London, out into the suburbs. It was too easy: forgotten relatives, lost letters, packets of photographs tied with black ribbon, documents, tape recordings, specialists in every field overwhelming her with arcane footnotes.

She had to step back from it, or be swallowed entirely. Lichtenstein joined an artists' group in Arad, Israel. But there was no relief. She had to return to Rodinsky, continue her task. She'd been brooding on her involvement in a show that was being staged at the Slaughterhouse Gallery in Smithfield for the launch of my book *Lights Out for the Territory*. She thought she might do a Rodinsky presentation, slides and projections. She would bring wrapped objects from the Princelet Street attic.

'I want to mount the photographs . . . in a very formal – museum archival – way & maybe to give them my own random cataloguing on top of his. I'm also very excited about the idea of a performance. . . . I've become obsessed with my many tapes . . . & thought it would be interesting to read, in a very BBC kind of way, from his diary – 2 people struggling with a language – yearning for home etc. What do you think? It's the beginning of an idea.'

What I thought, but didn't say, was that it might be the beginning of something else, a book. That it would be magnificent if Rachel could transport the material she had gathered to a territory far beyond performance, curation, installation. That the book, the story of the Princelet Street room, was the task for which Rodinsky had laid out all the elements of a mystery. The task for which he had chosen her.

BEYOND THE BOUNDARIES OF WHITECHAPEL

Rachel Lichtenstein

IN MODERN ETH[I

AMHARIC ግንዘ፡ፀ፡

RIÑI- እ ግ ር ኜ   A[ÃRÃ?]

AMHARINIA

እ ም ኌ ር ኜ

EITHER THE SAME AS

OR:

ካ መ ኂ ቢ፡

HA-MU-RA-BI

እ ም ኂ ፈ ሲ፡

A-M-RĀ-FĒ-L:

AMRAPHEL

The stench of raw flesh hung in the cold January air, reminding me of another trip only a few months ago, when I had weaved my way through the back streets of the Arab meat market in Jerusalem. That day now felt like a lifetime ago. The cloth-covered alleyways of the market had provided welcome relief from the intensity of the sun, which had been particularly uncomfortable because I was wearing a long, heavy dress. It was the appropriate attire for a visit to a rabbi's house. Now I was clothed in my London winter artist's uniform: black jeans, heavy boots, ex-army jacket and thick woollen gloves. It was only three o'clock in the afternoon but the light was already fading fast. By following Iain's hand-drawn map I wove my way towards the trading centre, realizing by the bloody trails that I must be close now, but the place was impossible to find.

I must have circled the deserted market at least five times before finding it. The exterior of the building appeared unmarked until I noticed the small brass sign just above the letter box. 'The Slaughterhouse'. I rang the bell. There was no answer; the door was open so I descended the narrow stairway to a large empty white space. The air inside was freezing and smelt of damp earth.

I called out, hearing a muffled reply that seemed to come from a cellar below. Scanning the deserted room for a way down, I saw a small iron balcony to my right. Over the edge I could see down to three cavernous, brick-lined tunnels that must once have housed the underground abattoir. As my eyes adjusted to the dim light I could make out two shadowy figures at the far end of the longest tunnel. They were Iain and the director of the Slaughterhouse, and they waved me down a precariously constructed staircase of wooden planks hidden beside the balcony.

A bright light shone violently into my face. Behind it stood Iain holding a torch. He was as pleased with the place as I was. For what I intended to do it was perfect. Far enough away from 'the room' for me to work in, and thick with an eerie atmosphere of past lives that would enable the performance to translate into this space. I had been allocated the smallest tunnel to the left, which was dark and enclosed, ideal for projecting the film I had been working on. I left the others and measured up. I had never been clearer about where the work would be placed. The photographs of Rodinsky's artefacts would rest on a bed of blue velvet on the wall opposite the entrance. A large wooden table would be used to cover the exposed hole in the floor that led directly to the vast labyrinth of London's Victorian sewage system. The table would become my stage, mirroring Rodinsky's own table, and I would bring in his green tablecloth from the synagogue to complete the effect.

Less than a week later I was standing nervously on my makeshift stage with a large, silent crowd before me breathing hot mist into the damp night air. I began, echoing the film behind me: wrapping books in blue velvet with white-gloved hands, lighting red sealing-wax, dripping hot drops on to knots of silk ribbon before placing the wrapped articles in archive boxes. As I continued my actions, taped voices filled the room, urging the crowd to look up to the wall behind me where archive footage of Rodinsky's room was being displayed.

Iain Sinclair's taped voice spoke over the images:

I think whatever happened happened in a multiverse, the same
thing occurring many times in an instant. He walked out of the
room and went down into the street and had a heart attack in
some obscure alley and was swept aside like a social derelict and
was never seen again, that's one. I think, two, he had reached a
point in his cabbalistic studies where he had begun to achieve
the Great Work, a kind of invisibility or moving into another
dimension, and he disappeared that way. Three, he's still there
and it's the room itself that has disappeared so when you go into
that room you don't see him, another space has been created.
Four, he got deeply into debt collecting such a vast amount of
books and had to do a runner, simply took off. Five, he was
wiped out by the CIA and secret state.

Then Val Williams, a writer and curator, said:

> I first found out about Rodinsky from Alan, who told me the
> story about how his room above the synagogue had been found
> after twenty-five years. I always remember the first image I had
> of that room was of the people going up there and finding it
> and finding the tea leaves were still there in the cup. And I
> think it was just that one little detail that really made me think
> about the way that we leave things and a fear I have always had
> about maybe going out in the morning and never coming back
> and all the little traces of you that would be left behind. It has
> always been something that has made me feel very anxious.
> Rodinsky's room, it made me think, if you died, and people
> found the things you'd left behind, photographs, the letters
> people had written to you, what kind of a picture would they
> make of you?'

The voice of Alan Dein, a local historian and tour guide:

> My first impression of the room was of a place where someone
> had lived for a long time, I had no idea who it was at all. I
> wandered in and stumbled over towering piles of extremely old
> papers, the *Star*, the *Herald*, the *Evening Standard*, papers dating
> back to the First World War. Climbing over the papers I looked
> over to the other side of the room, where there was a bed, roughly
> made, unkempt, filled with dust. My first impression was that a
> man had literally disappeared and turned to dust in the room.

The voices stopped, the images faded to white.
Then my voice in the cold tunnel:

> I was born in 1969, the same year that David Rodinsky, an
> orthodox Jew of unknown descent, mysteriously disappeared
> from his decaying East London loft. He lived above the
> synagogue where my late grandparents were married. His

abandoned room was left undisturbed for over a decade, a reflection of the end of an era, the deserted Jewish East End.

I have been told that when his room was finally opened in 1980, a solidified cup of tea sat next to his unmade bed. On the greasecaked stove stood a near-fossilized pot of porridge. His clothes hung in the wardrobe, heavy with dust. An empty spectacle case, his handwritten name inside, rested on the mantelpiece next to a calendar, the date fixed at January 1963. Towering piles of newspapers were stacked in corners and against the wall. Old 78 rpm records, empty bottles, and all manner of accumulated junk filled all the space that was not consumed by books. Every surface overflowed with books on subjects ranging from the Talmud to the study of hieroglyphics. He appears to have been a competent linguist as the evidence in his room reveals his self-taught knowledge of at least fifteen different languages, many of them no longer spoken. Clothing, books and the remains of food tell us he was

religious in his beliefs, but other evidence suggests he was as
interested in Irish drinking songs as in the mysteries of the
Zohar. Taped inside many books are numerous inserts by
Rodinsky: hand-drawn maps on the backs of cigarette packets,
a ten-rouble note, a faded photograph of a synagogue in
Prague, bubblegum cards from Iceland and Venezuela,
chocolate wrappers covered in Arabic text. Numerous
handwritten notebooks were also found containing Phoenician
tables of time, cabbalistic diagrams, bizarre poems, and
humorous anecdotes. All these abandoned possessions,
appearing like the consonants of a forgotten language, bare
bones of meaning, waiting for Rodinsky's return to receive
their full expression.

Some undeniable facts are deducible from the evidence he
left behind. Rodinsky lived in the attic on 19 Princelet Street for
at least thirty-seven years, as he stated in this letter dated 18
August 1961. The letter was never sent.

Dear Sir,

In reply to your second letter to me, I must inform you that I
have been advised by a solicitor that I should pay no rent
until I have consulted a Citizens Advice Bureau. Would you
kindly explain this. If I am not the recognized tenant then
who is? After all, I am my late mother's son and I lived here
with her since 1932, apart from the time I was in Broadstairs
and in other places, but this was my home.

Yours faithfully
D. Rodinsky

Rodinsky's learning capabilities appeared to be astounding, he
seemed to have spoken numerous languages and appeared
generally interested in the formation of language itself. I shall
read to you from one of his notebooks:

The earliest reference to writing in the Old Testament is Exodus 17:14, where Moses is commanded to write in a book an account of the victory just gained over Amalek at Rephidim. This may have been the first entry in the Book of Wars mentioned in Numbers 21:14. In Exodus 24:7 Moses reads the Book of the Covenant, i.e. Exodus 20 to 23 inclusive, in the audience of the people and afterwards ascends Mount Sinai to receive the two 'Lhiot'. From this point onwards the references to writing occur with increasing frequency, but it is always as a means of storing and preserving. The art of writing is a possession of the few and the diffusion or publication of literature takes place orally. But in Judges 8:14, the fact that by chance a prisoner was able to write down an account of Succoth for Gideon seems to point out that reading and writing were known generally. But in view of the late date now assigned to most of the earlier Old Testament books it's maintained that statements such as these are valid only for the period in which the author wrote and not that which they treat. Yet, the word which later came to signify 'scribe' is found in the Song of Deborah (Judges 5: 14–15), 'Out of Mashir came down governors, and out of Zebulun they that handle the pen of the writer.'

Rodinsky appears to have worked alone, rather than with a *havrusa* (study partner), the traditional *yeshiva* style of learning through debate with another. But maybe he did receive rabbinical visits to his room. Whether real or imagined the only evidence of outside contact in his solitary lifestyle seems to exist in his handwritten 'English to Hebrew Conversational Dictionary'. I will read an excerpt of the English he chooses to translate:

My sister isn't well today. She has pains and is feeling limp. The doctor says there is nothing to worry about. It is only a mild complaint from which many new immigrants suffer. It

should pass in three or four days. We must give her only light
food such as semolina pudding, rusks and weak tea.

Did he prescribe a medicine?

Yes, to be taken three times a day.

I hope things don't turn worse. Chin up! Don't take it so
hard. Cheerio then, see you soon.

Someone's knocking at the door. Somebody's ringing the
bell. Go and see who it is. It is Rabbi Amitov. Let him in,
please come in, welcome.

I haven't seen you for ages. I have missed you. I am pleased
to see you. I am very glad. I was in the neighbourhood and
thought I would drop in (for a chat). You're welcome! You're
always welcome (offer the man a chair). Please sit down. Will
you take your coat off? What brings you here? How are
things? How are things at home? Our household is strictly
Hebrew, does your wife speak Hebrew?

Yes, her English is very poor I'm sorry to say.

Why, that's marvellous! I thought I'd have to twist my
tongue trying to talk English, if you can call it that!

What a nice place you have here. What fine modern
furniture.

Please sit on the divan. Won't you sit down a while. We
seldom see you. Why do we no longer see you with us?

Rodinsky's insatiable linguistic curiosity was put to a wide range
of uses. The study of Japanese, Greek, Chaldean, German,
Accadian. It is my belief he was trying to write a book on the
structure of language itself. Here is an extract from another of
his notebooks:

So you see if you are to master the Accadian cuneiform you
may ask what a way to write why didn't they invent an
alphabet or some other signs with only one reading? The
answer is they did at the time when the lingo was dying out

but this was not to facilitate Accadian, but only to preserve
Sumerian. Earlier the Uganites of Ras Shamra had invented
one alphabet from these cuneiforms and at a later date the
Persians invented another which was partly alphabetical and
partly syllabic with a few makeshift word signs . . .

Numerous notebooks were found with such writings and many
others were discovered full of peculiar poems and songs:

> get your hair cut
> have a Yul Brinner
> if I have a Yul Brinner
> You'll grinner

> I SCREAM, YOU'LL SCREAM FOR DAN DURMA ICE CREAM
> My old man will keep on drinking
> wasting his money on beer
> So I told him
> Hit the road Jack
> Beat it
> And don't come back here

I shall finish with another excerpt from Rodinsky's 'Hebrew to
English Conversational Dictionary'. In this section it is Rodinsky
who retains the right to question our morbid fascination with
his private story. I shall read the English he chooses to translate:

> Who are you?
> Where are you?
> What are you doing?
> Where are you going?
> Where did you come from?
> Where are you staying?
> How old are you?
> What do you wish for?

What is your pleasure?

Can I help you?

What are you saying?

What is wrong?

Is it true what they say?

What has happened to you?

What is the matter with you?

Did you hear?

Did you understand?

Are you serious?

Where did you get off?

How far is it from here to Jerusalem?

Who are you looking for?

What are you looking at?

Who do you think I am?

Do you understand Arabic, Turkish, Maltese? I know some
    Russian ...

I had intruded into Rodinsky's personal life, rummaged through his belongings, discussed his personality and possible whereabouts with many people, but the truth was I did not know if he was dead or alive. I decided to call Saul Issroff, the only person I could think of who might be able to help me find out.

I had met Saul the previous October after giving a lecture on my work at the Spiro Institute, a London institution for Hebrew and Jewish studies. Saul is the director of the British Jewish Genealogical Institute and has carried out a considerable amount of research into his own family background. He took a great interest in my art work and commissioned me to make a sculpture based on his mother's life history for her ninetieth birthday. We became friends as well as work colleagues, and when I first told Saul about my search for Rodinsky he offered to put out a request for information about him on the Jewish Genealogy Society of Great Britain's website. Within a week I had received two emails. The first was from a Dr Robert Rodensky from Toronto, a physiologist, translator of Russian, and amateur genealogist. Dr Rodensky emailed me for my address and then sent me the following: a three-page printout of vowel permutations on the name Rodensky, a quirky newspaper clip about Morris 'Red' Rudensky, a safecracker who worked with Al Capone and died in 1989, and a Xerox of a photograph in a book, *The Career of Frank Licht*, captioned 'A view of Charles St.' (Providence, Rhode Island, USA, around 1900) showing a storefront sign with written on it 'L. Rodinsky. New-Second Hand Clothing.' A second, intriguing email arrived from a 'Jim', who also had been researching the name Rodinsky and claimed that there are many family members in Hartford and other parts of Connecticut as well as in Boston, Las Vegas and Argentina. He thought the Rodinskys originated from Grodno or Bialystock.

Saul suggested a visit to St Catherine's House – the Office of Population Censuses and Surveys – to try to locate a death certificate for David Rodinsky, and he was kind enough to offer to accompany me there. The following week we met at Holborn tube and made the short walk to St Catherine's House. Saul warned me that the chances of finding a death certificate, without even knowing the year of death, were extremely small. We entered the main hall of the building to be confronted with row upon row of oversized leather-bound books. Two large signs hung over the aisles, DEATHS and BIRTHS; we took a right into DEATHS. Tired, suited figures were pulling the heavy volumes from the shelves and painstakingly scouring the pages for information. Every few minutes a piped announcement would come over the loudspeakers: 'Please keep all your personal belongings with you, pickpockets are known to be operating in this building.' The only other sound was the rhythmical banging of the giant books being slammed shut, dragged off the shelves and plonked on to the desks. The air in the grey, stiflingly overheated room was thick with dust and sighs.

We had little to go on. I suggested 1969 as it was the year I had been born and from the evidence in Rodinsky's room I knew for sure that he had been alive until 1967. We located the correct aisle and each selected a volume at random, I opened mine roughly in the centre: Rodenskitzy, Rodins, Rodin, flicked the page, Rodin, Rodin, *Rodinsky, David, of 19 Princelet Street, London E1, DX 421235, March to April quarter 1969.* I looked over to Saul, nose buried between the pages, a well-trained finger rapidly moving across the small print. 'Saul,' I screeched (much too loudly; angry looks flashed over). 'I think I've found him.' He gave me a pleasant, patient smile, reminiscent of one I'd often seen as a child on my father's face after he'd told me some fantastical story and I'd believed him, but there it was, David Rodinsky. The death certificate would take a few days to arrive in the post and then I would know the cause, exact date and place of death.

On Wednesday, a thin brown envelope landed on the doormat. I rushed upstairs to open it. It took some time, my hands were shaking so much. While taking a deep breath I read then reread and reread the certificate. Surely there must be some mistake. This could not be the same David Rodinsky. The death certificate stated he died in Epsom in Surrey.

Name and Surname: David Rodinsky, no. 391, DX 421235

When and Where: 4th of March 1969. The Grove, Horton Lane,
    Epsom

Sex: male. Age: 44 yrs. Occupation: none

Address: 19 Princelet Street, E1

Cause of death: broncho-pneumonia, II epilepsy with paranoid
    features

Certified by J.S. Patmat MB

Residence of informant: D. Wiltshire, occupier, The Grove,
    Horton Lane, Epsom, registered the 5th of March 1969.

How did a Jewish scholar who never appeared to have left the square mile of Spitalfields end up in Surrey? It seemed unlikely, but surely there could not be two David Rodinskys of 19 Princelet Street? The only way to check would be to visit the house in Epsom and see if 'D. Wiltshire' could shed any light on things.

I drove to Surrey the following week, finding my way to Horton, a small district of Epsom a few miles south of the town centre. Horton consists of a triangular village green, surrounded by cottages, a pond

and a pub. I decided to stop at the pub and ask for directions. The
barmaid stared at me and shrugged while silently serving a flat lager
to the only other person in the room, a large balding man, dressed in
grey overalls, propped up against the far end of the bar. I was about
to leave when the man called me back. 'Whereabouts in Horton Lane
do you want?' he drawled. 'I've been driving up and down that lane
for the past twenty-five years, know everywhere.'

'A private house, called the Grove.'

He sniggered. 'I think you probably mean the Longrove, one of
the psychiatric hospitals on the lane.'

This information made sense of Rodinsky's strange appearance in
Epsom. The man went on to tell me that there had been five mental
institutions on Horton Lane, four of which were now closed down,
the Longrove being one of them. He moved closer and told me in
whispers that the Longrove had mysteriously burned down, along
with all its records, five years previously. The man said he had been
a driver of medical equipment to the hospitals in Horton Lane for
twenty-five years, then he lowered his eyebrows and told of strange
goings-on, unexplained fires, weird disappearances. I took out a
notebook and pressed him to go on. Big mistake. Panic washed over
him and he ran to the fruit machine, mumbling something about
'more than my job's worth', and refused to talk to me any more.

I decided to go to Horton Lane anyway. It was exactly as he had
described it: a long road winding through fields lined with tall fir
trees. There were no private residences to be seen for miles, only the
empty shells of the former institutions looming in the distance.
About halfway along the lane I saw a sign for the Longrove. I pulled
into the drive only to be stopped by a twelve-foot metal gate topped
with rolls of barbed wire. I got out of the car to read the orange and
black sign strapped to the gates:

PRIVATE PROPERTY
TRESPASSERS WILL BE PROSECUTED
TEL. SURREY HEALTH AUTHORITY ON 0126 445 876
FOR FURTHER INFORMATION

There appeared to be no access to the place apart from over the gate. Just as I was contemplating how to climb over it a huge salivating Alsatian hurled itself against the metal bars, jaws desperately trying to clamp themselves around my ankles. I jumped back, adrenalin pumping through my veins, and within seconds a grim-looking security guard appeared. No I could not go in, no I could not take pictures, no he did not know anything else; he pointed to the telephone number on the sign and asked me to leave. The following day I tried calling the number. A curt secretary answered: all records had been destroyed in the fire, she could not help.

Another dead end: I could not prove that the man who died here had been the same David Rodinsky. Some of the data on the death certificate contrasted sharply with previous information I had gathered about him, such as his age. The death certificate stated he died aged forty-four. But Bill Fishman remembered seeing him in his attic in the late Thirties. He described him as an old man bent over his books by candlelight. If we were talking about the same Rodinsky he would only have been in his teens at the time. Nor did his age tie in with Mr Katz's story about Rodinsky's elderly daughter, Mrs Lipman.

A few weeks later I was battling my way through the crowds of worshippers pouring out of the mosque on Brick Lane after Ramadan services when I spotted Mr Katz in the window of his shop, which is situated opposite the mosque. When he saw me he waved me in. 'Shalom, Raquel. You know when I leave Stamford Hill I feel like I need my passport to come here now.' He grinned at me through his long white beard, while gesticulating to the crowds outside. His shop was as devoid of customers as usual but there was still only enough room for one person as all the available space was taken up with large brown packages that I presumed contained the string and paper bags he must sell so much of to have been in business there for the last fifty-seven years. 'Raquel, remember the old lady I told you about, Rodinsky's daughter? She come in here to see me last veek and I told her about you and your project and she is villing to speak to you. I have her address somevhere.' I could hardly reply through excitement: this could be the best lead I had had yet. He disappeared into the back room. I could see him shuffling through a mountain of loose papers on his desk. 'It's here somewhere . . . ah . . . here we have it.' He handed me the small scrap of paper and I thanked him profusely. We spoke for a few more minutes in my broken Hebrew which always made him smile, and I left exuberant.

On receiving the address I went immediately to try to talk with the woman. She had left no phone number, I would just go and see if she was in: Mrs Bella Lipman, Dobson's Place, London E1. It took a while to find the estate, wandering through the narrow back streets behind Brick Lane. She lived in a graffiti-covered, crumbling Sixties council block. I could see her front door from the street but the only access to the building was via the intercom. I buzzed the number repeatedly: no reply. I tried the next-door number and spoke to a neighbour. She told me Mrs Lipman *never* went out and was probably in; did I want to come up and knock on the door? She let me into a dank stairwell that reeked of urine. I pressed for the lift and walked straight into it, completely preoccupied with my own personal mission and without noticing the gang of Asian teenagers with whom I was sharing the small metal cubicle. I stared blankly straight at them. Two boys, fourteen years old at the most, were holding open a large plastic bag while another tipped some white powder into it. Everyone froze. I could hear nothing but my own heart beating. A fourth boy, who was obviously starting to become disturbed by my presence, pulled out a small but sharp-looking penknife and thrust it in my direction with the words, 'Fuck off, we're busy.' I backed out and raced up the stairs. I arrived breathless at Mrs Lipman's door, knocking loudly while looking over my shoulder. Silence, no footsteps behind me, no answer from Mrs Lipman. After slipping a note through the letterbox I knocked next door. Eventually a beautiful pair of dark eyes appeared nervously at the letterbox. The woman spoke little English, did not know Mrs Lipman, had never seen her. The neighbour on the other side refused to respond. I was not surprised that Mrs Lipman never went out. I don't think I would have. I paced around the corridor, too afraid to go back down the stairwell, until I found a fire exit at the other end of the block, then I sped down and out, rushing back to Princelet Street to collect myself.

By now I was used to the strange whisperings of the synagogue. After so many hours spent there alone, gone were the days when the slam of a door or muffled footsteps would make me run out into the street with the hairs on the back of my neck prickling. Now the building had become a refuge, and I would often drop by on the way to the studio and go upstairs to Rodinsky's room to write, think, draw. On this occasion I sat in the synagogue trying to calm down. In all the years I had been in East London I had never before been physically threatened. But I was partly to blame. Inner-city areas are much like the desert: full of dangerous creatures that are rarely seen unless you become curious and start to overturn stones or poke about in dark crevices. If I had registered earlier what was happening, I would have been left alone. As I slowly came out of shock I became vaguely aware of a strange noise in the synagogue. I could hear something being dragged across the floor and it sounded as if it was coming from Rodinsky's room. I called out – no response. Slowly I began to ascend the stairs; the noise got louder. I tried to comfort myself with the theory I had once been told about old wooden buildings. They are always inhabited by rats and mice. The noise these creatures emit is too low to be properly registered by the human ear although a recognition of another presence is felt. This is what many humans confuse with the sensation of feeling a ghostly presence. If these were rats I was hearing, they were extremely large.

Just as I was about to enter Rodinsky's room, convinced that this was the time he had chosen to appear to me in a luminous glow, I heard a loud plummy 'hellooo ho, yoo hoo', then two women appeared from behind the door holding a large, strange-looking wooden object. They introduced themselves as Evelyn and Michal Friedlander, respectively the wife and daughter of the famous Rabbi Albert Friedlander whose *Riders Towards the Dawn* I was then reading. In the book Rabbi Friedlander 'enters into a dialogue with the

great Jewish writers and thinkers of our time – with Primo Levi,
Bruno Bettelheim, Elie Wiesel – and tries to move towards a concept
of humanity that includes evil as a component of our make-up, that
sees the glory of human existence in winning partial victories
against darkness, and that celebrates the hope that even a journey
moving into darkness has dimensions of hope within itself'. Rabbi
Lionel Blue says of it, 'Anyone interested in the future of Judaism
and, after the Holocaust, in their own humanity, should read this
book.' His wife and daughter turned out to be as dynamic as Rabbi
Friedlander himself; Evelyn is an expert in Jewish textiles, founder of
the Hidden Legacy Foundation as well as being involved in numerous other projects, and Michal is the curator of the Jewish Museum
in Berkeley, California. The object they were holding turned out to
be a specially crafted stand for taking pictures of Torah mantles
[protective coverings for Torah scrolls, often highly decorated]. They
had been in Rodinsky's room taking photographs of the synagogue
artefacts in the hope of trying to secure some funding to restore the
fragile objects. I had heard about Evelyn from Samuel Melnick who
told me about the marvellous restoration job she had conducted on
the most precious of the Torah mantles in the Princelet Street
collection. It was made of rare silk and covered in pearls. Sam told
me it had been made from a former wedding gown. I asked him if
this was kosher and he laughed and said he would have to consult a
rabbi.

I told the two wonderful women a little of my work and we went
for a coffee in Rossi's in Hanbury Street, Rodinsky's spoon-playing
haunt of the late Fifties. I told the Friedlanders about this and other
stories about Rodinsky. They were fascinated and promised they
would try to help by putting up posters in their synagogue and
asking former East Londoners from their congregation if they had
known him. I sat in Rossi's with my new friends and we talked for
hours. I told them about my recent experience at the Kosher
Luncheon Club, and they were keen to help me house the abandoned artefacts. Evelyn was involved in a project that was trying to
set up a safe house for Judaica in London. Her partner in this was a

David Jacobs, a name I had heard before – from Rosemary Weinstein at the Museum of London – in connection with the Princelet Street synagogue. I felt sure that Evelyn would be a great help to me in my quest for Rodinsky.

After five attempts to contact Bella Lipman, I had nearly given up hope when I received a telephone call. Bella had been in hospital, she had only just received the note I had left and was willing to see me after Shabbat. On the phone, she sounded frail and upset, and she began to tell me of her various illnesses. We made an appointment for the following Monday morning.

I began to fantasize about rescuing Bella Lipman from that dreadful estate. I imagined her alone, terrified, with no help. I took a trip to Grodzinski's and arrived armed with kosher cakes and biscuits. Bella answered the intercom this time, and I entered the hallway which had been washed down with strong disinfectant. No one was in the lift. As I arrived on the first floor I could see a small head, framed by an amazing halo of bright red hair, peering out of a blue door. Bella waved me in. As I approached I had that feeling of being a giant I've often felt at Jewish functions. Like most of my relatives, Bella only came up to my armpit.

Her flat was spotless, in stark contrast to the surrounding environment. I was honoured with a grand tour that started in the kitchen. Bella proudly showed me her large 'modern' fridge and sparkling but ancient stove. All cupboards were opened for my inspection and the sweet-smelling paper lining was admired, as was her extensive stock of kosher goods which filled the cupboards to bursting point. She scolded me for bringing the cakes, she had plenty of food, her home help always got her shopping and pension and her niece regularly visited with supplies. She made me take the cakes back. I already felt humbled in her presence: Bella was more than capable of looking after herself. She was bright and articulate, but I noticed that her eyes were clouded and she obviously found it difficult to see clearly. She showed me the large collection of pills she needed to take daily and then held up her hands. The tops of her fingers were bent. 'I can't peel potatoes, open a tin of salmon, nothing. The home help comes and does it for me.' She ushered me into a sparsely decorated lounge and asked me to sit at the round, lace-covered table in the centre of the room. 'Sit here, dear. No, here is more comfortable. Now what do you want to know, what have I that's interesting to tell you?' I again explained why I had come and asked Bella if I could record the conversation. 'No, I don't think my family would like me to be recorded.'

I felt like an intruder, there under false pretences. Bella did not want to talk about Princelet Street. She wanted to know about my family, my trip to Israel, was I married? 'No – why not!' She wanted to show me photographs of her niece. 'Look how beautiful she is, my favourite, such tiny feet, you can tell by her daughter, such an angel.' She wanted company, not an interview. When I pressed her again about her former life in the Princelet Street synagogue, her eyes filled with tears and her voice wavered. 'I lived there all my life, with my dear husband, God rest his soul, may all good Yiddisher girls find such a man as he. I was married there, my sisters and my brother were married there, my brother was bar mitzvahed there, God rest his soul, it was the only *shul* I ever knew.' Bella lived in the rooms above the synagogue (the next floor down from the Rodinskys) for nearly all of her married life. She was not Rodinsky's daughter – she laughed when I suggested it. 'He was never with a woman as far as I know, the mother wouldn't allow it; she was very strict, very protective.'

Bella and her husband had left the synagogue in the summer of 1981. Bella was already an old lady by that time and very dependent on her husband. Against his wishes, one sunny afternoon in July of the same year, she had taken her first trip alone to the market in Whitechapel High Street, just a five-minute walk from their home. While purchasing some vegetables she had been viciously attacked from behind and knocked unconscious in the middle of the street. Bella had been mugged for the contents of her small leather handbag: the few pounds that constituted the remainder of her weekly pension, a green plastic comb, photographs of her wedding day, and the colourful array of her daily medications.

Fortunately Bella remembered nothing of the event itself; the first memory she had was of waking up, at the London Hospital on the opposite side of the road, to the sound of her husband's hysterical crying. When she awoke she found her world had been irrevocably changed: she could not see. Limited sight later returned to her right eye, but the attack rendered her permanently blind in her left eye. The incident alerted social services to the Lipmans' dreadful living conditions and soon after, they were rehoused at Dobson House. Bella's husband passed away a few years later. It was understandably painful for Bella to talk of these things, and equally painful for her to recall her happier memories of Princelet Street. When I mentioned David Rodinsky again, her eyes filled with tears. 'Poor David, of course I knew him, *alav ha-shalom*. I feel he is dead now.' In her opinion he was no genius; in fact, she described him as almost retarded. 'He did have a job, he worked in a shoe factory in Princelet Street. The mother was extremely protective of him, and had little interest in the daughter.' Bella remembers Rodinsky's older sister, Bertha, as 'brilliant'. 'She was always collecting books, hundreds of books, she was very shy and never married and sadly ended up in a mental institution, *alav ha-shalom*.' The mother appeared never to have let either child have relationships, and they lived an extremely orthodox lifestyle. 'She saved all his earnings for him, she was a good mother, do you know a bad mother?' Bella recalled a day in 1961. 'The mother was like a stick, she was *krank*. She came downstairs to me and asked me to go and buy a chicken for David and kosher it for him, it was a big *mitzvah*, so of course I did it for her. That same night an ambulance came and took her away. David walked all the way to Bancroft Road Hospital. When he returned he came to see me; she was dead, cancer.' Bella and her husband knew David would not survive long after her, with the sister away also. 'Please, this is wrong to talk ill of the dead.' We stopped the interview and Bella stood up wincing. 'My hernia, look at my stomach, I was always a fit woman.' Then she showed me her arms, bent and twisted, 'osteoporosis'. Bella went into the kitchen to refill the plate with tiny cakes and make fresh lemon tea.

I began writing furiously, as she wasn't comfortable with me making any transcriptions while we talked. My eyes rested on the freshly polished mantelpiece. In the centre stood tiny brass candlesticks with the candles and matches ready; a well-cared-for hand-crocheted dolly sat beside them, and to the right of the dolly a flower arrangement of blue and pink plastic carnations. On the other side of the candlesticks stood a faded picture of the present King and Queen, an enamelled ashtray from Israel, and a small brass carriage clock. Bella poured me tea and passed the cakes. 'Eat, eat and be well. I can't have any, high blood pressure, more illness I have than are in the books.' Bella began to talk about her family again, all now living in North London, more photographs. I felt angry: how could they leave her here alone? I had underestimated Bella Lipman. 'Let me tell you something, dolly. Never live with your family. My family want me there, but here I have my independence, and that's the most important thing. My own bed, my own flat, my independence, it is everything.'

We went back to talking about Princelet Street. Bella remembered one happy *Seder* night at Princelet Street that she shared with the Rodinskys, 'Just the once, after the war, we spent *Pesach* together in the top room. She cooked, the mother, and we sang and ate till late into the night. David was quiet but he was happy, it was a happy time.' Bella's eyes filled with tears again. 'I have no *Seder* night now, because I'm orthodox and I won't travel, it is the way I was bought up. There is no one here to share it with now. I say my *Shema* every night, I *bensch* over the candles, I kiss all the *mezuzahs* before I sleep and God is good to me, this is what I can still do.' We talked about the gradual closure of the Princelet Street synagogue. I knew from Samuel Melnick that it had officially closed in 1963 although I had heard that, even at that time, on many a Shabbat morning someone would be standing outside or knocking on doors to find enough people for a *minyan*. Bella told me the synagogue was in a shocking state even in the early Fifties and in desperate need of repair. Although the last service was held in the early Sixties, the remaining community set up a *bet midrash* in the building, and study groups continued alongside services when a *minyan* could be reached right up to the late Seventies. I presume that David took part in this learning but Bella couldn't be sure. Suddenly Bella switched back to talking about David. 'I never went up to the room after the mother died, he didn't want it; we'd say hello, good morning, this was all. Sometimes he would disappear for days. I would hear the key turn in the middle of the night, terrified I was that some *nebish* would run in. He started to eat *treyf* at the Indian restaurants, terrible. I think he used to drink, he couldn't look after himself. Please, we can't talk ill of the dead. I know he went regularly to the picture house on Brick Lane, he was often out and about after his mother died. She wouldn't let him out, you see. He did have money, the night she came to see me before she died she showed me a post office book of his with what she had saved for him. God only knows what he did with it.'

I remembered Bill Fishman's description of David Rodinsky as a *tzaddick* who was always going out into the streets with pockets full of change practising *tzadokam* by giving away his money to the poor. Bella didn't want to talk about him any more; I felt she was getting tired. She invited me back any time. I was sorry that I couldn't see her for three months as I was leaving in two days' time for Israel and then Poland. I felt afraid that Bella Lipman would not last until my return, but Bella, 'a tiny little bit', as she described herself, was much tougher than she looked.

In many ways the interview with Bella confirmed that the death certificate I'd discovered belonged to David Rodinsky. But it seemed impossible that I would ever be able to confirm this indisputably, as all the records at the Longrove had been destroyed in the fire. Confirming his death was not the only reason I had become so interested in the death certificate. Not only did David Rodinsky die in the year of my birth, but he died a matter of days before I'd been born. Dates of birth and death have great significance in cabbalistic thought, and I made a mental note to explore this during my forthcoming trip to Israel.

The following week, on arrival at Ben-Gurion airport, I took the number five bus to Dizengoff to visit my friend Liz. She's a curious American, who had made the decision to stay in Israel despite the recent bombings, receiving terrible pay, not speaking a word of the language, and despising the Israeli male population. Liz was employed as a model maker for an animation company in Tel Aviv, and she'd asked me to meet her direct from work as she wanted to introduce me to her British boss. As soon as I met Jeremy and heard his clearly recognizable North London accent we began to fire names at each other. The London Jewish community is not so large. I could almost trace the street he grew up in from his voice and had a fairly good idea of the other Londoners living in Israel whom he might know. The first I mentioned was Johnny Kamiel (a friend from university who was now living in Tel Aviv) who turned out to be a close friend of Jeremy, and who was currently staying in his house. Liz and I were invited to join them later that evening.

Jeremy lives in downtown Tel Aviv in a former industrial area called Florentine, now fashionably slummy and inhabited mainly by artists. Liz and I wound our way through the darkly lit back streets for hours before eventually locating Jeremy's small Arab house, recognizable by the round turquoise window he had told us to look out for. The house consisted of one small, white arched room downstairs with a tiny kitchen attached. Above the kitchen, to the right, there was a blue-and-gold-tiled balcony that concealed an exotically decorated bedroom, covered in Bedouin tapestries and brightly coloured muslin drapes. A small spiral staircase positioned at the base of the bed led up to the roof, where it was possible to see the port of Jaffa and the minaret of the nearby mosque. It was strange to see middle-class Hendon boys in this setting, reclining on numerous deep red camel-hair cushions, getting slowly stoned on a *nargila*, the water pipe used traditionally by Bedouins for smoking tobacco and hash. Johnny was amazed to see me, but barely able to speak in consequence of overindulgence in the large bubbling pipe in front of him. And who could blame him? Tomorrow he was to start his *milluim* guarding the border on the West Bank. It was hard to imagine small-framed, softly spoken Johnny marching side by side with tough, muscular, well-trained Israelis. He proudly introduced me to his 'new best friend', his rifle, which for the next month would never leave his side. While giggling hysterically, he unsuccessfully attempted to lift the giant hunk of metal above his chin, his laughter rapidly fading with the act. Jeremy had little interest in pandering to Johnny's melancholy mood. Liz had told him about the Rodinsky research I was conducting, and he was curious to know more. He sat me down, serving me cups of strong Turkish coffee and asking many questions. When I told Jeremy about the date of Rodinsky's death and my birth he became increasingly excited and suggested I visit a rabbi he knew of in Jerusalem

who specialized in the study of cabbala. Jeremy had been to see the
rabbi himself and he told us he had a remarkable, if fanciful, story
about the man and how he came to be a great cabbalist. He held us in
suspense, promising to tell the story after a supper of omelettes and
salad. With the heat of the cooking, the humid, still air inside the
small room became unbearable. Trying to find a whisper of wind, we
moved up on to the roof, and Jeremy told us his story:

A young man was driving down a street in Jerusalem when he
was flagged down by a bearded old Hasid. He stopped and let
the old man get into the car, and asked him where he wanted to
go. He asked to be dropped off in *Mea Shearim*. As they drove,
the bearded stranger inspected the young driver carefully, and
after many minutes in silence he told him he had special and
mystical talents unused as yet. When they reached their
destination, the old man gave the young man a blessing and left.
The driver laughed the whole event off, but all night he lay
awake thinking about the words of the old man. What had he
meant by special talents? He decided to return to the address the
following day to ask him to explain. On finding the house he
was surprised to see it boarded up and unlived in. His curiosity
aroused, he knocked anyway, but there was no answer.
Eventually a woman from a neighbouring house came to her
window. When he enquired as to the old man's whereabouts,
she told him that no one had lived there for the past fifteen
years – since the former owner passed away. The driver asked
his name, but she did not know; all she could tell him was the
man had been a rabbi, and a well-respected cabbalist. The driver
tried to forget the incident, but over the years the rabbi's words
continually played on his mind. About ten years after the event,
to his horror, he awoke one morning to discover he was
completely paralysed from the waist down. During the days,
months and years he spent bedridden, he began to study
cabbala. After many years of study he became a well-respected
cabbalist of great mystical abilities.

Jeremy claimed to have heard this story through a friend of a friend called Yossi who had gone to visit the cabbalist a number of years previously. According to Jeremy, Yossi, a falafel-stand owner in Tel Aviv, had been experiencing an increasing amount of bad luck. A friend of his suggested he visit the cabbalist. On his first visit the rabbi told him he had ten objects in his house that were creating the bad luck; they were to be removed immediately and burned in the yard. The rabbi described the exact objects and their precise position in the house in incredible detail. Yossi was amazed and terrified and did exactly as the rabbi commanded. Yossi's problems stopped immediately, and he returned the following week to thank him.

When Yossi entered the rabbi's house, he saw food and drink on the table and many people laughing and talking in the room. The people turned out to be the disciples of the cabbalist; they had gathered there to hear him give a lecture. Suddenly the merrymaking stopped as all eyes turned towards a distressed couple who had just entered the room. They went straight to the rabbi and told him through a flurry of tears the problems they were having with their seven-year-old daughter. She was foulmouthed, abusive and violent. They could not understand her behaviour and were beside themselves with worry. The rabbi promised to help, and he ordered them to bring the child to him immediately. The table was cleared of food and drink and a white cloth was laid on top of it. The girl was dragged in by her parents; she spat continuously whilst hurling vile abuse at everyone present. The rabbi gathered his disciples close to him and ordered the girl to lie on the table. He then placed an open book of *Zohar* over her face and began to chant softly. As his voice became louder, his disciples joined in. They were repeating over and over the same three secret words; words that are never used in prayer. As they chanted, they began to move in circles around the girl, three times one way and then three times the other. Suddenly the girl's rantings ceased. At the same moment, the candles levitated above the candlesticks. The lids on top of the fizzy-drink bottles flew into the air and a watermelon on the table exploded.

The young girl threw her head back violently before emitting the most inhuman, high-pitched screams. Her mother was hysterical, but the rabbi would not let her pass into the magic circle they had formed. The chanting increased, the demonic screams became louder and louder. Yossi could bear no more, and ran from the room and up the street. Heart pounding and hands shaking, he managed to find the keys to his car, and once inside he hung on to the steering wheel for dear life, resting his pale face against it. Paralysed with fear he remained in this position for hours. Yossi never returned to the rabbi's house.

Whether I believed the story or not was irrelevant. I was too curious not to pay the rabbi a visit myself. Jeremy gave me his details and I telephoned the following day. A young female voice answered. I was told it was not possible to make an appointment, but the rabbi had an open-door policy between four and seven on Sundays. I could come and wait, and if I was lucky I would receive an audience. She suggested arriving early.

The rabbi lived in the heart of the old city, in the Jewish quarter of Jerusalem, a labyrinth of ancient narrow sandstone streets. It is impossible to distinguish one street from the other and, unless you know the territory well, it is easy to take a wrong turn and accidentally cross the border into the Arab meat market, surrounded by decapitated goat heads and dripping blood. To avoid this grisly sight I allowed myself, for the price of a few shekels, to be led by a small, dark-haired boy out of the maze and back into the Jewish quarter. I then felt safe to ask in Hebrew for directions.

'You want to see the rebbe?' said a toothless, headscarved woman, straight out of my nostalgic fantasy. She hobbled with me a few streets further and pointed to a small doorway around which a lot of action was taking place. Seated on a small wooden stool in front of the entrance was an artist, dressed in a wide-brimmed panama hat, with a magnificent handlebar moustache and sharply creased linen slacks. He was deeply absorbed in reproducing in oil paint the picture-postcard street scene before him. A horde of dogs, children and neighbours surrounded the painter and blocked the stairway to the rabbi's house. As I approached, a number of small children darted into the doorway before me, but when I entered they seemed to have disappeared from sight.

The brightness of the streets had dazzled me: I could see only vague patterns inside which gradually came into focus as an exotic jumble of cloth. It looked as if a volcano had erupted in the centre of the room, spewing brightly coloured miniature clothes over every surface. A cascade of them erupted down the narrow stairwell, spilling on to every furnishing, hanging from the balcony railings and between the cupboards. I had difficulty working out where the walls, and the various levels of the tiny home, started and stopped – it was impossible to see an inch of uncovered floor space. A particularly large pile of dresses to my left began to heave, and two bright-eyed smiling boys with long soft curly earlocks emerged. To my right I heard a suppressed giggle; three more small children appeared from under the table, proudly holding a bottle of Coca-Cola while they sang in unison, 'Rak b'shabbas, rak b'shabbas' (only for the Sabbath, only for the Sabbath).

A large woman entered the room from behind a curtain at the far end. She was wearing a bright red flowery dress and a long dark wig and carrying young twins, one resting on each broad hip. She introduced herself as the rabbi's wife. I asked if there were any more children hiding in the room, and she said she expected so, they had a total of twelve. It was impossible to imagine where they all slept. She pulled back the curtain at the far end of the room and led me into a long narrow space where a number of people were patiently waiting to see the rabbi. This room was orderly, in sharp contrast to the outburst of colour and chaos next door, sparsely decorated and lined ceiling to floor with books. In the centre of the room was a long wooden table around which about eight people were sitting waiting to see the rabbi.

I sat down and waited with them. The majority of the other customers were small plump Sephardic housewives, whispering urgent prayers from frayed leather-bound books. The clock at the far end of the room ticked away, and people drifted slowly in and out of the rabbi's office. Thankfully there were no ominous sounds escaping from its walls.

Jeremy had told me to think of a question to ask the rabbi, as this was the standard format for someone visiting a cabbalist. My question was clear. My return to Israel had been more than just a holiday. The last time I had been in Jerusalem was only a few months previously. I had spent an eventful year living in the country, leaving reluctantly for England to see my family, to exhibit a piece of sculpture at an exhibition and also to perform in the Slaughterhouse show. Originally, I had intended to be in London for a couple of months and then return to Israel. But after agreeing to write this book I was very unclear about which country I wanted to live in and what path to take next.

During the long wait to see the rabbi, I spent the time reflecting on how I had come to this point in my life. I had left London for Arad in the summer of 1995, relieved at the opportunity to escape from my city life and the addictive pull of Rodinsky's room. I had arrived there, sickly and thin, my chest weakened by pneumonia, hopeful that time spent in the pure desert air would strengthen my bruised lungs. The damp and dusty environment of the Princelet Street synagogue had irritated my condition and the Holocaust exhibition I had completed for West London Synagogue had entirely drained me, both physically and emotionally.[1] The exhibition had taken up most of the previous three years, and was the most difficult task I had ever completed. After years of research the exhibition was finally constructed in the basement of the abandoned Princelet Street synagogue. A painful labour of love. Slowly, I stitched together hundreds of printed linen panels that told in brief the story of the Shoah. It was damp in there, and the weight of my task hung heavily on me. The hushed whisperings of my ancestors, thick in the air of the old synagogue.

[1]   The completed exhibition is permanently installed at West London Synagogue.

To counteract this painful daily activity I spent my nights indulging in the underground rave scene of Dalston, in a former cinema now aptly named the Labryinth. It consisted of a complex network of low-ceilinged smoky black rooms, eerily lit by laser lights and crudely painted luminous cartoons. This place became my refuge, the stabilizer of my sanity, my projection into modern life from the basement of my synagogue. The club fascinated me. In another time it would have been terrifying. But this was the Nineties. The thuggish-looking characters who filled the dance floors were temporarily transformed into smiling, winking, gentle beings, obediently pumping away to hypnotic hardcore, occasionally stopping to give you a sweaty hug. I loved it – at the time it was the one place in my universe where things made sense. I would dance furiously for hours on end, dancing until my toenails went black from the pressure of my trainers mercilessly thumping on the concrete floor.

This was the creature that arrived in the sleepy desert town of Arad, determined to regain my health and establish myself again as a full-time artist. The day of my arrival I went directly to my studio, situated in the artists' quarter of the town. I took with me a small suitcase containing some tools, paints and two envelopes. In one of the envelopes was a selection of the photographs I had been taking in Rodinsky's room over the past few years. I put them up on one wall of the studio and every morning I would find them curled up on the dusty floor, the desert heat melting away their fragile Blutack support. I felt as though Rodinsky was telling me this was not their place – they needed to return to his room to be understood. Some of the other students in Arad became fascinated with the images, and I would often talk about Rodinsky with them. My Hebrew teacher became interested in one photograph of Rodinsky's notebook, convinced from what she saw that Rodinsky had been a great cabbalistic scholar. And Amos Oz, the Israeli writer, whose beautiful and flamboyant wife was the director of the arts project, would often visit me. The interesting discussions with Amos himself probably first gave me the idea of assembling the Rodinsky research into a book. But at the time I had another preoccupation. The other envelope contained a single photograph. It had been taken in Poland in the 1920s and was the only record of the entire Kirsch family to survive the war. Out of the twelve family members in the picture, there were only four survivors. One of them was my grandmother. The picture had always hung above the fireplace in my grandparents' house and now it hangs in my parents' hallway. My uncles both have copies, and during my travels I have seen the picture in the homes of relatives in New York, Poland and Israel.

In the relentless heat of the desert I sat in my studio, inhaling the oxygen-rich air, lungs slowly recovering, while I stared at the images in front of me. On one wall sat Rodinsky's artefacts, strangely separated from their attic tomb, floating in the midday heat. I left them alone. The photograph from Poland haunted me day and night. I started to make sketches from the image, drawing every family member again and again until I could recognize all the features of their faces. I projected the image on to the wall, and painstakingly traced their outlines until they towered before me, life-size. My tiny studio was soon filled with hundreds of sketches of the Kirsch family. I did not know what to do with them.

The following week I went on a trip with the rest of the artists to an archaeological dig on the borders of the Negev and Hebron. We were digging in the catacombs, and nearly all of us retrieved some broken pieces of ancient pottery. I was amazed we were given permission to do this, but our guide explained that archaeological material in Israel is so plentiful that there are not enough funds or manpower to deal with it all. Not one of us had recovered anything of any real value, and we were asked to add our finds to a huge pile of pottery shards on the way to the cafeteria. I cheekily asked our guide if we could keep one of them. 'Take as many as you want, this is archaeological rubbish. We have so many pieces of pottery it is only the really rare or large pieces that can be reconstructed.' I could not believe my luck. I had come across the most incredible raw material that a sculptor could ever hope to find. Some of the pieces dated back two thousand years. I asked everyone in the group to fill up their rucksacks for me. I had an idea about how to use the shards in a piece of work.

On returning to the studio I began to clean the pieces and sort them into different shades and tones. I wanted to use them to reconstruct the family photograph, to create a life-size mosaic from the ancient shards. I began enthusiastically, but soon realized I did not have enough tiles to complete the project. I asked Nili Oz if she could help me contact another archaeological site, and she arranged a meeting for me at the largest site in the country, in Caesarea.

I arrived at Caesarea to be greeted by Yoram Saad, the manager of the site. He threw my bag into the back of his dirty jeep and asked how he could help. 'Please, be brief. I only have half an hour to spare.' Typical charming Israeli. We went to his office, situated in the middle of the Roman amphitheatre that was the heart of Herod's majestic ancient city of Caesarea. I told Yoram about my project and surprisingly he was very excited about the idea. He told me he was himself an artist and from a large orthodox family, not unlike the one in my photograph. He offered me as many shards as I wanted and said he would help in any way he could. We walked out on to the site, past the walls of the amphitheatre to a giant pile of discarded broken pottery. Yoram began to tell me of the problems of preserving the site and of the work he was involved in there. Two hours had passed and we were still on the pile of shards, talking and talking. He began to tell me a little of his life. He was the oldest of thirteen children of extremely orthodox parents. His mother came from Iraq and his father from Morocco. Yoram had been brought up in a very traditional way and had been unable to cope with the pressures of orthodox living. He had run away from home at the age of thirteen. He had grown up on a kibbutz with an aunt, living a completely secular life. For many years he had been isolated from his family, this separation increasing as he became first an artist and then an archaeologist. He confessed to me that he had been haunted by his rejection of his Jewish faith and in the past week had decided to start keeping kosher and Shabbat again.

I felt great empathy with Yoram's decision. While spending endless hours redrawing the photograph of my family in Poland I had reached a similar conclusion. I wanted to become orthodox. How did their deaths make sense, if I did not perpetuate the Jewish faith they had died for? However, this decision was far more complex for

me than for Yoram. He had the joyous support of his entire family
who readily welcomed him back on his 'return'. I experienced the
opposite response. My parents are far from orthodox. My mother is
in fact not Jewish, which means that in the eyes of the orthodox neither am I. To become truly accepted within the community I would
need to undergo a lengthy and difficult process of conversion.

Arad was the perfect place for me to begin my studies towards
conversion. I had the support of the local rabbi and began to study
with him every day. My time was split between the synagogue, the
studio, Hebrew lessons and the rabbi's front room where we would
discuss Torah late into the night. This process had been going on for
a number of months when I met Yoram. I was already dressing in an
orthodox way, covering myself from ankle to neck, and had just
started to observe Shabbat and recently, with the help of the rabbi,
I had koshered my kitchen. He had arrived at my tiny flat, armed
with a huge samovar, some tongs and four large stones. I had boiled
all my kitchen utensils and crockery the night before and separated
them into two piles, one for meat, the other for milk. Under the
rabbi's instruction I filled the samovar with water and began to boil
it on the gas ring. In the flame of the remaining ring I placed the
four stones. When the water had boiled and the stones were red-hot
the rabbi lifted the huge steaming samovar and told me to take the
stones with the tongs and drag them across the kitchen surfaces. As
I did so, he poured the boiling water over them, creating a tremendous amount of steam and noise. The utensils and crockery were
then placed in the boiling water and my kitchen was officially
koshered.

After eight months of study I was ready to go to *yeshiva* to finish
my conversion. This coincided with the completion of the mosaic. It
had been a difficult and laborious task in the relentless desert heat.
The finished art work weighed over half a ton and measured nearly
two metres high and two metres wide. With a lot of help I managed
to transport the work to four different galleries in Israel; it came to
the attention of a London curator, and she invited me to exhibit the
work at the Barbican Art Gallery in a show entitled 'Rubies and

Rebels: Jewish Female Artists in Contemporary British Art'. It was
then that Iain Sinclair asked me to exhibit some work about
Rodinsky at the show he was organizing at the Slaughterhouse
Gallery. I decided to return to England to exhibit in these shows,
knowing that when I went to *yeshiva* there would be little time to
pursue my artistic career.

In Israel my new lifestyle had made perfect sense. Back in London
I was having an extremely hard time, particularly with my parents
and friends, who found the change in my dress, manners and behaviour difficult to accept. As at so many other times in my life I turned
to my art for solace, working day and night in the studio to complete
the Rodinsky work for the Slaughterhouse show. I made a film, took
photographs and wrote a performance all based on David Rodinsky.
After my time in Israel I felt that my connection with him was even
stronger than before. For the first time, I could truly relate to his
struggle between living the orthodox life he had been brought up in
and his attraction to the secular world around him. I was thinking of
Bella Lipman's descriptions of him eating in Indian restaurants, his
fascination with foreign languages, and the many empty bottles of

beer found in his room, alongside the Irish drinking songs copied into his notebooks. Maybe we had more in common than I had at first thought.

Now I had come to see the cabbalist hoping the visit might help me to decide what direction to take next. Should I remain in London and write the book about Rodinsky, or should I return to live an orthodox life in Israel? Then it was my turn to go into the rabbi's room – my heart was racing and my palms were sweating. The room was claustrophobically small and most of the space was taken up by a large office table, behind which the rabbi sat. The walls were lined with books and a few framed images of strange geometric patterns I did not recognize. The rabbi was an impressive sight, wearing a glamorous purple silk robe, majestically set off by a long dark beard. He stared at me solemnly as I entered and gestured briefly with his eyebrows for me to sit down. As I did so he casually placed an open palm in front of me, coughing politely, until I, with eyes averted, gently laid a fifty-shekel note inside it.

The rabbi sat back in his chair, sighed deeply, and asked me why I had come. Didn't he know already? I asked him my question, explaining nothing of my background or who Rodinsky was: should I come back to study in Israel, or stay in England and write the book? The only piece of information I added, when asked, was the date of my birth and the date of Rodinsky's death. The rabbi wrote down this information then began to make a strange chart in pencil on a large piece of paper in front of him. I strained in my chair to take a look but could only make out a confusing-looking configuration of Hebrew letters. I was desperate to own that piece of paper but too shy to ask; it did not seem appropriate. After about ten minutes he stopped, looked at me, took a deep breath, and then closed his eyes while resting his hands together as if in prayer. He stayed in this position for a long time. Finally he opened his eyes, threw down his hands on the table and looked straight at me. Slowly, in disjointed English and carefully chosen words, he began to speak. 'You need to spend time in nature alone.' Long pause. 'You are in some ways fragile, but have a strong *nefesh* and a thirst to discover the depth in things. You are always searching for disappearing things; most of the time you do not find them, sometimes you do. You are connected to the *olam hasod*, the secrets of the earth, you are the one that peels back the layers of the earth, like an onion, to find the meaning. This man, Rodinsky, his *neshama*, his soul, is connected to yours, you must continue your search, it is this search that will lead you to the right path.' His last words had made the hairs stand up on the back of my neck. Maybe he was right, that it was my destiny, my duty, the will of God for me to find out what had happened to David Rodinsky. The rabbi stopped talking and we sat in silence. After trying to ensure I was being polite by sitting for the appropriate amount of time, I thanked him and stood up to leave. My legs were weak beneath me; as I stumbled shakily towards the door he called me back. 'Wait. I want to give you a blessing so you will succeed in your journey.' He asked me to stand near him, and again he closed his eyes, muttered some words under his breath, and raised his hands towards my face. Slowly, he opened his eyes and smiled up at me, nodding graciously as I thanked him again. I left the room elated, and clear in my mind about what to do next. I would return to London and finish the book. I hoped that the other issues I was struggling with would become clear through this process.

WHO CARES FOR THE CARETAKER?

Iain Sinclair

> no more than a breath between
> there and not there
>
> Paul Celan

A man, a human being, almost certainly dead. A man whose story lives in other men's mouths. A rumour monger who exists only in rumour. One of three brothers (or half-brothers); an immigrant Whitechapel family, Russian Jews, as neatly dispersed and divided as in a Wesker play. All of them have ambitions to write, to interpret, to remember, to shift themselves somewhere beyond the accident of their birthplace. (This was a large family. The mother, like David Rodinsky's in the Princelet Street garret, was described by one of her sons as a 'resident ghost'. There were four sons from the first marriage and five children from a second.) The senior brother 'escapes' to Highgate and is respected as the author of sturdy works of history and biography, one of which, *The Burning Bush*, is an almost-500-page discourse on 'Antisemitism and World History'. Another brother, now tucked away in Mecklenburgh Square, Bloomsbury, produces novels and television plays, edits the journal *Jews in Eastern Europe*. The third brother publishes nothing but is glossed by the painter and film-maker Donald Cammell as 'one of the great conversationalists and one of the great improvisers, what we call a "chat artist" – he could chat fantastically in East End lingo'. This

biblical younger son, the nominated black sheep, drifted between
worlds, disappearing for months at a time. He haunted Chelsea, the
demi-monde, scuffling around the gamey fold of the map where
bent aristos and old Etonian chancers snorted the feral energies of
the underclass. He was a wit, a *pasticheur*, a joker. A gambler, pander,
storyteller. A sexual opportunist, a predator, a victim. A conduit.
He brokered introductions at a period when Ronnie Kray and Lord
Boothby held court in the Grave Maurice public house, opposite the
London Hospital in Whitechapel Road, auditioning likely prospects:
rent boys, fight game novices.

It's too easy in retrospect to see this life as a representation of its
era, the shapeshifting, the multiple identities, the slippage between
high and low culture, between east and west of the city. The man was
a writer who didn't write, a character who was permanently 'on',
busking for his supper. His booze, his chemical supplements. His
borrowed wardrobe: a scarlet-lined jacket from some rock star, a pair
of Cordovan loafers from a society portraitist. His career was pre-
fictional. He had to die to launch himself, to come into his own. As
Cammell, another unfulfilled man, explained in an interview
recorded in Los Angeles (14 March 1992), the vision of the city that the
group associated with the film *Performance* attempted to bring into
focus mixed William Burroughs with the viscid interiors of Francis
Bacon, Jorge Luis Borges with Mad Frankie Fraser: hallucination,
derangement, violence, self-destruction (a style that would eventually
find itself deconstructed in Campari ads). Sounds and artefacts stolen
from North Africa. The envelope of identity turned inside out like
Yeats's cosmic egg. Then scrambled with Worcester sauce.

'I've filched ideas from a couple of Borges's stories,' Cammell
said. 'He believes in people taking on each other's personalities. . . .
It's not a Buddhist idea though it partakes of transmigration . . . the
eternal souls.'

The story of the third brother becomes an analogue for the myth
of David Rodinsky, the vanishing Spitalfields cabbalist. It begins in
the same immigrant quarter of London. It ends, across the river,
with an obscure death. A man shifts from his proper territory. And

in the process he is stripped of his humanity; his biography is constructed from unreliable anecdotes, grey and smudged photocopies of a portrait by the Australian artist Brett Whiteley. (Metropolitan ironist as longhaired, round-bellied monk perched on the edge of a table while he enjoys a blowjob). He was also drawn by Lucian Freud, a tribute in which the subject's name is not revealed. (The key to Freud's B-list.) This work, now catalogued as *Man in a Headscarf* (1954), was known as *The Procurer* – until its subject took violent objection. The man didn't want his best shot at anonymous immortality to be tagged with a bad joke. Market values, the potential conversion of louche art into serious money, sprinkles stardust on the most erased lifeline. Titles, in a culture addicted to text, confer a terrible potency. Freud's sketch is low-key, ambiguous. Hooded initiate or athlete in sweatsuit? Downcast eyes, a chipped nose and a small, tight mouth. Intelligent gloom. A moment of self-reflection for an average sensual man? Or boredom, barely controlled, before an outburst of cynical laughter?

As he is footnoted by hip culture pundits, this man loses his place of birth. He is deprived of the privilege of narrating his own history. Jonathan Meades in an essay on Christopher Gibbs, a patron, a man who made a career out of good taste, unforced charm and a nice line in socks, profiles the lost brother in a brisk para. Lesser journalists amplify and repeat Meades's improvisations. So that the few 'facts' appearing in lifestyle magazines, or wafted at film symposia, father a generation of Chinese whispers. The Chelsea chancer is placed by Meades as 'the scion of a liberal Jewish Highgate family'. In effect, he becomes his brother's son. His birthplace, Hare Marsh, Whitechapel, as in some sentimental Dickensian transit out of poverty, is exchanged for the shining house on the hill, the second-generation stability and status of his brother Barnet's family. His role as trickster, fraud, social comedian is downgraded. He is not allowed to construct his own fabrications, the 'lies' or little improvements that turn a 'genius' conman into a living novel. David Rodinsky, equally fretted by researchers, essayists, had the advantage of being associated with a single set: 'Rodinsky's room.'

There was no convenient location to visit in search of this other man. He is reported in clubland, in Cheyne Walk, at the dog track; suspended, head shaven, throat gashed, from a flat near Derry & Toms (a scene paraphrased in the film *Villain*). The character played by Ian McShane in Michael Tuchner's gangland saga owes much to the deracinated brother. It's not difficult to find the connection: Donald Cammell. Cammell, in the early stages of an eccentric film career, wrote a script for Ian La Frenais (*Villain*'s author), one of those standard lost works that even the author has trouble recalling, a Gerald Kershian bagatelle 'about a wrestler'. Cammell, pressed by his interrogator, can't bring the title into focus. Was it *The Pleasuredome*? No, that was Kenneth Anger. *The Touchables*? Who knows or cares? The director, Bob Freeman, was last seen in Hong Kong and the script might have been an early draft for *Performance*: 'a low life character, a couple of girls'.

But here at last, in the transcript of the Cammell interview, is the name of the third brother. Except that all these names, transcribed by some unfortunate secretary, are dyslexic approximations. Jean-Luc Godard's cameraman Raoul Coutard is rendered as 'Putard Raoul', Borges is 'Luiz Borges', David Cronenberg is 'Kronenberg'. And the brother is introduced as 'part of Francis Bacon, Lucien (sic) Freud's band of, you know, the East End world that encroached on the real world'. The name, David Litvinov, when he finally receives it, is not quite his own. But then why should it be – Meades also goes for the 'Litvinov' reading – when the geography of London has been stood on its head, and Cammell and James Fox imagine that the Old Kent Road and the Thomas à Becket pub are somewhere deep in the East End? East Street Market in Walworth is seamlessly connected to Brick Lane, and all parts beyond Chelsea, Kensington, and Knightsbridge are interchangeable reservoirs of geezers, boxers, lovable razor-striped rogues with a gobful of chat.

The elder brothers, Barnet and Emanuel Litvinoff, are published with their surnames spelt in the way they prefer. But David, having no books to his credit, had to take his chances; being remembered as the provider of additional dialogue for *Performance*. Cammell thought of him as a 'dialogue coach', a lurker in the shadows who helped the actors towards a proper sense of stylized authenticity. Litvinoff introduced Cammell to 'a lot of East End people ... including the Krays ... or two of them'. But he was much more than an obliging social secretary, a man with useful phone numbers. Meades fingers him as 'a piece of very rough trade' who obligingly 'topped himself' at Davington Priory in Faversham as a signal that the curtain was coming down on a dodgy era. The Priory, then in the hands of Christopher Gibbs, was later sold to Bob Geldof and Paula Yates. (The truth of this episode was more prosaic. Litvinoff took an overdose of sleeping pills. Three and a half years in Kent was enough for anyone. He left careful instructions for the dispersal of his collection of blues tapes.)

Where I was concerned, the quest for David Litvinoff, a detective story unravelling the mysteries of a life without evidence, a life recalled in contradictory monologues, was twinned with Rachel Lichtenstein's furious pursuit of the other David, Rodinsky. Litvinoff had gone out into the world (making regular returns to nocturnal Whitechapel), but he had made himself over, so that even the sound of his voice on the telephone gave nothing of his background away. He was like Harold Pinter, the actor, doing Goldberg in *The Birthday Party*: fast, ingratiating, ruthless, angered by some unintended slight. A grammatical error. An inadequate pause. An insult that can never be repaired. Litvinoff talked in inverted commas. A collage of customized quotations and compulsive puns. Like Pinter, he enjoyed breezing in for cameo appearances in his own scripts. Except that Litvinoff's scripts were untranscribed. They only existed if he could persuade a drunk, a society cruiser, or a journalist to remember them. And there was something much worse than Pinter's notorious pique, the glasses of whisky flung in the face. Litvinoff's reinvention as a Chelsea face involved real violence. According to George Melly, he understood very well the sexual excitement at the root of any act of brutality. He beat a suspected informer (innocent) and was himself slashed across the mouth outside a tube station. 'He was an animal,' said Cammell. 'He didn't care.' Many of the best Litvinoff

stories take place in hospital. Feeling himself slighted by the underground film-maker and Crowleyite, Kenneth Anger, he cycled across
Regent's Park to deliver, in person, a good thrashing. And to receive,
in exchange, Anger's curse. A year later he was dead.

From time to time I met people who claimed to have known
Litvinoff, their stories never connected. There were no fields of
superimposition. No hologramatic portrait ever emerged. Colin
MacCabe, in an essay on *Performance*, writes of James Fox and
Cammell, as schoolboys, meeting Litvinoff in Soho. They could be
talking about different men with the same name. Fox recalls 'a latter-
day Fagin teaching schoolboys to pinch cigarettes'. Rachel
Lichtenstein heard the same language applied to Rodinsky, the
shorthand for Jew as alien. Black rat of the city sewers, corrupter of
innocence.

One Sunday, at a book fair in the Royal National Hotel,
Bloomsbury, Hilary Gerrard limped up to my stall, working his way
through the mob, his cane brandished with the insouciance of Julian
Maclaren-Ross. Gerrard was a collector of Sixties memorabilia. He
had warehouses of the stuff, scattered around three continents, psy-
chedelic ephemera kept in cryogenic suspension until it achieved its
inevitable stock market quotation. This compulsive hoarding was a
way of holding on to a past that might never have happened.
Gerrard was a bit of a secret in the trade: no address, rumoured to be
Ringo Starr's accountant, paid cash on the nail. His discourse was
swift, Tin Pan Alley negotiated by house-trained hipster. A motor-
mouth who could pick your pocket while he charmed you with an
unforgiving cascade of gags. A man very comfortable in his well-
tailored anecdotage.

Gerrard had heard about my interest in Litvinoff. He not only
knew him, he'd been his best friend. (Litvinoff was everybody's best
friend, he specialized in it. That was his profession. In your company, he was the perfect audience: witty, up to speed with the gossip,
seductive – always with a certain edge. Then he was gone and you
were holding a phone number for an address where nobody had
ever heard of him.) Gerrard and Litvinoff knocked around together

in their poverty days as East End lads on the make. They slept on late-night buses. They opened a fish restaurant in Soho. A cellar with no kitchen and no licence. When anyone was foolish enough to try the place, one of them bunnied at the table while the other slipped around the corner to the chip shop.

They were wide boys, provocateurs, conceptualists. They stayed on the move. Their need, every day, to raise the wedge had the effect of concentrating their minds. Soho life was *The Small World of Sammy Lee* with laughs. Litvinoff managed to scandalize the audience at the Institute for Contemporary Arts (which had been set up for that purpose) with an early performance event involving a now-orthodox display of full-frontal nudity. (His brother Emanuel achieved the same effect at the same venue by having the courage to read a poem accusing the author of *The Waste Land* of anti-Semitism before an audience that included Eliot himself. Stephen Spender, ever the politician, abased himself before the great man by announcing that 'as a poet as Jewish as Litvinoff, I deeply resent this slander'.)

My obsession with Litvinoff, the nagging sense that his story, the story of the brothers, was a necessary one, became part of the script for a documentary film I was making with Chris Petit. The film was called *The Cardinal and the Corpse*. Petit shared my belief that the official map of the culture, at any time, would always fail to include vital features. Too many good writers were left out of the canon. This was particularly true of East London proletarian novelists. We found out in the course of our researches that though Alexander Baron and Emanuel Litvinoff were both still writing, neither had much expectation of being published. Baron, the more modest of the two, declared that he didn't know who the publishers were any more. He didn't have any numbers to call. Litvinoff wouldn't have seen himself as an East London writer. He was a 'lost' European; the district where he had grown up belonged with 'Warsaw, Kishinev, Kiev, Kharkov, Odessa' and not with the rest of London. So he told us, when interviewed on the highsided iron bridge that connects Hare Marsh with Pedley Street; a bridge that is itself a kind of checkpoint, a too-obvious metaphor for translation between zones, market and green field, past and future, life and death.

That's how Emanuel Litvinoff pitched it to Patrick Wright, when the essayist walked him back through Whitechapel in search of memory prompts, fossils of childhood. Wright contrived their excursion, this annotated drift, to finish in Princelet Street, in the decommissioned synagogue. The name David Rodinsky meant nothing to Litvinoff. He had his own experiences of hunger, poverty, cabbalistic scholarship, abandoned epics of mysticism. He'd been visited in his solitary room by the exiled Elias Canetti. He was labouring on an 'interminable' novel. Lack of food and a solitary existence given over to deranged feats of concentration left him in a 'trancelike' condition. 'I spoke of the need to shape one's life into an instrument through which the voice of God would utter, a trumpet of prophecy, of my dream that an angel stood at my shoulder while I wrote the story of my generation on to the page in illuminated letters like the Book of Kells.' He existed, so he explained to Wright, in a state of perpetual hallucination and breakdown, conjuring with 'psychometry, automatic writing, meditation and seance-like attempts to re-enter past lives'.

Brought to the synagogue, Litvinoff acknowledged that the building was 'full of ghosts', but he was too absorbed in the fiction of his own life to engage with Rodinsky. That would be asking too much. Each visit, each twisting ascent of the dark staircase, is a sort of test. It is a way of defining the visitor, adding something to the portrait of Rodinsky, by a process of elimination. Each visitor scrapes back some of the soot, blackens a finger. This is a long-term project. A biography constructed through erasure. By learning what we should forget, we make the space for Rodinsky to return. Litvinoff cannot afford to become involved with the vanished caretaker. That would be a collaboration he was not prepared to tolerate. Once, when times were hard, he had ghosted novels for Louis Golding. But not now. Time was too short. By writing about Rodinsky, he would *become* Rodinsky. He would have to accept that dictation, give himself over to a place he had escaped. The place (and the family) that haunted everything he wrote. As Wright concludes: 'This myth of the de-materializing immigrant hardly detains Litvinoff, who understands Jewish disappearance in the incomparably greater terms demanded by the Holocaust.'

Petit and I had to work hard to find anyone who could remember David Litvinoff. The price for membership of that exclusive club seemed to be burn-out, premature senility or suicide. The sad troop foregathered at the Carpenters Arms in Cheshire Street (a site that conveniently doubled with another gangland strand in the story). By now there were rumours in the London book trade about a set of Litvinoff diaries. Had he been working on these in the Priory during that undocumented period before his death? Did the diaries (what a tale they had to tell) incriminate figures from the homosexual/drug/gambling subterranea? He had apparently shared boyfriends with Ronnie Kray. He was always turning up, after one of his unexplained absences, with wads of ready cash – which he dispersed with characteristic generosity. So many of the cast and crew of *Performance* had already stumbled into madness, messianic seizure, violence, obscurity and death, that the film had the reputation of being a psychic vortex. It fed so successfully on the demonic energies of the period that it heated time, sending a portion of London into a terminal tailspin. And Litvinoff was the guide, the messenger. He reworked dialogue as part of a mythic project. ('Was your old man a barber?')

Our bringing together of some elements from a spurned and displaced literary life – Grub Street visionaries, street poets, remittance men banished from their own past – was a curtain-call for the reforgotten. Some of them (Robin Cook, Michael Moorcock) successfully ignored the camera and small crew. They were what they were: remorseless narratives of lives composed as they were lived. Inhabited faces. They were possessed by visible emotion. Cook stood against a wet window and conjured up the presence of death, 'the general contract'. Moorcock, recalling Gerald Kersh, found his eyes moistening as he moved from tender sentimentality into tales of roguery and faked signatures. But any of them, asked about David

Litvinoff, dried up, muttered, opened some book in the hope of
finding a prompt. Cook would have busked it; give him an hour and
a couple more pints of Guinness and he'd have the story perfected.
Emanuel Litvinoff had nothing to say. His brother was a subject
that couldn't be discussed. Gerry and Pat Goldstein, a pair of West
London notables – book hunters, memory brokers, social whirl-
winds – tried to push Manny into admitting that they'd all met at
David's funeral. But it was no use; Manny stood facing the pub, his
back to the wall, signing the books Gerry pulled from his bag. Pat on
one side, Gerry on the other . . . and these books that he hadn't seen
for years, books that were no longer to be found, and were now to be
upgraded with an inscription and a flowing signature.

Nobody had any dirt on David. No whisper of the diaries. To
take it any further would be to force a narrative far beyond any reasonable justification. We let it drift. Perhaps we'd got it all wrong: the
Carpenters Arms, after all, was part of another story, the murder of
Jack the Hat. Later, of course, in the way these things go, I discovered
that by chance we'd begun our investigation in the perfect place. The
Litvinoff home, the Fuller Street tenement, was across the road from
the pub. Emanuel had gone to school in Wood Close. We had
launched our quest just a few yards from the true starting place of
the Litvinoff story. And Gerry Goldstein, who had been a close
friend and partner in David's Chelsea adventures, knew far more
than he was prepared to reveal under the interrogation of a television crew. Joining our search for the mythical journals, he played
dumb, realizing all the time that the very thing we were looking for
was safely tucked away in his Shepherd's Bush flat. There were no
written journals, but Gerry was one of a number of people (Nigel
Waymouth was another and a third lived in Cheero Point, New
South Wales) who guarded a large collection of Litvinoff tape
recordings.

Six or seven years after the film was completed (around the time it
was being reshown on Channel 4 in the dead reaches of the night),
Gerry contacted me. He fancied a walk. Pat had an interest in a bomb-
site parking lot near Tower Bridge. We could hit a few bookshops,

drop in on the odd caff, and swop a yarn or two. (By now Gerry was a multiple, a self-impersonator. He'd flashed through the histories of punk as Malcolm McLaren's best mate and gopher, and was known to be a chum of Sandy Lieberson who produced *Performance* and the high camp, but moderately disastrous, film version of Moorcock's *The Final Programme*. Moorcock had even cast his fellow Mervyn Peake fan as 'a well-known underworld character called Jerry Silverstein' in an episode of *The Metatemporal Detective*, produced for DC Comics. Gerry, like Litvinoff, existed in a state of virtual unreality. His pension would have to be earned by rehashing edited highlights in documentary films. He and Pat were available, cash in hand, as the last witnesses for whatever you wanted to hear about the Sixties and Seventies. You hum it, they'd play it.)

Gerry had been with Litvinoff at Davington Priory and they were returning to London by train, to Victoria Station. Litvinoff found himself in a position analogous to David Rodinsky (but in a far grander style). He was the keeper of a property that was not his own. He had the time to pursue his own interests. He *had* to pursue those interests, there was nothing else left. But Litvinoff was a rogue philosopher, not a mystic. He needed society. He needed somebody to annoy. Jonathan Meades described him as 'a caretaker'.

Before my walk with Gerry began, he left me a copy of one of the Litvinoff tapes. We tried it on various half-broken machines and produced a few helium giggles and psycho-acoustic moans. It was only later, on my return, that I worked through my collection of abandoned and outdated players and recovered the Litvinoff voice. It was shocking, after all this time, to hear someone so buoyant, so fast, so manipulative. Litvinoff had rigged his phone to a recording device so that he could create and control a comedy of manners and misunderstandings. He had bugged himself to provide us with a posthumous diary. Live performances, untranscribed, unpromoted. For the delicious pleasure of the author/director and a few of his friends. *Krapp's Last Tape* meets J. Edgar Hoover.

This was the scenario: Litvinoff and Goldstein had been accosted by a mad-eyed vagrant, a Welsh, Neo-Romantic, storm-and-blood

booze-hound. A sentimental anti-Semite. A memory man who trea-
sured every slight, every missed appointment, every run-in with the
Old Bill. The tramp, John Ivor Golding, got more than he bargained
for when he hit on this pair. He was inducted by Litvinoff into the
play of the city. He was given drink and money, sent around to
plague such figures as Mick Jagger and Eric Clapton. He was introduced to the counter-cultural illustrator Martin Sharp, told to
report, in the guise of 'a professor of philosophy from Swansea
University', to a lunch party at the Pheasantry in King's Road.

Golding, webbed up with Donald Cammell, Christopher Gibbs,
Litvinoff and Jagger, was a weird concept to grasp. It was like Pinter's
caretaker blundering on to the set of *Performance*. And that, clearly,
is how Litvinoff read it. A tumbled world where past fictions, uncast
archetypes, could cohabit with rock stars, petty crims and
shapeshifting drug fiends. The dialogue from old scripts and forgotten musicals could be laced with the latest Chelsea/Whitechapel
neologisms.

The tramp was persuaded to phone Litvinoff – who then taped
the entire production, and played the straight man, pushing Golding
into wilder and wilder excesses. Listening to this dialogue, I was
drawn irresistibly back to *The Caretaker*. Litvinoff has exactly the
Pinter manner of indulgent sarcasm, absurdist flattery that turns, on
the beat, into lethal accusation. He plays Mick to Golding's Davies.
(I began to imagine the three characters in Pinter's play as the
Litvinoff brothers, struggling for possession of the memory of the
room, the home place. Danny Gralton's magnificently cold-eyed
photographs of Rodinsky's attic, the clutter, the dust, seemed like a
precise transcription of the set for *The Caretaker*.)

David Litvinoff begins by chiding Golding for missing the previous evening's party, where they'd been served a 'lovely Biafran wine'.
Golding responds that he was delayed in a public house waiting to
keep an appointment with the non-appearing Gerry. The dialogue,
the fencing for position, is ersatz Pinter.

LITVINOFF: You're very reserved.

GOLDING: It's all right if you meet the right company.

LITVINOFF: Do you get to the moving cinema a lot?

GOLDING: I've worn the tails, top hat, white gloves . . . I've worn better garb than you see me on.

LITVINOFF: Your attitude on philosophy is very . . . very breathtaking. Very abstract.

GOLDING: Well, I have been a big reader in my days of solitude and melancholy.

Social niceties taken care of, they move on to a subject of mutual interest: the iniquity of the police, whom Litvinoff describes as 'frustrated tailors – they're always stitching people up'.

GOLDING: Don't they know the difference between a bona fide citizen and an undesirable?'

LITVINOFF: You're a man of splendid bearing.

GOLDING: I know the weaknesses of equity and utility. Whatever the qualm or equivocation.

LITVINOFF: I saw the light burning in your eye after closing time in Victoria.

GOLDING: I could have been a licensed surrogate. At Llanelli in Carmarthen. It could have made a difference in the mollycoddling of Mick [Jagger].

LITVINOFF: There's a Victorian light in your eyes after closing time . . . Midst all the people hying and scurrying around Victoria, you alone had the dignity of the Third Eye. Your eyes were a magnificent sight, even allowing for the bloodshot bits in various parts of them.

GOLDING: You understand me, don't you?

LITVINOFF: You looked in extremely good health and fairly expectorative and splenetic when I saw you. You don't have any infectious diseases – like anthrax – do you?

GOLDING: I can assure you . . . I use the highest order of discretion. As no doubt you would observe.

LITVINOFF: You can keep a confidence? You won't tell anyone, will

> you. I'm trusting you like a brother. I can rely on you
> implicitly?
> GOLDING: Better than these walls.
> LITVINOFF: I'm afraid I'm rather keen on the grape. I've drunk
> four bottles.

And so it goes, on and on, for more than an hour. Act One. Golding talks of his days on the road, waiting to get his papers from Lord McAlpine. Another wasted evening in the Royal Oak, Commercial Street, Newport. Like Pinter's tramp, he suffers from selective amnesia: fantastic details, addresses, times, produced to confirm a story that will never otherwise be believed. McAlpine has confiscated Golding's carrier bag with his 'shaving gear and papers'.

The conversation drifts to Gerry. 'I'm very worried about Gerry,' Litvinoff confides. 'He doesn't know if he prefers the company of boys or girls.' Is Golding prepared, if necessary, to share a bed? He is. 'I'm involved with a very strange synagogical church syndrome,' he mumbles in justification. 'There's a synagogue in Cathedral Road. I've been to a lot of boys' parties there.'

The conclusion is unexpected. Litvinoff decides to float the notion that Golding was the original for Pinter's Davies.

> GOLDING: I have done work for a scriptwriter.
> LITVINOFF: I know about that, *The Caretaker* play.
> GOLDING: I did that with complete philanthropy, but I don't
> worry about that.

He is unconcerned that his surrogate has moved on to such fame in the world, while he is left out in the cold at the mercy of a sadistic constabulary. Litvinoff is his last hope. He doesn't know that his conversation is being recorded and he probably doesn't care. He is being directed. In Litvinoff's parallel universe, Golding *is* the caretaker. He precedes Pinter's theatrical creation. He's full of chat, rant, theories, memories of an Arcadian past peopled with vipers. He sees himself on *Desert Island Discs*.

GOLDING: You read *The Caretaker*, didn't you? You understand
me. I'm very precarious. I know what I'm talking about.
LITVINOFF: Do you accept sterling?
GOLDING: I have an amnesia for it.

Golding vanishes. He is not heard of again. There is no place,
like Rodinsky's attic, to sustain his memory. Nothing to hold him in
life. No photographs, books, clothes, witnesses. He is a blustering,
pathetic voice on a tape that was once passed around as a joke, a
specimen of improvised comedy. His papers had gone. He was no
caretaker. He was unhoused, on the move, forced to make his pitch
on a daily basis, to present himself as a character in search of a
drink. It was Litvinoff who became the caretaker, with only a single
grudging screen credit, the mythology of his friends, and a few
unauthenticated tapes, as his epitaph. He was left with Jonathan
Meades's cynical obituary: 'Litvinov [sic] succeeded where the Krays
had failed; he topped himself on the premises.'

After I had listened to the tape, Gerry obviously decided that no
great harm could be done by offering me access to another friend of
Litvinoff, the film producer Sandy Lieberson. Lieberson lives, with-
out ostentation, in a quiet street in the hinterland between Camden
Town and Primrose Hill. Gerry had some difficulty in remembering
the right number. We stuffed notes through the wrong door before
I noticed the freight of books, Richard Hamilton prints, Angus
McBean and Bill Brandt photographs in the adjacent property.

Lieberson, courteous and soft-spoken, denied that Litvinoff was
ever a writer, even by proxy. 'What David did, he knew literature and
he loved it. But any opportunity he had to do something himself, he
wasn't able to do it. I gave him the chance to write the Lenny Bruce
book and ultimately he never came through with it. You'd have to
say, in the end, he was a bit of a petty thief, David. He nicked some
pictures from Robert Fraser, things like that.'

Gerry remembered the episode, he'd been in on it. 'Well, that was
a stroke David pulled. What he did, he went along to Robert Fraser's
gallery and I was with him. And he had some old out-takes of the

Rolling Stones. He said . . . you know he was a big Dylan freak, David . . . he said, "I've got this really rare Bob Dylan album, just come out. Like the Basement Tapes, but better." So Robert took the pictures off the wall and he gave them to him.'

Litvinoff, according to Gerry, had done some Grub Street hacking from time to time. 'He used to work for the *Express*. When he was younger. On that William Hickey column.' The usual agenda: misinformation, bent gossip, black propaganda. Fiction with headlines. Fiction that paid by the word. Anything to avoid the horror of confronting a blank page, taking down the voices in the head.

There were letters from Litvinoff in Lieberson's files, scraps, fragments, drafts, cancelled beginnings. He spoke of the Chelsea chancer with great tenderness. He produced a photograph, taken in the last years, a break from the caretaking assignment at the Priory. A colour print, ornately framed, had pride of place in Lieberson's library. I took my own shot of Gerry holding up this final portrait, the vertical scar in Goldstein's left cheek catching the light. Litvinoff in an alcove, in some French church. Blue jeans, white shirt. A notebook, or collection of papers, cradled on his lap. The right arm bent in a gesture that is obviously ironic; a quotation, a reference to an heretical original. The pale stone tracery behind him becomes an enchanted forest. Litvinoff as scholar and seeker, floating in his niche like Dr Donne in St Paul's Cathedral.

Before we left, thanking Lieberson for his time, Gerry returned to the notion of Litvinoff as author or diarist. 'When we were living in the country, he was writing bits of stuff down.' Nothing was finished and Gerry didn't know what had become of it, where it had been dispersed. Everyone remembered Litvinoff as a different man. Perhaps our invented journals were still out there. We discover whatever we need to sustain our fantasies. Litvinoff the conversationalist, the lover of literature, the con man, the bruiser, fades from the story in the guise of a caretaker. A keeper of secrets.

But to see David Rodinsky as another caretaker would be a mistake. Douglas Blain, in his *A Brief and Very Personal History of the Spitalfields Trust* (1989), describes the condition of number 19,

Princelet Street in terms of Rodinsky's disappearance. He gives the Trust the credit for 'uncovering an interesting piece of local history'. The state of repair and the story of the last inhabitant were woven into a single strand. 'Nothing had changed here since 1963 when the Elders of the United Synagogue departed, leaving in residence their caretaker and his wife, together with a Mr Rodinsky, scholar and inhabitant of the garret.'

Rodinsky was never a caretaker. That is a role that has, in the aftermath of Pinter's successful play, been grafted on to him. The notion of caretakership belonged to the Spitalfields Trust, protectors of the fabric, the detail of the buildings. They wanted not so much to keep these properties intact, fixed in time, as to shove them backwards into an entirely imaginary past: into the cobwebs and recorded voices that Dennis Severs ringmastered in Folgate Street. The Princelet Street building, Blain asserted, 'remained unscathed by the dreadfully squalid and lately destructive passage of time in this part of Spitalfields'.

This quaint notion seemed to accord with one of Peter Ackroyd's conceits: that time moves at a different pace in different places. That there are privileged zones (for Ackroyd, these would include Clerkenwell, Limehouse and Whitechapel) where peculiarly sensitive voyants, 'Cockney visionaries', can surf the vortex, move without constraint between historical periods employing a kind of temporal Esperanto, where nothing is real and everything is pastiched. There is no here and now. Time becomes obedient to the will. And the lives of such as Rodinsky are optioned as fable.

THE MAN WHO
NEVER WAS

Rachel Lichtenstein

I returned from Israel to a number of excited messages from Saul Issroff. It appeared that the rabbi's blessing had already started to work. Saul had received a telephone call from the manager of a Jewish old people's home in North London, who informed him that he had located a cousin of David Rodinsky. Saul gave me the telephone number, and I rang straight away. The manager was reluctant to give me any information about the mysterious cousin. He said he would pass on my details to Mrs X and, if she was interested, she would get in touch with me. I waited patiently for five days until I could bear it no more. I rang back. The official told me he had passed on the information and this was all he could do, hopefully she would contact me soon. Goodbye.

Another week passed. Late on Thursday afternoon I received a telephone call from a Mrs Carol Wayne. She apologized for not phoning sooner but she had been busy making costumes for a show. Carol told me she was formerly Ethel Rodinsky and that she had grown up in Princelet Street. She was a cousin of David and remembered him from when she was a child. Reticent at first, Carol warmed to me when I told her my own grandparents had also lived in Princelet Street and had a shop there. She remembered the shop and invited me over for tea the following week. She told me she had moved from Princelet Street in the late Thirties to Stamford Hill and from there to Hendon where she now lived with her husband. Her family were originally from Russia. Carol had continued in the family business of hairdressing which began in a small village in the Ukraine in 1845. Carol and Alvin were hairdressing until the year before our conversation, 'four generations of specialized Jewish hairdressers, we made *shaytels*, cuts, perms, sets, everything. It was very successful.' When they gave up hairdressing they ran a charitable business conducting mime shows. Carol made all the costumes, designed the posters, the lighting, and took the bookings, while Alvin performed the one-man mime show, mainly in Jewish old people's homes. As they were leaving one of their regular haunts, Sobell House in Brent Cross, Carol had spotted a printed A4 sheet on the noticeboard. The director of the centre had printed off the request that Saul had placed for me on the Jewish Genealogical Institute's website and placed it on the noticeboard, knowing that many of the visitors to Sobell House were originally from Whitechapel.

The following Thursday, after a long bus journey from East London, I arrived at Hendon Central. It should only have taken another few minutes for me to walk to the Waynes' house, but I got lost. The houses all looked the same and the street seemed to go on forever. Eventually I found their home, a far cry from Princelet Street. I walked up the neatly kept gravel path, past their smart car and well-tended flowerbeds, and rang the chiming bell. The door was opened by a petite attractive woman with bright ginger hair and a friendly smile. I felt instantly at ease: it was like stepping into my Aunt Lily's house. The walls of the hallway were covered with family photographs: various small faces of smiling grandchildren sitting on the knees of Carol and Alvin, pictures of elderly friends and relatives in shorts and loud shirts against the backdrop of a Florida golf course, or sombre characters from Russia in faded sepia and grand gilt frames. Carol ushered me into the front room and sat me down beside an immaculately laid lace-covered table, weighed down with home-made cakes and biscuits. Immediately we began to talk about David. To the left of her chair, resting on the floor, was a large plastic bag.

Carol pulled out of the bag a fading paper covered in large biro text. I recognized the handwriting instantly. 'This is the letter I found from David, I haven't got any photos of him. There is another letter, a bit nasty, just can't find it, there's things about me in it. He was very very clever, brilliant, I only remember him from when I was a child. I know he used to go around in this dirty cap. My mother tried everything to make him make a real person of himself. He dressed like a beggar. He was very thin, taller than me, not terribly tall, but very thin, I remember his mother and his sister, his mother was Haicka and his sister was Bertha, called Brendall. They lived in squalor, ugh, it was awful.'

I hardly needed to ask any questions, Carol was readily digging up her memories of David. I asked her if she remembered his father as I had been unable to find out any information about him. 'I never knew what happened to him, I never remember him being around, maybe he was killed in Russia, because I think it was my grandmother who brought his mother over. They all came from a small village near Kiev, that's where my parents came from. I can't remember the exact name of it. I'm sure that David was born here though. He used to speak to us in Yiddish, but I think he was born here. He was only a few years older than I am I think. As far as I know he always lived in the rooms above the synagogue, I don't know exactly how old he was. I was born in Princelet Street and I was about seven or eight when we moved to Fashion Street and about two years after the war started we moved to Clapton. I think that David's mother was related to my grandmother, we used to call her *mimuke* Haicka but she wasn't a true aunt. My surname was Rodinsky, so I imagine she was a cousin to my grandmother. We were a very big family, they had nobody here except us, we looked after them. There was just the three of them.'

Carol confirmed for me that David had never married. 'I don't think he ever went out with a girl. He wasn't that type, he was very withdrawn and very, very religious. He was very clever.' When I asked about his appearance her response did not surprise me. 'He didn't dress nicely, he looked like a beggar; he wore old clothes and always this cap, he never looked clean. That room at the top, it was full of rags and wooden boxes. I remember going up there as a child. It was full of rubbish and we tried and we tried to get them to clear up but they wouldn't. They were happy like that and they didn't like you telling them about it either. All three of them lived in the one room. They weren't looking after the synagogue, I don't know how they got it. They definitely didn't look after the synagogue, but they might have rented the room. Look there's two letters here, this is dated 1961, he says he's all alone.'

> Do not expect to find my room as you suggested if you come
> again. My late mother was a very *frum* woman and she wanted
> me to observe the whole eleven months so I'm doing so. I will
> keep anything that meant anything to her in her sacred memory
> and I'm not concerned with the value of it, it symbolizes my
> home and my strong sentiment. Some *shmatter* may be cleared
> out in time but you must understand that I am a human being
> of flesh and blood and not a calculating machine. You must
> appreciate my lost years from five to sixteen when I was torn
> away from my home and you only languished hardship and
> misery, longing only to be reunited with the remaining
> members of my own family.

The letter was as curious to Carol as it was to me. She was unsure what he meant by his lost years and thought that maybe he was talking about time spent in Russia. She continued to read from the letter.

> You will remember that during those years you did not give two
> hoots about me. And when my mother asked for your advice
> you said, *Haicka nem dein gelt elvif elrose den veinder*. That

means Haicka take your money and throw it out the window. You never at any time gave us any real help, although you showed some friendship, do not think I'm ungrateful for what you did do or tried to do, but remember that I like you do not like being ordered about and that your intentions would be far more appreciated if you did not mistake vanity for quality especially at a time when I have lost what can never be replaced. Money cannot buy what I have lost and vanity does certainly not make up for it. If you cannot appreciate my sentiment then leave me alone. I regret using such language I thought you a *mensch* and if you have the decency to respect me and not use me for your own benefit under the guise of *rachmones* I do not want your sympathy only real guidance and respect for my feelings, just like anyone else would. Yours truly, best regards to all from David.

'This is very sad,' Carol Wayne said. 'He was so eccentric, that was his response to my mother's help. My mother was a real old-fashioned Yiddisher mama. She just tried to help him. He was so attached to his room, he couldn't leave. I remember, I think, they slept on the floor with the rags. I can't remember a bed, only the wooden boxes. I remember my mother telling them it was a fire-trap. They used to eat off the boxes. God forbid if there was a fire, they would have been burned alive. The room was cluttered with everything, especially books. My strongest memory is of me going with my mother up to their room and trying to help them. They took food if we brought it, but to try and get them to better the way they were living they didn't want to know. I remember his mother going around in the very long heavy clothing that would have been worn in Russia, layer upon layer upon layer of clothes because it was so cold up there. They just had an oil lamp to keep them warm.'

I asked Carol if any of the Rodinskys had worked, but she seemed to think not. 'The mother definitely didn't. To me she was always very very old, she may not have been, to me she looked it. Whether his sister worked I can't remember, she was also a very clever person.

She died young, I think she was in a mental home, I'm not sure.
They had a terribly hard life, they could have bettered it, they
wouldn't let anybody do anything for them. They didn't want anything better. They were all quite reclusive. Apart from us, as far as I
know, they didn't see anyone . . . I can't even remember the synagogue, all I can remember is climbing up all the stairs, narrow
staircase, very dark, very scary, to where they lived at the top. I just
remember the rags and the wooden boxes, terrible, and the windows
were high up a bit, very dirty, I can't remember any furniture only
the wooden boxes and all the *shmatter* lying about everywhere . . . I
remember him even coming to see us here in this house. He was
very withdrawn, very quiet, he was a soul I felt very sorry for. He
never talked about his studies or what he was up to. As far as I know
he only knew us; my aunt who would have known him died about
six weeks ago unfortunately. She lived in Old Montague Street with
my grandmother, they both knew about him. I think he just wandered around, picking stuff up, he must have got money from
somewhere. He didn't work, I'm sure he didn't. His sister might
have accumulated the books, she was very clever, spoke a lot of languages. She was much older than us; when I was a child she seemed
very grown up. Neither of them ever got married . . .'

Carol's gentle voice began to blur into a distant hum – for the first
time I realized that maybe it was the sister who had been the real
genius. She might have collected all the books, been the true linguist.
Certainly the notebooks found in the room were written by David.
But what did they prove? It was possible the information inside
them had been copied directly out of textbooks. I thought again
about his death certificate. It stated that David had 'epilepsy with
paranoid features'. I had discussed this with a doctor friend of mine
who thought it a misdiagnosis of autism. This would make sense of
the repetitive nature of his notebooks, the transcribed diagrams,
long lists and tables: all classic features of autism. Maybe Bertha
had been the real linguist. Having to hide her talents, this level of
learning – particularly of such a secular subject as languages – being
strictly forbidden for orthodox women. Bella Lipman had also told

me that it was the sister who had been the brains; she had described David as 'appearing a bit retarded'. How typical it would be to witness all the paraphernalia in the Rodinskys' room and to assume that the scholar must have been a man. I thought back to my time in Israel, my strong desire to study, all the wonders of Jewish learning. And then my mounting frustration at discovering that the intellectual world of Jewish law was not open to me.

I thought back to the series of photographs, expressing my frustrations, that I had produced in Israel. I had dressed in a traditional way, covering myself, in tights, long skirt, wrist-to-neck buttoned-through shirt and head covering and then crept down to the beach in the early dawn hours, where I added a pair of flippers, a snorkel and face mask to my costume. Slowly I entered the sea, asking a friend to record the experience with an underwater camera. The

images were ambiguous, in a certain light appearing like a celebration, a dance of defiance. This is how I first saw them until someone pointed out to me they looked like a woman drowning. 'Not Waving but Drowning'. Would I be able to breathe or would I drown? Discover a new world or a dark suffocating place where I would keep needing to come up for air? Did Rodinsky's sister battle with these same dilemmas? Why did she never marry? Why did she end up spending her last years in a mental institution?

My thoughts had taken me out of the pleasant environment of Carol's kitchen. She politely brought me back by offering another delicious home-made cake. I needed to focus back on Princelet Street, so I asked Carol what was it like growing up there. 'It was lovely, very happy, we had my grandparents, we all lived in two rooms at the top of the house, my mother had four boys and then me. The street door was always open, people went to one another, my grandparents lived a few doors away, the whole area was completely Jewish, the atmosphere was special. I remember at *Seder* night, at my grandparents', everyone came, everyone helped, I remember falling asleep at the table. It was a religious atmosphere, I remember *Erev Pesach* they used to go around with a barrow shouting out "*chometz, chometz*", they used to sell the *chometz* in the street, it was entirely different. It was safe for children to go out then.'

Carol became emotional when recalling these childhood memories, so we took a short break before talking about David and his family again. 'His sister was definitely more outgoing than him and his mother was normal, except she didn't like you to tell her to clear up. She used to come to our house quite a lot, his mother. They never came for *Shabbos* though, my mother would take them food, but they were too shy to come. I wish I could remember more.' The interview was interrupted by the telephone ringing and Alvin, Carol's husband, entered the room. Alvin and I talked a little while he made fresh tea. When Carol came off the phone she asked him, 'Alvin, you met David, didn't you? You remember, the one who lived in Princelet Street.'

'A strange boy, he did come here once on the bus. I remember the letter he wrote to your mother. Very naughty, very insulting, it seemed the mind went whoosh, you know, like he was in a spin . . . all of a sudden there was hatred. He was very bitter about life, losing his mother and his sister, he was a lost soul, eccentric and brilliant. He was a recluse. I remember how he lived. Floorboards, it was all eyuckky. They had rags, and cluttered with books, books, books and they were brilliant, lovely people, his mother was lovely, he was . . . odd.'

Carol told me that the last time she had seen David was in 1958 when he had made a rare visit to their house in Hendon. 'We lost track of him completely after that, so what happened to him even we don't know. He was only in his thirties or early forties but he always looked older.' Like Alvin, she described David as a 'lost soul'. 'My mother used to give him money, food and some of my father's things that she still had here, some old clothes. He looked like a tramp, a beggar. If you tried to help him he would bite your head off, you know.'

Alvin believed 'someone did something to him or he simply vanished'. 'Like I said, we never heard of him again after he visited here, we tried to find him but nobody seemed to know where he was. A mystery.'

I was starting to feel sick. I hadn't prepared myself for this. Carol and Alvin also had no idea whether he was dead or alive. The information they had given me about his age seemed to tie in with the dates recorded on his death certificate. I had to tell them. With my stomach in my shoes I said, 'Carol, Alvin, I'm afraid I may have bad news for you. I think I have found his death certificate.' They both looked at me in silence. Twenty-eight years after his death I was the person breaking this news to his only surviving relatives.

When I showed them the death certificate Carol exclaimed, 'Surrey! Why would he be in Surrey?'

This was the most difficult news of all to deliver. I explained that I had visited Epsom, presuming the Grove to be a private house, and discovered that it was in fact a psychiatric hospital called the

Longrove. I told them about the fire that five years earlier had destroyed all the records, making it impossible for me to find out more.

Carol was sitting quietly fighting back the tears and Alvin had gently laid his hand on her shoulder. Carol excused herself and went to the bathroom, emerging red-eyed a few minutes later. She told me she was not that surprised. 'His mother went through a pogrom in Russia and I think she was molested. This affected them all, they had a very strange upbringing. Brendall was in a mental home, she had a nervous breakdown, she had several fits. They were one of those families that whatever they touched they never won.'

Alvin suggested we break for more tea and biscuits. We stopped the interview and continued with easily flowing conversation about their grandchildren, my recent trip to Israel, my father's shop in Hatton Garden and the people we both knew there. After a pleasant half-hour we returned to the table where Carol began to look through the plastic bag beside her. She found another letter from David. 'We lived here when he wrote that, he must have asked me if he could come and live here, in 1961, but we didn't have room. His mother had died but his sister was still alive. Rachel, do you have a photograph of him?' 'No,' I told her. 'I've never found one.' I was desperately hoping Carol might pull out a portrait of him from her plastic bag, but she told me she could not find one either. She promised to go through her mother's things once more.

Carol went on to tell me more about David and his family. She said, 'They were very religious. David he was very very religious. He must have gone to the *shul* downstairs, I can't remember him going to Machizke Haddas, he would have gone downstairs, or maybe like us to the Nelson Street *shul*. I'd like to be more religious; we keep a kosher home, and Alvin works *Shabbos* so we can't help that. My brothers were all away in the forces during the war, it was only me really who visited the Rodinskys, because I used to go with my mother to his room.' I asked Carol what she thought had happened to the mother. In a whisper she told me, 'When she was in Russia, she was raped.' Alvin could not cope with the silence that followed, and quickly broke it by offering me another sandwich or a cake. The subject was obviously closed for discussion and I did not want to intrude any further than I felt I had already.

I continued by asking Carol if she knew what year the family had arrived from Russia. 'They must have come the same time as Alvin's mother, and my father's family, he was a Rodinsky, it must have been before the First World War. They tried to send my father back to Russia. It was before the First World War they all came over, and Haicka was a very disturbed person then. A lovely woman, very retiring, quiet, she was a tall woman. If you clapped your hands she would run, a nervous individual type.' Carol had no idea what had happened to the father. 'He didn't come over with them, definitely not because my grandparents took Haicka immediately under their wing. I think he must have died or stayed in Russia and she came over here.'

They argued a little about David's birthplace, Carol realizing that since David was born in 1925 his father must have come to Britain after all.

'Not necessarily,' said Alvin. 'Maybe she had another gentleman, with due respect.'

Carol shook her head. 'Really, Alvin, I don't think so.'

He looked at me and winked. 'Well, a pregnancy can't last that long.'

Carol ignored him. 'Probably the husband came over and died here before I was aware of anything. I am sure David was born here.'

I asked Carol what David was like the last time he came to visit her.

'He seemed very lonely and unhappy. You got vibes of unhappiness. He was extremely shy.' I told Carol about the café owner who remembered David playing the spoons and making everyone laugh.

She was amazed. 'I can't imagine it. But he was a 'centric, very 'centric.'

Alvin interjected again. 'This person who remembers him playing the spoons, you could go to the police and they've got these things called identity kits, was he like this, was he like that, and you can build up a portrait of him.' I thought it was a lovely idea.

Alvin continued to describe him from memory. 'He had sharp features, a long face, a thin nose, very sallow complexion, definitely no beard, no way. No straggles. No moustache. Very shabbily dressed and that cap he wore and an old raincoat, but you could tell he was a religious Jew.'

I asked Carol what the Rodinskys did for the sabbath and the festivals. She said, 'Haicka must have cooked. She must have had a blue light. They would put a piece of steel over the stove. They never came to us, they didn't want to. I think they must have got money from somewhere, they lived near the market and people would give them things when they knew they were poor like that. The *shul* probably gave them food.' Carol did not think they had any visitors apart from her family.

The interview was again interrupted by the phone, and Carol left the room leaving me with Alvin. 'He was a 'centric from the sounds of him, a real 'centric, he didn't really travel, even to Clapton, he might visit there, he certainly didn't have a car and couldn't afford bus fares too much, so he kept himself in that area and if he was found in Surrey, where you said, he must have been taken there. Thank God it was before the days of the snuff videos but nevertheless he might have been abducted for whatever. You should make a film of this story: The Man That Never Was.'

Carol returned and began to look through the old photographs from the plastic bag. 'There's my father and my *zaida* Rodinsky. There's my aunty Genny, akin to Haicka. She quite resembled her in a way; see how they dressed, that's how I can remember Haicka with that thick heavy skirt, long, she didn't wear a *shaytel*, couldn't afford it. Look, that's me. Ethel Rodinsky, Fashion Street, 1934.'

'A real beauty queen,' said Alvin.

She found many more pictures. 'This one's from Buxton Street school. It was all Jewish pupils then . . . I'm trying to find a picture of David, I can't find it.'

Carol said she missed the East End. 'The atmosphere was special. As soon as you came in there was a herring on the table, a cup of lemon tea on a white cloth. You didn't have to make an appointment to see anyone, you just went in, you would go visiting, you just went, that was how it was.'

As she was looking through the bag, Carol found another letter David had written to her mother.

Betsy, if you were really concerned about me you would not offer to spend my money, in fact money would not come into it at all, you would send someone to help me tidy up. When I come home from work tired, as you know that I'm all alone and your motive would not be money. Since I'm big enough to look after myself as you told the neighbours downstairs and since you cannot be trusted, I showed you my post office book and my late mother's post office book in confidence and you had to tell them downstairs and lord knows who else. You are big headed, snobbish and stuck up enough to mind your own business and leave me alone. Don't pretend to be concerned about me or my sister if your alteria motive is your own benefit. I hate hypocrites and liars, David.

P.S. You are no relative to us, your late husbands grandfather and ours were only fourth cousins and that your name Rodinsky is the same as ours is only an accident. You told the neighbours downstairs you've never seen so many *shmatters* as are in our place. What about when you lived in Fashion Street and Ethel used to say 'I'll tidy up when the Queen comes.' Now you live in Hendon in a house that you didn't buy, you spend other people's money but not your own. You think yourself countess Pintansky. As you have no sense I won't waste any more ink on you.

Carol managed to laugh. 'Honestly, my mother was only trying to help. I mean really, countess Pintansky, we only tried to help him live decently. Now I realize there were people living downstairs.' I told her about Bella Lipman but Carol was too young to have remembered her. She showed me another photograph of her and her brothers. I asked if they would remember him but she doubted it. She suggested I try the 'Telex, no intertex'. I suggested the Internet. 'Yes of course, my nephew was on it and he told me he noticed someone there asking about Rodinsky.' It had been me. I remembered his name and the important piece of information he had given me, that the Rodinsky family had originated from a small shtetl in the former Ukraine, not far from Kiev, called Kushovata. Carol expected this was correct but couldn't be sure. She continued shuffling through the papers in the bag. 'I'm trying to find out if he went to school. I don't think he did but he was brilliant. His Hebrew was superb. I remember that.'

Alvin chipped in. 'I remember my Hebrew teacher, he would chase the boys over the desk with a cane. Ooch.' He grinned at me again.

Carol sighed. 'I'm trying to think if there's anyone else in the family. Aunty Clara would have known.'

Alvin could not resist another comic opportunity. 'Excuse me, Aunty Clara,' he called out to the heavens. 'Can you hear us, no she can't.'

Carol was sorry she couldn't help more. 'They're all gone I'm afraid.' She was trying so hard to help. 'I can picture him now, tall and thin, taller than me, long very sad face, sallow complexion and the cap . . . I can't believe he played the spoons, amazing, you see he was two people . . . was he sychisofrantic? The person I remember wouldn't have done that, never, I can't ever remember seeing him smile.' This was amazing to me, and I told her about Bill Fishman's very contradictory image of him walking the streets with pockets full of change, giving out money to the poor. Carol found it hard to believe. 'Where did he get the money?' Carol believed if they did have money they were happy living as they did, in a peasant style. She said, 'They weren't typical, my mother was very poor, but everything was scrubbed, white, everything sparkled, just two rooms for six of us but it was clean, we had to go down to the yard for the toilet. We washed in cold water in a sink in the corridor, shared it with other families. We used newspaper for toilet roll, had it cut up hanging on a hook. I never remember seeing anything like that room, it made such an impression on me.' I asked Carol how his mental health appeared to her when she last saw him. 'He was logical, he knew what he was talking about. I never remember him talking about what he did or didn't do. I'm sorry I can't help you more.'

After the interview with Carol and Alvin I still had no answers as to who Rodinsky's father might be. I wrote up the interview and realized I'd forgotten to ask Carol about Hyman Rodinsky, the name I'd discovered in the register rescued from the Kosher Luncheon Club. I took the crumbling book carefully out of the protective acid-free wrapping I'd encased it in, and looked up the page again. The handwriting was very unclear: it might be *Rodinsky* or *Rodensky*, I couldn't be sure. Carol told me there was a Hyman in the family, 'Uncle Hymie', but he had definitely not been David's father.

I went the very next day to St Catherine's House to look for David's birth certificate. I knew from his death certificate that David had been born in 1925. The visit would also provide me with an opportunity to trace the newly discovered Hyman and Esther Rodinsky from the Kosher Luncheon Club register and maybe find some more pieces of the puzzle.

I arrived at the records office and met Stanley, an artist friend who had recently become a civil servant and, conveniently for me, was now the manager of BIRTHS and DEATHS. He proudly showed me around. We reached the aisle for 1925 BIRTHS. Stanley randomly picked a book off the shelf and instructed me how to search, turning the great heavy pages of the book. From his top pocket he produced a small metal ruler and a magnifying glass. 'Tools of the trade. Start in the left-hand corner and work your way down the small print, using the magnifying glass and the ruler to help you concentrate.' He began to read out the names: 'Rodan, Roder, Rodes, Rodin, Rodins, Rodinsky, Ro——' I stopped his hand before the ruler covered the name. We had found him: David Rodinsky born February 1925, Whitechapel district, London Hospital, ref. number 60X34.

The exhausted solicitor beside us went visibly green and told us, 'I have been here for nearly three weeks searching for one birth.' I sent off for the birth certificate, impatient for its arrival, knowing that in a few days' time I would have the name and occupation of Rodinsky's father, who had been impossible to trace up to that point. The search had confirmed that David had been born in England. With the main objective achieved so quickly, I told Stanley of my wish to find Hyman and Esther Rodinsky. He took me to the microfiche room and I began to search. Hours later I had found no trace of another Rodinsky.

I left the room, unable to do any more that day. As I made my way towards the exit, I noticed a familiar figure hunched over some books, wearing an embroidered *kippa* on his head. He slowly moved his hands across his pointed white beard in concentration and then turned his head in my direction. 'Sam?' He twisted around sharply to see who had called him, nearly falling off his chair in the process. 'What are you doing here?' It was Samuel Melnick. Over the years since my time in residence Sam and I had spent many hours together up in Rodinsky's room, attempting to archive the collection, translating material and discussing the future of the building. Sam had written a book on the history of the Princelet Street synagogue, *A Giant among Giants*, that took ten years to complete. His grandfather was the last rabbi at the Princelet Street synagogue and, oddly enough, he had married a Leah Lichtenstein, so Sam and I always joke about being related. Sam was one of the first people into Rodinsky's room and helped the Museum of London to dismantle and store it. Unfortunately for me, Sam had little interest in Rodinsky and had written him off as an eccentric lunatic. He is a meticulous researcher and was in the records office tracing some lost relatives for a family in Australia. I told him about my morning's work and the recent events at the luncheon club and synagogue in Greatorex Street and he was very upset about them.

A few days later I was sitting outside my local pub, the Pride of Spitalfields in Heneage Street, when Gerry, an artist I know, walked by. He told me he had been invited by the Commercial Gallery to make a piece of work for an art event that was happening in Greatorex Street. He had gone down there and found a room 'full of incredible Jewish textiles and books, all sorts of things, just dumped in a corner'. He said he had no idea what they were and was interested in using them, if appropriate, to make a piece of work, and he wondered if I would come down and identify things for him.

We went together the following day. It was good to see the synagogue in the day: soft rays from the glass roof bathed the building in light, washing away memories of my previous visit. Gerry took me straight to the cupboard adjacent to the ark and we began pulling out heavy, dust-laden objects and spreading them about on the synagogue floor. We found a huge blue velvet ark curtain, hand embroidered in gold thread, in good condition despite its covering of cobwebs. Slowly rotting underneath it we discovered a pile of exquisitely made gold and white silk Torah mantles, two heavy black cantors' robes, *tefillin*, boxes of prayer-books, bags filled with *talliot* and *tzitzits*, and various other pieces of synagogue memorabilia.

Gerry was understandably nervous about using these artefacts in a work of art. He asked my opinion, and I decided to call Sam Melnick as he would know exactly what the material was and the best place to house it. I sat on the steps of the ark in the empty synagogue, kicking a few cigarette butts out of my way as I did so, and called Sam on my mobile phone. He agreed to meet us there the following afternoon. Gerry and I went back to his studio and spent the rest of the afternoon discussing what to do with the artefacts. We decided to hijack the next art event with an uninvited installation.

The following morning was spent in a frenzy of collecting. Gerry biked over to the West End to pick up the acid-free tissue and archival boxes we'd ordered, and I went to the printer's to retrieve the museum labels for the boxes. We reconvened at two o'clock on the steps of the Kosher Luncheon Club, and when Sam arrived the three of us went back into the abandoned synagogue. We spent the rest of the afternoon identifying the artefacts, wrapping them in acid-free tissue, placing them in archival boxes and labelling them.

That evening the artists descended upon the building again. A large
crowd arrived in the main synagogue at about seven o'clock and
began to install PA systems and a bar – for the rave party that
evening. But they had a problem, because Gerry and I had installed
the boxes containing the artefacts all over the floor and we were
projecting images of Sam and me boxing the material alongside an
audio tape of Sam describing the objects. I told the DJ he could not
possibly set up in there, it would interrupt my art. We argued but I
won. The synagogue was quiet again that night.

The following day Gerry and I took the artefacts back to Princelet
Street for safe keeping. I remembered Evelyn Friedlander telling me
about the project she was setting up with a man called David Jacobs:
to find a safe house for Judaica in London. I left a note for Evelyn,
telling her I would get in touch on my return from Poland. I was
leaving the following day for Kraków and would be away for a
couple of months.

The morning before I left, the birth certificate arrived. It told me
that in February 1925, David Rodinsky was born at 73 Hanbury
Street. 'Father: Barnett Rodinsky, Tailor.' Barnett Rodinsky had
signed the certificate. He had definitely come from Russia with his
wife. I could find out no more than this about him, but aimed to
visit Kushovata, the original home of Haicka and Barnett Rodinsky,
during my visit to Poland.

'MOBILE INVISIBILITY':
Golems, Dybbuks and Unanchored Presences

Iain Sinclair

I am told of certain Stars, in the Chinese system of
Astrology, which are invisible so long as they keep moving,
only being seen, when they pause. Might thy Golem share
this Property?

Thomas Pynchon, *Mason & Dixon*

Rumours of Rodinsky spread outwards, in slow circles, from the
Princelet Street synagogue. The series of photographs taken by
Danny Gralton defined the set. Defined number 19 Princelet Street
as a set. Slow light processed through a large-format camera nudged
Rodinsky's attic out of the mundane stream of time. It was removed,
fixed in the eternal now, anchored by a catalogue of particulars.
Shimmering particles revealed the board ceiling with its warped
timber; a dusty bottle of medicinal wine, strategically arranged rugs
and rags, the *Angelus* print like a pious window. Gralton foregrounded newspapers that acted like subtitles: ISRAEL REBORN. Sorry
shards of scholarship were heaped on the table. The photographer's
gift for documentation was at odds with an expressionistic impulse
towards direction, arrangement, presentation. The room provoked
this very natural response. It was a dim interior, untouched for years,
in which a correct display of objects would expose some terrible
narrative secret.

Staring at Gralton's prints, a sumptuous entropy of detail encourages this, locks the observer into a dark space. The light source, the
shuttered window, is occulted. We wait so long for the drama to

begin. And then, very gradually, it breaks on us: the room *is* the drama. Rodinsky will never appear. There is nothing he could say. He is an absence. He doesn't belong in his own story. The incontinent clutter of things, uncollectable sub-antiques, displaces his consciousness. He is represented by whatever has survived his disappearance. The room is the map of a mind that anyone capable of climbing the stairs can sample. Rodinsky's life has been sacrificed to construct a myth, mortality ensuring immortality.

Gralton's photographs appeared in all the places where Spitalfields, Colin Ward's 'zone of transition', was defining itself. On the cover of the *London Review of Books*, in Robert Hewison's *Future Perfect*, and in *The Saving of Spitalfields*, which was put out by the Spitalfields Historic Buildings Trust. All these opinion-forming publications used the genuine forgeries that Gralton produced as a way of clinching an argument: Spitalfields was special because it had trapped time in a bottle. The dingy streets held residues of Georgian London, cloacal smears from the victims of Jack the Ripper, poverty statistics customized by Arthur Morrison. This was where the gothic imagination was tamed by social reformers. (If you want to understand the power of Gralton's retrievals, compare and contrast them with Dan Cruickshank's photographs, as they are featured in *The Saving of Spitalfields*. Cruickshank positions his camera to make useful slides for his next lecture: 'carpenter's marks', 'box cornice', or 'weaver's garret beyond repair'. The image is subservient to its label. Nothing is allowed to retain a patina of mystery.)

Contemplation of the Princelet Street set, and the convenient absence of Rodinsky, gave licence to film-makers and essayists. Spitalfields must not be allowed to drift with the rest of London, it must not be abandoned to the vulgar imperatives of capital (from which it had emerged in the first place). Special interest groups were frantic to establish squatters' rights for the coming recolonization. Dan Cruickshank, Mark Girouard, Colin Amery and the other New Georgian activists wanted to plug the district (or a favoured sample of the district) into Huguenot time. Spitalfields would not be connected to any of its surrounding territory (neither the clubbers, scrubbers and gay ecstatics of Shoreditch, nor the coarsened commodity brokers of the City, nor yet the leather hustlers, transvestite prostitutes, scab artists and horror-sampling tourist processions of Brick Lane). The heritaged streets around the partially demolished Spital Square would spurn their proximity to Broadgate with its frosty towers and its pastiched New World walkways, and choose instead to claim kinship through vertical time and not unboundaried space. By an incestuous act of will, they merged with an earlier version of themselves, spurning other relationships – except where the lowlife picaresque provided a source of cheap artefacts to authenticate their restored properties.

Raphael Samuel, a longtime resident of Elder Street, was a much more subtle propagandist. A scholar of place with strong family associations (Hebrew publishers and booksellers in Wentworth Street), Samuel clearly felt that his ties with the territory were of a different order to those of the New Georgian incomers. He enjoyed the moral superiority of the underprivileged, the disadvantaged, the labouring poor. (Even if, as an intellectual, widely published essayist and Oxford don, this was a proxy status.) Many hours of his life had been spent in recording the stories of those who had lived here. His account of the career of a Brick Lane villain, *East End Underworld : Chapters in the Life of Arthur Harding*, is a wonder of transcription and sensitive editing; offering, as incidental benefits, the freshest portrait of the Jago, a criminal taxonomy of the Lane, and the strategies of survival required to duck and dive from late Victorian times to the establishment of the Kray twins as voodoo deities. Samuel earned the right, through hard-won knowledge, to describe Spitalfields on his own terms. He had a sentimental attachment to a number of items in the bibliography of East London: Israel Zangwill's *Children of the Ghetto*, Jack London's *The People of the Abyss*, Arthur Morrison's *Child of the Jago*. Like Emanuel Litvinoff, he interpreted the area around Brick Lane in terms of the ghetto; he linked it with settlements in Poland and Russia, never with Islington, Hackney or Southwark. 'Spitalfields' was a gentrified flourish, a statement of validation for Nicholas Hawksmoor's Christ

Church (which is why Peter Ackroyd's *Hawksmoor* was so prescient in its timing, being published just as Gralton was invited to break into Rodinsky's sanctuary).

The New Georgians didn't much care for Ackroyd's sinister pastiche, his notion of satanic sacrifice; the submerged paedophile agenda of cruel phallic towers, murdered children, and redeeming boy angels. But that book was everywhere. I remember visiting a writer/director who had restored a Huguenot house in Fournier Street. This man, Rodney Archer, had recently staged a play in what he described as 'the Old Synagogue, Princelet Street'. The play was *The Harlot's Curse*, a ritualistic circling around the swishing coattails of Jack the Ripper, through rhyme, song, movement. 'Running through the play like a river is Blake's *London*,' said the *Observer*. One myth underwriting another. A ghost performance in a house of ghosts. A subdued audience shuffling into a building that overwhelmed them with its loud silence.

'A church bell strikes the hour. A man sharpens the knife – a scrape on each stroke of the bell.' So Archer's notes for the play instruct. From his first-floor sitting room, it is possible to peer directly down into the rectory, at the east end of Christ Church, and to see Hawksmoor's original staircase; to look across the bulk of the church itself and up at that sharply angled and dominant steeple. Archer's room, unfinished, is decorated with Ian Harper's Neo-Romantic backdrop for the play, brought here from Princelet Street. The fireplace, Archer tells us, once belonged to Oscar Wilde. Or so the rumour goes. A covert trophy rescued from his ruin and passed on, generation after generation, through the hands of the sympathetic few. On the mantelpiece are a pile of yellow-jacketed books. All one title: *Hawksmoor*. Each visitor to Fournier Street brings the Ackroyd bestseller as a gift, provoking unworthy thoughts of coal and Newcastle.

Raphael Samuel, halfheartedly renovating his property in Elder Street, prising the hardboard from the fireplaces, hopes to dig out publications of another kind. '*The Black Dwarf* or some fossilized specimen from the days of "weaver radicalism".' No such luck, the best he could come up with was 'a token of the London Corresponding Society . . . found in the floorboards.' 'United for a Reform of Parliament 1795.' Samuel was delighted to discover that his house had 'once been tenanted by an English Jacobin'. We excavate the history we need, bend the past to colonize the present. Even Samuel, the radical, the retriever of working-class memories, wants to force the territory closer to his reading of it. Spitalfields must be a shtetl of the last days. Working on his house he felt 'the panelled walls cocooning us, the firewood blazing in the grate'. 'We seemed,' he wrote, 'to be suspended in time and space.' Given over to place, the Jewish leftist and Peter Ackroyd, the former literary editor of the *Spectator*, are one. Ackroyd's Hawksmoor 'traced his name in the dust along the windowsill and then erased it . . . As he sat in the middle of the room sometimes he could see moving shapes, just out of the corner of his eye, but they were as indistinct as shadows on water and when he turned to look at them they were gone . . . And as Hawksmoor's voice reverberated around the room, some coins fell off the mantelpiece.'

Alongside his essay on *The Pathos of Conservation*, Samuel includes his own photograph of Elder Street. He has presented himself, with some conviction, as a more sophisticated version of David Rodinsky: Jew, scholar, excavator of mysteries, debunker of gentrifying pretensions. A man who has found his place. Samuel's photograph of his house, number 19, offers a near duplicate of another building with the same number: Dan Cruickshank's portrait of the Princelet Street synagogue. But the two properties were travelling in different directions. Elder Street was, for the first time since the Sixties, in 'family occupation'. The synagogue remained in limbo, no longer a place of business, no longer a site for worship, and not yet a museum. Princelet Street's passivity was an affront. The building demanded new narratives.

When Samuel died prematurely, leaving so many projects half-finished or half-begun, his partner, Alison Light, edited a series of posthumous papers under the title *Theatres of Memory*. In introducing the second volume, *Island Stories*, Light describes the Elder

Street scholar's curious filing system. She could be talking about Rodinsky. 'Raphael's files are crammed with reused paper of all shapes, textures and colours: a motley of notes stuck on the backs of scrap (from college memos to drafts of friends' articles, all themselves interesting, if distracting, reading); cut-ups from xeroxes and press-cuttings agencies, shreds of paper napkins from restaurants where a conversation was hurriedly written down and later dissected. . . . Cliffs of ringbinders in every available space . . . excitable, ever-mounting piles of file-cards . . . packed uneasily into old Oxo tins, teetering on dusty windowsills or lurking beneath chairs. Since everything could, in theory, be reused, nothing could be thrown away.'

Legitimate research, combined with limitless passion, contrives another Rodinsky analogue. The Spitalfields house of paper. The incomplete masterpiece waiting to be written. An hallucinatory tonnage of fragments seductively exposed in the hope that some future acolyte will complete the Great Work. Samuel, pen and notebook peeping from the pocket of his denim jacket, roll-up occupying busy fingers, wild scoop of hair scarfing across the creased brow, peers with affectionate irony (for Stefan Wallgren's author portrait). He's safely placed among rafts of books and documents, but the chair in Rodinsky's attic is forever unoccupied. There once was such a man, here are his words, his testament.

In 1991 a young woman arrived at the Princelet Street synagogue hoping to research her family history. Her grandfather had his first shop in this street, before moving east to the fringes of the London Hospital. Rachel Lichtenstein, to achieve balance in her own life, had to secure her past with documentation, hard evidence. She was as much a curator as an artist. Her instincts were forensic, archival. The synagogue, she hoped, would be a treasure store of dusty records, relics, scrolls, photographs. Coming in from the business of the streets, the hustling leather traders, the shuttered properties, she was unprepared for what she would find. This was a pivotal moment. A step that changed all her received notions of family and place.

Cobwebs. She remembers those. Sprayed across every corner, hanging from the brass candle-holders. Imported dust. Instant antiquity. The ruin dressed as a ruin. The synagogue with all its ritual impedimenta: a vision of the end of time. This was how a building *should* look, when it is opened to the light after years of slumbering inattention. Faked, set-dressed, parodying its distress and woeful neglect.

Rachel had walked in on the shooting of a film, *The Golem of Princelet Street*. The director, Brett Turnbull, was a student at the National Film School. The production was advised by the East End omnivore Professor Bill Fishman. One of the underemployed gophers followed her around, feeding her appetite for myth, explaining that the plot of the film was based on the legend of a man who had lived *in the very attic where they were now standing* – and who had disappeared. His name was David Rodinsky.

The building in its gothic trim, the vanishing Hebrew cabbalist: here was everything Rachel wanted. An antidote to Southend, the suburbs. A riposte to the comfortably nihilistic conservatism of student life in Sheffield. Here were the legendary spectres out of Meyrink and Leo Perutz. The film, responding to the mood engendered by Danny Gralton's photographs, to rumours of black-and-white documentaries of unknown provenance, attempted to reinvoke the compensatory fable of the Golem. But this was a heritaged golem, a Welfare State golem, a golem with a pension book – a toothless emanation. Turnbull's short film blended the local sentimental tradition of Wolf Mankowitz with a pinch of mysticism and a nip of reality. *A Kid for Two Farthings* meets *Dr Caligari*, by way of *Bicycle Thieves*. Rodinsky the solitary scholar, the caretaker who is about to be expelled into the streets, forms an alliance with a rag trade Bangladeshi boy so that they can make a golem. This sad monster, modelled in the heavy clay of a rain-sodden building site, is closer to an unfired version of Antony Gormley's *Brick Man* than to an expressionist automaton. Botched magic. Magic without correct ritual observation. Magic detached from a community of belief. The film ends with Rodinsky being taken away from the synagogue in an ambulance. With a conspicuous flourish, a crane-shot climbs above a weary Princelet Street, distancing itself (and the viewer) from this humble anecdote of the ghetto.

The conversion of David Rodinsky from golem maker to golem signified the movement of the story from whimsical documentary into apocalyptic millenarianism. When the ghetto is under threat, Rabbi Judah Loew ben Bezalel comes forward to reveal his homunculus, or to shape a giant servant out of river mud, a guardian for the poor and the oppressed. In Turnbull's film the golem is required to fend off the bulldozers, but the attempt is hopeless. The actor David Graham invests Rodinsky with the pathos of a figure from Yiddish theatre. He scratches at his cabbalistic tables in a gesture of nostalgic reverence, knowing that those days have passed. Now a golem can be nothing more than a heap of dust, a few unidentified rags in a forgotten room.

In the best fiction, in tales as vertiginous and strange as Gustav Meyrink's *Der Golem* (1915), the creature is already a memory; it belongs in a fabulous but longed-for past. The golem is that which has been banished, an atavistic cartoon. A dream companion. The ugly shape of something that has gone and cannot be recalled. A dark absence whose strange gravitational field sucks in the spectres of anxiety, paranoia, impotence. Miss Havisham is a golem. So is Mr Rochester's first wife (and her pale avatar, Daphne du Maurier's eponymous *Rebecca*). Strange how the English like to gender-bend their golems, turn them into women. The cobwebs of English romanticism are wisps of an unblooded wedding dress, *memento mori* for a mad bride in the attic.

Gustav Meyrink translated Dickens into German. Kafka and Meyrink, Prague contemporaries, drew on the fantastic, labyrinthine city of Dickens's fiction: the river of corpses, a geography of dust heaps, bone shops, candlelit domesticities enacted against a curtain of fog. *The Trial* is a pared-down translation of *Great Expectations*; the frantic subplots, the adjectival luxuriance hacked back. The Law and its ghosts. Spontaneous combustions in houses stuffed with rags and papers. The hierarchic structure of Dickens's tales insists upon a spook in the garret, a half-demented creature who belongs to another age; some wounded thing who can inspire patronage from the careless young. Provocations of mystery. Tolerated pets, eccentric in their feral gentility. They are defined by the pathetic objects that surround them; birds in cages, memories that overwhelm their feeble understanding of present time.

Meyrink, the charlatan, occultist, café conversationalist of Prague, sought out characters who had emigrated from the novels of Dickens into the close lanes of his own mythopoeic city. He wanted to repossess them, restore them to fiction. Angelo Maria Ripellino in his delirious homage, *Magic Prague*, tells how Kafka's executor, Max Brod, remarked in his memoirs 'that Meyrink numbered among his friends a collector of dead flies and a second-hand bookseller who resold rare books only with the consent of a tame raven with clipped wings'.

Meyrink's golem is that which survives, unfulfilled, deactivated, forgotten in an attic above a boarded-up synagogue. If the automaton (giant, revenger, Spring-Heel'd Jack) steps outside the limits of the ghetto, he is doomed. His ungainly rage will betray him. Like Frankenstein's monster (his new Adam), the golem, released from his temporal prison, will be driven to the extremities of the known world, some desert of ice where language freezes into a howl of pain. He must learn patience, wait. Stay, hidden under the eaves, in the half-dark, suffocating beneath the blankets of the last caretaker. In obscurity the golem is immortal. He defines the singularity of place. 'Something which cannot die haunts this quarter of the city,' writes Meyrink. When the golem's hiding place is uncovered, and his myths are made public, then the ghetto loses its integrity. Fables of compensation and impotence become the trophies of developers.

Chayim Bloch in his book *The Golem (Legends of the Ghetto of Prague)*, published in Vienna in 1920, writes of the death of the Golem: 'He was covered with old prayer robes and remains of Hebrew books, which according to Jewish custom were stored in the garret of the synagogue.' A reversal of profane usage: the cellar becomes the attic, relics and decanted libraries float overhead. By

tradition the golem was to be found in the attic of the Altneu synagogue in Prague. A thing of mud, dredged from the Moldau river,
crumbling back into dust. In Whitechapel the immigrant is tainted
by his time on the river, his arrival, penniless and without possessions or property, at the Irongate Steps, alongside the Tower of
London. (One of the fables of the old city tells of Jews, expelled by
Edward I, being put aground by a ship's master on a sandbank under
London Bridge. Let them wait for a more favourable tide. Their
cries, so compilers of mysteries claim, can still be heard, on certain
reaches of the river.)

From mud, the story emerges. Meyrink, influenced by Paracelsus,
deranged by his long concentration on narratives that shifted
beyond his grasp, subtexts breeding subtexts, began to comb
through the sewers of Prague for the philosopher's stone. Or so it
was whispered. Nocturnal expeditions, wading through shit, a
yellow poultice clinging to his boots, in search of an instrument of
transformation. The point where his quest for the Golem would
fuse with his attempt to understand the metaphor of alchemy. But
this gossip was itself a metaphor for the way that Meyrink's dubious
novels appeared to the literary journeymen: a dabbling in filth, a
useless stirring up of waste. A quest with no other purpose than to
demonstrate the madness of its perpetrator. Meyrink, burrowing in
tunnels beneath the ghetto, dredged for the substance, the
alchemist's *magisterium*, that would, according to Ripellino, cause
'the creation of the Golem and the search for the philosopher's stone
to converge'. The Golem, formed from primary matter, would be
alchemized into gold; a quality of light that would haunt the ghetto
for generations to come.

How does all this concern David Rodinsky? Rodinsky the scholar,
the caretaker who was not a caretaker. The New Georgians were
keen to install him as golem in the attic, a presence to sanction the
collecting of his books and furniture. Carol Wayne (the former Ethel
Rodinsky), in conversation with Rachel Lichtenstein, said that 'he
looked like a tramp, a beggar'. She warned, 'If you tried to help him,
he would bite off your head.' So was he an unacknowledged version

of Mac Davies, Pinter's peppery vagrant? That was not how Rodinsky saw it. 'If I am not the recognized tenant who is?' he wrote in a letter of 18 August 1961. Tenant, guardian. Keeper of place. Rodinsky wasted no time on his appearance. He dressed in charity-shop hand-me-downs. His head was always covered by a flat cap like those worn by the labourers in the fruit market. Heavy jackets, long in the sleeve, shiny with use, were still hanging in the wardrobe when Danny Gralton began his photographic survey of the attic rooms. But nobody could describe Rodinsky's appearance. Rachel, after all her investigations, all her visits to elderly relatives, did not turn up a single photograph of the man. He eluded her. Meyrink in *The Golem* writes of a 'rather queer card', a visitor who, despite his 'eccentric appearance', cannot be described. 'Golem stories are all hard telling. Pernath, here, just now was telling us he knew quite well how the stranger looked, but he couldn't describe him. More or less every three and thirty years something takes place in our streets, not too out-of-the-way startling in itself, yet the terror of it is too strong for either explanation or excuse.'

So the golem, and Rodinsky's identification with this figure, is a matter of eternal recurrence, cyclic time. The metaphor is activated when it is needed. In movement the golem is unseen, only when he comes to rest is he vulnerable. 'It stalks through the Ghetto,' says Meyrink, 'with a queer groping, stumbling kind of gait, as if afraid of falling over, and quite suddenly – is gone.' Sudden invisibility is a consequence of recognition. Speak of him and he isn't there. But any new telling of the tale can only begin from this disappearance. The disappearance represents the moment when the golem breaks off from his random circuits and fixes himself in one place. 'Usually,' Meyrink notes, 'it is seen to disappear round a corner. At other times it is said to have described a circle and gone back to the point when it started – an old house, close by the synagogue.'

It's too tempting. The golem has drawn in the essayists, the busy-bodies. They have to know what the house contains. They must describe it, list its contents, photograph everything – if only to prove that the thing in the attic no longer exists. The myth must be drained of its potency. Meyrink's mob searched the house in the Altschulgasse 'from top to bottom'. Only by hanging washing out of every window, to demonstrate how that particular room was clear, do they discover that 'there was a room inside the house with no entrance'. 'A room with no doors.' And this, we should understand, is a very different thing to a room without doors. This is a proud boast, a loudly asserted negative: *the room had no doors*. A narrow room, tailored to a single purpose; a room such as the one depicted on the cover of Margaret Cox's *Life and Death in Spitalfields (1790–1850)*. A studded chamber held upright by a skeleton and decorated with the mocking inscription: 'An Apartment for a SINGLE Gentleman.' A room in which to be buried. A vertical coffin.

But that is just one aspect of this 'room with no doors'. The Edgar Allan Poe nightmare has a secondary reading – as poverty hutch. A room with entrances and exits, the necessary apertures, but without the extravagance of door-hangings. A more primitive kind of space. Dan Cruickshank and Peter Wyld in *London: The Art of Georgian Building* run to an entire chapter on doors; baroque, extravagant, cantilevered and carved. Doors represent status: those who possess them are allowed a measure of privacy. They can remove themselves from their servants, supplicants or creditors. The door is a border, framed and presented. The impoverished, the vagrants of the city, know them only from the outside. Spaces to which they are granted access have no doors (unless they are doors to keep them in, doors of prisons or madhouses).

H. Leivick in his play *The Golem* (1920), written for the Habima, a Hebrew theatre company that emerged from post-revolutionary Russia, sends his blundering giant, Joseph Golem, to lodge in the Fifth Tower. The other towers belong to the cardinal points of the compass; this tower (like the Fifth Quarter, the ghetto of the Jews) is nowhere. It exists as a zone from which there is no escape: it is the ghetto of the ghetto. Here sleep the beggars, the sick, the demented, the freaks and the rogues. The stage directions for the scene in the Fifth Tower (Scene IV. Beggars) could be describing Rodinsky's room, in the period before its partial restoration by the Spitalfields

Trust. 'A large room, a shambles . . . One wall has been broken through. The others are blackened, covered with cobwebs, soaked by the rains. No doors, shaky thresholds, broken windows.' *No doors*: a condition of existence for the Golem. For Rodinsky. A man whose life is open to all. A man who has attempted to erase the barriers between worlds, states of existence. A man who has successfully vanished while, at the same time, persuading others to launch a lifelong quest for his biography.

The search for Rodinsky is as driven and as dangerous as the forensic excavations carried out in the crypt of Christ Church, Spitalfields. As if the measuring and photographing of mummified remnants could bring back those lives, powder the air with lost time. The archaeological project, excavating the vaults beneath Hawksmoor's church, analysing bones and artefacts – around one thousand skeletons were 'recovered' – took place between 1984 and 1989, during the period when the Museum of London were interesting themselves in Rodinsky. Photographs of coffin frills and shrouds double for the contents of the Princelet Street wardrobe. Dentures could date from the early nineteenth century, or they could have been issued, in the wake of post-war benevolence, by Nye Bevan's National Health Service. The Spitalfields streets (featuring, if at all possible, the Christ Church steeple) appear in accounts of the excavation of the crypt as well as in books of heritage, all those gloatingly arcane encyclopaedias of detail. Fournier Street, Spital Square, Princelet Street: unpeopled, without cars, carefully framed in black-and-white plates of remembrance.

How feverishly the memory thieves fell on Rodinsky's maps, his marked-up copies of the *London A–Z*. Perhaps these charts would show the peregrinations of an invisible man? If his walks could be repeated, might he be brought back to life? What did his curious symbols mean? Were these walks prophetic? Would they reveal the letters of some cabbalistic code? Or did they simply record the small journeys he had been prompted to undertake? And why was 'Spitalfields ("Itchy Park")' marked as 'No. 1'?

The maps were unknowable, but the clothes in the wardrobe

could be carried over to the light and photographed. The drabness, the recessive colours. The colours that were no colour: dead water under a leaden sky. Pre-golem silt. Lifeless wool. Dim synthetics saturated with dust. Street sweat left to dry in the dark. Even Rodinsky's jackets were keyed to the mood of the golem fable. The Golem of Chayim Bloch (and of Leivick) dressed, as befits his origin, in mud colours. The Thames or the Vltava on a bad afternoon, liquid khaki. Shit in a jug. The Golem wore the clothes of a sexton or *shames*. Rodinsky, through his status as unofficial caretaker, is therefore inducted into the golem tribe. But he has outlived his rabbi, his people. Through him, another way of life, different beliefs, a more demanding ethical system is mythologized.

Our assumptions become reckless: a man, the facts of his life barely known, is adopted as a symbol for the reimagination of a special district of London. After publishing, in the late Eighties, a speculative essay on Rodinsky ('The Man Who Became a Room'), I received a letter from someone who had known him. A Mr Ian Shames of Stoke Newington. Shames (the sexton brought to life) remembered the last days of the synagogue. Remembered Rodinsky as two people: the idiot and the scholar. There was no way of understanding the transition between these states, from autistic incoherence to fluent ease in areas of knowledge to which he had no obvious access. Had the reclusive scholar completed the Great Work, the rush of enlightenment? Could this explain his sudden extraordinary breakthrough, his gift for languages? Gustav Meyrink, in his Dr John Dee novel *The Angel of the West Window*, describes this condition of exhilaration, achieved wisdom, very accurately:

Does not an unearthly light, yes: light, announce the fiery messenger? Are not secret things made manifest? Does not Kelley speak in tongues, as did the Apostles of the Lord on the Day of Pentecost? I have long established through careful, nay, cunning, trial that Edward Kelley knows scarcely any of the Latin he speaks when the spirit is upon him – not to mention

Greek and Hebrew, or even Aramaic! All his speech concerns the noble mysteries of perfection, and often it seems as if the great masters of the ancient world were speaking through the unconscious Kelley – Plato, King Solomon, Aristotle himself, Socrates and Pythagoras.

Shames wanted to temper my excesses. 'I knew him when young,' he wrote, 'a pasty-faced chappie who always looked undernourished. . . . He was a tenant together with his mother in two rooms let to them above the Princelet Street synagogue, not a scholar, his sustenance was given to him and his mother from Jewish charities.' There must be no talk of golems, cabbalists, interdimensional voyages, invisibility. Rodinsky was a man to be pitied, an inadequate. 'He kept himself interesting during his short life, but unfortunately attained nothing, this was due to his low IQ. With people like him, they know not of having an ambition nor the initiative to get somewhere in life. David invisible? Definitely NO!'

Invisible? Rodinsky is only invisible in the sense that he is absorbed by the room in which he was the last tenant. The Golem is closer to that room than to Rodinsky the man. The stature of the mud giant, his huge but disconcertingly featureless face, grants licence to those who would project their own terrors on to him. And the abandoned room in the Princelet Street synagogue shares this characteristic: it is a dressed set, it solicits narrative.

There is a cycle of golem tales in which the creature acts as a primitive detective, solving local mysteries, revenging injustices, false accusations against the Jews of the ghetto. In these tales, Rabbi Loew and Joseph Golem are early prototypes of Sherlock Holmes and Doctor Watson. Loew is neurasthenic, burdened with knowledge; a rabbi of eccentric practice whose wisdom can be interpreted by outsiders as trafficking with occult forces. (The Prague of Rudolph II encourages this reading: Dr Dee and Edward Kelley were another pairing whose conjurings depended on congress with the realm of spirits.) Loew broods in his study, while Joseph Golem blunders around the scene of the crime. The rabbi has conveniently provided

his mute servant with an amulet that grants invisibility. According to
Chayim Bloch: 'some regarded him as a spectre of Rabbi Loew'. The
servant, the *shames*, represents the authority of his master. The
Golem has greater potency: he has been given life by Loew. He is
Loew's projection, his fiction. These folk tales founded a genre.
There is a direct line of descent to Sexton Blake and Tinker (and to
Michael Moorcock's *fin de siècle* deconstruction of these characters:
as Seaton Begg and his sidekick, Doctor 'Taffy' Sinclair, in *The
Metatemporal Detective* for DC Comics).

The Golem was one of the first in a long line of ethnic detectives,
the forerunner of the currently fashionable investigators created
by Walter Mosley, James Sallis and Tony Hillerman (or, more perti-
nently, Jerome Charyn with his Isaac Sidel and Manfred Coen). He
operated within the ghetto. He protected his own people, defending
them from racist conspiracies. He solved the case of the pig wagon,
when a spiteful debtor tried to smuggle the body of a Christian
child into the house of a Jewish moneylender by stitching the tiny
corpse inside a slaughtered animal. In beating a confession out of
the terrified miscreant, the Golem establishes the hardboiled tradition of getting your retaliation in first. Stomp the punk and ask
questions later. Dead men, ventriloquized by necromantic arts, have
no reason to lie. They are the purest witnesses to the drama of
death.

One of the classic mysteries is the locked-room killing, a sub-
genre that traces its descent to Edgar Allan Poe's *Murders in the
Rue Morgue*. (Another early example, *The Big Bow Mystery*, was
written by Israel Zangwill, a master of Spitalfields picaresque,
author of *Children of the Ghetto* and *The King of Schnorrers*.)
Fantasists would like to enrol Rodinsky's garret into this catalogue.
His disappearance has all the elements: the half-devoured meal,
the open diary, the occult conjurings. There are no reliable witnesses. The detective, a young woman, has much more invested in
the case than she cares to acknowledge. She's a returnee, coming
back to territory that is under the threat of development. She
believes that solving this mystery will unlock all the secrets of the

city. She's from a comfortable background but decides, perversely, that she must live and work in the lower depths. Old people talk to her. She's threatened by teenage hoods, glue-sniffers with knives. She makes amazing discoveries, but there is no final solution. She gives up, tries other countries, is tempted by religious orthodoxy. She receives offers of marriage. But all the time she is haunted by the face of a man she has never seen. A man of whom there is no photograph. A man whose story is the story of a sealed room. The room is his doctored autobiography. It contains all the clues, everything he touched and arranged. Solitary, haunted, obsessed, she takes to spending long hours in that room, the dim attic. Clairvoyance. She's waiting for a voice. She wants Rodinsky to dictate his story. She tells me that treating her quest like a detective story brings the Spitalfields investigation into a parallel relationship with her Talmudic studies. In Israel her teachers taught her to make numerous readings from three sentences. Weeks, months in the desert, picking the same words apart. Letters as numbers. Words broken and reformed. The search for truth, illumination, and the meditations on Rodinsky were indivisible acts. The scholar had vanished into the text.

Rachel Lichtenstein becomes an emanation from Meyrink's fiction: 'brooding on past events . . . that strange recurring dream I kept having that I was in a house containing a certain room the door of which was locked to me'. 'I had been mad,' says Meyrink's protagonist in a moment of terrible self-revelation. 'They had, in short, locked up a room which communicated with certain chambers in my brain; they had made me into an exile in the midst of the life that surrounded me.' The madness, the heat of the vision, moves out into the streets; the geography of the district is skewed. Anyone who visits the room, a cell of memory, is affected. They become essayists, tale tellers, literary detectives. They have one piece of the story. They search out fellow sufferers, trying to assemble a complete narrative. The room is a false memory, a projection. It held one revelation: that a man had vanished. Rodinsky was redundant. He had persuaded another person to complete his story. The legend of the Golem, according to Meyrink, recurs, returns when it is needed. 'He dwells high above ground, in a room with no door, and one window only, through which mankind may not recognize him. Whosoever can both banish and *purify* him, that man will be reconciled with his own self.'

> If all are dead,
> One must remain.
> Let that be you.
>
> H. Leivick, *The Golem*

A new version of *The Golem*, written by Peter Wolf (with 'scenes' by Bonnie Greer and Chiman Rahimi), was staged at the Bridewell Theatre early in 1998. The event had several attractions for me. It might be useful to see a play that dealt with archetypes that were becoming increasingly familiar: Rabbi Loew, his pupils, his daughter, and his contrary, the implacable Brother Thaddeus. These characters were like letters from a hidden alphabet (in my mock-cabbalist reading): it was a question of watching the dance, seeing how the shapes fell across the stage, granting the shadows a life of their own. This theatre had once been a place of recreation for printers, then a venue for performances and presentations. I had been here before, taking part in a week-long series of readings, interviews, shocks and shows, entitled *Subversion in the Street of Shame*. Emanuel Litvinoff held a public conversation with Patrick Wright. The sculptor and poet Brian Catling crawled beneath the stage, moaning inarticulately in the character of the Cyclops (the space had once contained a swimming pool). What was peculiar about the Bridewell was its consanguinity with the Princelet Street synagogue. Atmosphere, ambiance. 'Vibes' as the old hippies used to call it.

Places where the temperature changed as you stepped in from the street. Places with an undeclared history and a disturbing sense of potential: that something should be enacted in present time to mollify an unresolved past. These theatres of memory took the breath away. Visitors tended to sleepwalk for a few moments, touching the walls, and then flop on to a bench in a state of exhaustion. If they came to do an interview, they were soon reduced to silence. (Catling moved on from the Bridewell to give a reading, in the character of a sexton, in Princelet Street; opening and closing the proceedings by lighting and snuffing the candles on the brass chandeliers. It was a bitterly cold night and the audience, split between those who elected to stand against the walls of the synagogue and those who went upstairs to the women's gallery, were glad of their shots of complimentary vodka. In the entrance hall a smoking slide-projector imposed New York exteriors, other mysterious spaces, over the crumbling plaster. The building was turned inside out. Professor Eric Mottram sat in the guest of honour's seat, a tape recorder that refused to function on his lap. His head nodded, he dozed; the atmosphere was heavy with the guttering candles. It must have been one of the last of many, many strange readings that Mottram attended. He died a couple of months later.)

Watching Wolf's play was like being back in the synagogue. I panned around the room, taking in the arrangement of chairs that surrounded the actors on three sides, the balconies that overlooked the body of the hall, the pillars – and I was aware of the echoing vault beneath the boards, the former swimming pool. The action, at first, seemed unexceptional, a minimal cast struggling to hold a small but voluble audience. The play was in part sponsored by Jewish Care, 'Anglo-Jewry's largest social services organization'. A charity that, in the tradition of Zangwill, prided itself on 'providing a wide range of services for the elderly, people with mental and physical disabilities, their families and carers, the unemployed and survivors of the Holocaust'. The audience were, I should guess, eighty or ninety per cent Jewish, with a smattering of outpatients and Americans who couldn't believe there was nowhere around

Fleet Street where they could get a steak on a Saturday night. But the area was dead. You had to search to find a pub (the Cheshire Cheese), let alone a restaurant. Nobody passing through the deserted streets would have guessed that anything was happening at the bottom of this secret lane at the back of St Bride's Church. There was plenty of animation among the paying customers, before the play started; debate, discussion, consultation of programme notes. What followed was something of an anticlimax, much less theatrical than the congregation, the respectful seekers who had come hoping for much more than the actors could deliver.

Wolf's problem, or so it seemed to me, was to strike a balance between mystical elements and the desire to treat this folk tale to a purge of social realism. Wolf is aware that he is writing his play on the far side of the Holocaust, the black spider at the heart of European consciousness.

> When I was interviewing Holocaust survivors for our previous
> production, *In Extremis*, I spoke with one who told me of how
> he had seen a Golem in the concentration camp. . . . At night he
> would lie in his barracks and a shadowy figure would appear in
> the doorway which he recognized as the Golem from childhood
> stories. This figure was not a protecting, Superman-type, but
> rather a frightening monster who might attack him at any time.

Wolf's Golem 'represents Fear'. And here the experience of sitting in this room, a synagogue-like space, surrounded by galleries, becomes difficult. A gathering, largely Jewish, is watching a secular performance with powerful ritual elements. In a synagogue that is not a synagogue, we see a group of actors re-creating Rabbi Loew's house and place of worship. Only when, with the crude conjuring of a Victorian penny gaff, Loew swirls his cloak to bring the Golem to life, or to make him vanish (through the trapdoor down into the swimming pool), does the charade come to life.

In that state of drift that is the experience of sitting in the half-dark, letting some curious performance unravel, I find myself moving from reverie to instants of attention when the actors, or their gestures, trigger a memory. In Wolf's golem play, Rabbi Loew's study is suggested by towers of rather uninteresting-looking books: the Rodinsky connection is obvious, but there's not much I can do with it. The books have been assembled by a set-dresser who had to take whatever he could pick up. The intriguing (and unexpected) moment, as far as I was concerned, came when the rabbi's daughter, Jessica (played by Catherine Cusack), flew at these unsupported columns and scattered the books across the stage. (My wife, at this point, had a nasty glint in her eye.) Jessica was revealed as the brightest of the rabbi's students, but, being a woman, she was denied access to books and to dancing. The males, from time to time, flung themselves about in a *Fiddler on the Roof* frenzy. But she was condemned to stand in the doorway, fetching and carrying for her father. The righteous anger, the spirit in the play, belonged to Jessica and not to the golem. Simon Dubnov in his *History of the Jews* (1967–1973) explains that 'the entire system of education rendered men ne'er-do-wells. Women would be the breadwinners while their husbands went wool-gathering in the house of study or the Hassidic synagogue.' Under the rabbinical system, girls received no schooling. The Jessica in Wolf's drama displays an anachronistic feminism in her justified passion for knowledge and ecstatic dancing. Her rebellion is of a different order to that of her namesake, Shylock's daughter, who marries out. ('What heinous sin is it in me, / To be asham'd to be my father's child.') Shakespeare's Jessica is a trophy wife for a gentile, depicted in engravings by such as the Dalziel Brothers as lush and dark; desirable forbidden fruit.

The Golem, deactivated, broken up, is locked in the attic: the word inscribed on his brow, *Emeth* (Truth), has become *Meth* (Death). The door has been locked, 'barring anyone from entering ever again'. A breeze from elsewhere, the spirit of risk, has been absorbed by the young woman. Jessica, like Miriam (the daughter of a holy man in Meyrink's *Der Golem*), is thought to be possessed. Miriam says that 'when they realized how earnest I was they would have liked to call me mad, and were only prevented by their belief that I was what they called "learned", for they knew I had studied Hebrew and Aramaic, besides Midrashin and the Targumic writings.' Miriam, in other words, is a prototype of Rodinsky. An autodidact, a scholar who transgresses the accepted boundaries of scholarship. Her fierce learning, this swerving progress between orthodox doctrine, parental duty, mysticism, numerology, coincidence, vision, hysteria, is where the daughters of invention, the wild girls, engage with eternally recurring golems, with wraiths like David Rodinsky. By their acts, they offer themselves up and are patronized by dim and timid fathers. Miriam complains that these old men 'adopted an expression which means precisely nothing at all'. They called her 'highly strung'.

For these subjugated creatures, with their impertinent questions, the Golem is a suitor: a primitive male, impotent and urgent, hangdog, heavy-handed, dumb with desire. A stooge without language. An awkward lumpen stumbler, destroyer of domestic harmony. A thug, neutered by sentimental desire, who longs to be cuffed into domesticity.

It's an unrequired relationship, a parody of the father/daughter fix from which they are determined to escape. The daughter of a rich man is his greatest treasure. One of Chayim Bloch's golem legends concerns a rich merchant, a dealer who 'carried on his business with unbending rectitude and punctilious honesty'. This man has an only daughter, Rahel ('beautiful, virtuous' etcetera); a daughter who, horror of horrors, elopes with a Christian. And then, under the influence of the fanatical Thaddeus, converts.

> The balmy evening breeze, which wafted to her the sweet
> fragrance of the rustling linden trees, intoxicated her and
> robbed her of the courage to refrain from taking a mad step. She
> crossed the bridge. . . . Thither the wild longings of her soul
> drew her.

By her actions, she loses her father – and without a father the play cannot begin. Febrile Prince Hamlet waits on his ghost. Rachel

Lichtenstein nominates her own 'father', in the shape of Rodinsky. Her investigations force him to speak. She ingests this *dybbuk*, the elective ancestor. It's a form of willed possession. She wants to complete some unfinished business. Rachel, like Leye, the heroine of S. Anski's *The Dybbuk*, finds herself living the 'unlived life', wondering what happens to words that are left unspoken. 'How, then, can the unconsumed candle of a life be put out forever? How can that be?' Leye's wealthy father spreads out a feast for beggars and vagrants, because he knows that one of them might be a holy man in disguise, the prophet Elijah returned to earth. Any ragged wanderer, or wild-eyed caretaker, squatter in a derelict site, might – who knows? – be revealed as one of the Thirty-Six Just Men, the Illuminati, keepers of the doctrine. Within the ghetto there is respect for scholarship, however eccentric; respect for those who exchange worldly position for the spiritual quest. Madness is an ambiguous blessing. Any spittle-flecked ranter might be a millennial messenger, one of those possessed by an unfulfilled ancestor. It is the business of the living, as W.B. Yeats wrote in *A Vision*, to 'assist the imagination of the dead'.

The *dybbuk* is such a visitation, a more benevolent form of incubus: an entity selective about its host body. Possession by a *dybbuk* is frequently a kind of blessing: but there is no shirking the responsibility of the task for which the recipient has been nominated. Something was absent in such lives, there was an emptiness, until this contact was recognized. Anski's Messenger explains: 'The souls of the dead do return to the world, but not as disembodied spirits. Some souls must go through several incarnations before they achieve purification. . . . And there are some souls that enter a new-born body and achieve purification by means of their own deeds.'

Rachel Lichtenstein was attracted by these notions, inspired (though not without a proper sense of the occasion's absurdity) by her visit to a cabbalist in Jerusalem. At the level of metaphor, she saw herself as blessed by the spirit of David Rodinsky. And also haunted – this sense grew on her as she moved deeper into her investigations – by Rodinsky's sister. Perhaps it was, as those who

knew the family remembered, the sister who was the scholar, the hot
intelligence? Was it not the sister who built up the library? The sister
who, in an orthodox family, was frustrated and unfulfilled. The sister
whose photograph Rachel had traced and made into a curious postcard. This card, superimposing a face, printed across what looks
like an identity card on to a creased white sheet, is open-eyed,
ambiguous. The figure avoids the gaze of the camera. Lichtenstein
has called her work *Portrait of Rodinsky*. I had fallen into the trap,
assuming at first that this, at long last, was David. But, no, it was the
other Rodinsky. The sister who ended her days in an asylum. The
sister whose fate drove David Rodinsky into a frenzy of letter writing, into making hand-drawn maps of the suburbs, the half-country
where the madhouses are sited. The zone where urban nightmares
are earthed. A rim, scattered with golf courses and boarding kennels
for dogs, where Rodinsky would end his own days. For the ghosts of
the ghetto, the M25 became an *eruv*, a mysterious borderline that
captured their dreams; a perimeter fence they would never be
allowed to breach.

Well, he once told me he knows spells that can create a
golem, revive the dead, make one invisible, call forth evil
spirits, even Satan himself. (*Spits.*) I heard this from his
own lips.

S. Anski, The Dybbuk

The story drifts, murky, then lit for a moment by the dance of
sunlight, but it always flows back to the room, to Danny
Gralton's photographs. Gralton, like Arcimboldo, has turned
Rodinsky into an effusion of objects: domestic, mystical, decayed.
And what objects these are! Rachel Lichtenstein's archive has enough
material to fill a dozen Shoreditch Biennales. But Gralton sees the
room as theatre. He frames his compositions so that the folds of an
old curtain hang at the right extremity, while daylight creeps in
from the left. The two figures in the Millet reproduction are dupli-
cated in a postcard on the table. A hard chair waits for an unseen
actor. Several open scripts solicit his attention. The corked bottle of
stout is a misplaced prop from an underground production of
Krapp's Last Tape.

All the objects belong to the apocrypha of last days, a house of
dead souls. Rodinsky's room is a reversed vortex, spinning time
backwards. The Hasids knew, as David Hartnett writes in *Black Milk*,
'that in the last days there must be many darknesses, many mysteries.' There are objects peculiar to these days, to the millennial set: a
discipline of chaos. From the interrogation of such objects – books,

candles, the magician's wardrobe with its hidden depths – wise men recognize that we have come to the end of the cycle. But Rodinsky's room is not as simple as that. Here the objects *bring about* an entropy consciousness, a half-delirious appreciation of apocalypse. Revelation out of dust and corruption. A story that can only be told at the end of time. The room promotes 'unmanifest existence'; its fanciful arrangement of objects is intended as a sequence of biographical prompts for the unwary. Touch any book, rifle any of the diaries, and you are hooked.

The room has waited, through the fifteen-year limbo of sequestration, to nominate its author, some latter-day Kafka, Borges, or Meyrink. Waited for Rachel Lichtenstein. She had no choice. She speaks of finding herself spending longer and longer periods alone in the attic, writing a little, falling into reverie, letting the furniture warp and shift as the light failed. The body of the synagogue was always too cold, but under the eaves there was a musty warmth, the heat of a single candle.

The shape that cannot be seen, the golem of the room, remains in perpetual movement. An old woman, trapped in a council flat, remembers some of the story. A cabbalist in Jerusalem suggests that important chapters are still to be written. The nominated storyteller, Rachel Lichtenstein, having dutifully chased all these rumours, made the phone calls, paid the visits, logged the evidence, has returned to her starting point: the partly occulted history of her own family. Who is she? Where does she come from? What is her task?

When the quest is broken off, as it has to be, the arc of movement, Rodinsky keeping pace with Lichtenstein, will be damaged. While he was tracked, there could never be a definitive resolution; documents or half-truths were revealed as and when they were needed. Now that Lichtenstein was travelling to Poland, coming back to her original researches, the fate of the story was critical. Movement ceasing, or falling out of synchronization, hobbles time. The gift of invisibility is no longer credited. The spell that has been cast on the room is broken and the story is in danger of crumbling into incoherence.

Mystics talk of an 'unmanifest existence'. An existence that is now at risk, threatened by conservationists, meddlers, money men. Aleister Crowley suggested that the locations of the bodies of the five victims of Jack the Ripper were arranged in a pentagram star that would confer invisibility on the perpetrator of those crimes. Invisibility is the ultimate goal of the magician: to be present, unseen, in future times. Unchallenged in your spurious immortality. Rachel Lichtenstein was wearied by these notions. Rodinsky's was the invisibility of the unnoticed, not of the Nietzschean assassin, the self-willed superman. The scribbled marks on his map recorded humble domestic quests and not the sites of sacrifice, past or future. To break free from this overwhelming rush of facts, the impedimenta of a short and troubled life, Rachel had to make a journey of her own. Leaving the Princelet Street room behind was the best way of understanding the essence of the teasing narrative that was hers, and hers alone, to complete.

WHO WILL SAY
KADDISH NOW?

Rachel Lichtenstein

And so it stood, unprepared and unfinished, in an
accidental intersection of time and space, without closing
of accounts, without reaching any goal, caught in a half
sentence as it were, without full stop or exclamation mark,
without trial ...

Bruno Schulz, Kometa

I woke as we began our descent, the green fields and forests forming a serene patchwork of colour below. Suddenly my stomach
contorted and I had to force myself not to vomit. It wasn't the drop
in air pressure that was making me feel sick but the images that
were now flooding into my mind. Photographs retrieved from cardboard boxes in Warsaw, Jerusalem, London, New York. Images that
burn into the skull and cannot be erased. Naked women clutching
children, standing on the edge of ravines in forests.

My dark mood swiftly passed as I disembarked and felt the heat
of the sun on my face, a great relief after weeks of drizzle and gloom
in London. As I entered the dingy terminal I smiled to myself, yes I
had definitely arrived. My last visit had been six years previously,
the final year of the communist regime. Everything was brown
then, and grey. I passed swiftly through passport control and then
took a brief taxi ride to the student dormitory, an ominous-looking
concrete institution in an ugly suburb of the city. I checked in and
took the small, metal-lined lift up to my room on the fourth floor.
Two tall men entered with me and I felt vulnerable. I had heard that
Poland had changed and crime had increased with capitalism. The

businessman I had shared the taxi with had warned me to hide my laptop: such an object was still worth a year's wages in Poland. The lift stopped with a thud, one of the men got out and opened the door for me, gesturing my way with a small bow. I felt myself blush slightly and managed to mutter a feeble thank you. I stepped into a dimly lit corridor, never-ending rooms to either side, and walked defiantly down, footsteps echoing. The room looked remarkably familiar, very much like my room in Israel: hard wooden single bed, one chair, one table, bare white walls, the only decoration being a thick strip of dark wood running around the wall just above the bed. I sat on the bed waiting for the rest of the group to arrive, aware this could be my only time alone for the next few weeks; overcome by the heat, I fell asleep. I woke suddenly in the middle of the night, cold and startled. The weather had changed dramatically and the air was icy and damp. After dressing in every warm piece of clothing I had brought with me I stepped out on to the balcony, staying close to the window to avoid the rain that was coming down fast. The noise of the rain was suddenly drowned out by a deafening clap of thunder. That night I witnessed the most fearsome forked lightning I had ever seen light up the dreary Kraków skyline.

I stayed on the balcony until early dawn, amazed at the scene emerging from the grey half-light before me. The advertising hoardings and wide variety of Western cars had been completely absent during my last visit. Moreover, I had never seen rain in Poland before. During my previous trips the sun had shone relentlessly. I had travelled in the blazing summer heat from one end of the country to the other, on the old steam trains that were still used then in Poland and Russia. The trains were cheap and busy – only a privileged few had cars – and the stations were operating twenty-four hours a day. My favourite time to travel was the early morning, but only once did I ever manage to get a seat. Most often I would be standing in the corridor, my rucksack tightly wedged behind my knees, while I tried to breathe the fresh air from the open windows, avoiding the strong cigarette smoke produced by the vodka-drinking Polish farmers. I caused quite a stir in those days, a young Western girl travelling alone, easily recognizable by my Nike trainers and colourful T-shirts and shorts. People would always talk to me, or try to. Few spoke English and my Polish consisted of a few necessary niceties. They wanted to know why I had chosen Poland, they thought it amusing. Unlike them, I could travel anywhere I wanted with my British passport, so why come to Poland? Naïvely, much to the terror of my Aunt Guta, I used to tell them freely the purpose of my trip: to reunite with family and to visit Jewish sites. Sometimes my intrigued new Polish friends would ask more questions; once a young student began to cry and asked to come with me around the old Jewish quarter in Łódź. Other times the conversation would stop abruptly and they would walk briskly away. Once I was spat on. I did not care, I was nineteen years old, idealistic and completely alone for the first time in my life. Back then you could change money on the black market and receive over ten times the legal amount. I could afford anything I wanted, not that there was anything to buy: the shops were empty and long queues for bread, sugar and petrol were a common sight. No one knew of my whereabouts. The phone system in Poland was very basic then and it was impossible to phone abroad. My poor mother.

I took trains all over the country, often crossing over the same territory numerous times, just because I could, and I enjoyed many happy hours quietly staring from the window, soaking up scenes of rural Poland that my ancestors would have seen. Fields and fields of yellow sunflowers, haystacks shaped like pyramids, lazy peasants trundling slowly past on dusty roads with carts full of hay. When I reached my destination I would head straight for the Jewish quarter of the town or city, most often ending up in the cemetery. I took hundreds of photographs: tombstones covered in foliage, empty synagogues, Poles selling spice boxes on a market stall in Gdansk, Aunt Guta's granddaughter playing in the orchard, anti-Semitic graffiti on the wall of her flat. These trips had been intensely personal, and the images and scraps of abstract information gathered were translated into art work on my return. And now I was back in Poland, years later, to participate in an academic conference with dozens of other people, led by experts in the field of Polish Jewish history. Would I be able to cope with this new realism?

The distinctive sound of a New York accent in the next room: 'Lee-li, *wake up*, time to go, geerl.' I quickly showered, then ventured downstairs to breakfast. The breakfast hall was huge and full mainly of Polish students learning English for the summer. I needed no introduction to find my group. The level of noise from the two tables in the centre of the hall was unmistakable. Two dozen American Jewish academics are not hard to spot in a room full of Polish students. I sat on the edge of the group nervously. As soon as I opened my mouth I was hit with a barrage of questions. Why was I here? I couldn't answer them precisely. I had returned again for many reasons: to see my family, to experience Poland in the Nineties, to visit the unusual sites the conference would allow us access to, and to continue with my search for Rodinsky. I wanted to trace the information I had received in an email from Carol Wayne's nephew, who told me that as far as he knew, the Rodinsky family had originated from a small shtetl situated in the Ukraine called Kushovata, close to the Polish border. When I replied asking for further information about Kushovata he sent the following:

Regarding Kushovata, I know as little about it as I do Anatevka [the shtetl in *Fiddler on the Roof*] – and it may be as fictional. I was told about it by my grandmother, who must have been vaguely related to your David Rodinsky. The only way to determine if such a town with a name homophone to Kushovata ever existed is to examine a pre-Revolutionary map of Russia or go there yourself!

That was exactly what I planned to do, hoping that the professors and archive facilities at the Judaica Centre would be able to help me achieve this.

Our timid Polish guide was failing miserably to be heard over the din of the group. Eventually somebody noticed her 'HEY GUYS, LET'S GO' and slowly we moved outside. The scene that confronted us was very different from that the day before. The previously dust-covered and hot pavements were now awash with leaves and debris that had poured down from the surrounding mountains during the night. The yellow, dried-out lawn had turned into a sodden lake, impossible to walk past without soaking your feet. By the time we had got on the bus we were all wet through.

The rain was coming down so hard it was impossible to see any-thing of Kraków from the window, but within ten minutes we arrived at the Jagiellonian University. In the courtyard of the build-ing, sheltering from the rain and deeply engrossed in conversation with two other professors, I saw Felek. I ran straight over to him and

we embraced warmly. His gentle, calming voice, thick with traces of his Polish past, set me instantly at ease, blowing away any doubts I may have gathered from the morning about attending the confer-ence. Felek reminded me of my grandfather, whose rich guttural voice also never lost its Polish roots. But unlike Felek, my grandfa-ther never spoke a word of Polish or set foot on Polish soil after he left in 1930; he had no love left for Poland. Felek, on the other hand, is most rare for a Polish Jew of his generation.

Jan Blonski, in his introduction to Felek Scharf's collected essays *Poland What Have I To Do With Thee?*, describes him in this way:

A former pupil of the Hebrew High School, in his youth an ardent Zionist, who on his way from Poland to Palestine paused in London, fell in love, married and has taken upon himself the role of the Guardian of Cracovian and Jewish memory. The last witness, he bears authentic testimony to the character of the city and the Jewish community.

Felek still possesses a deep love for Poland and the language.

I am thinking what would be left of me if by some ungodly edict I were to be stripped of all that is Polish in me. First, of the language, which – although somewhat rusty and neglected – remains part of the furniture without which the inner space would be empty; of the poems and verses with which I lull myself to sleep; of the recollection of the landscape, its singular sights and smells. (Janusz Korczak remarked, during his stay in Palestine, that the eucalyptus speaks to him differently from the pine.) Were one to lose the link with that language and landscape . . . one would feel bereft, impoverished, incomplete.

And Felek has an intense relationship with the three countries I am constantly returning to. He told me, 'I look upon England as a wife, on Israel as a lover, on Poland as a stepmother.'

When I first met Felek there was an immediate mutual attraction, I was deeply impressed by his love and knowledge of Polish romantic poetry and Jewish history. I was dazzled by his gentlemanly manners, sharp dress sense and brilliant mind. He was fascinated and moved by my story, particularly of the mosaic of my family from Łódź I had made whilst in Israel. We met at the Spiro Institute in London. I had been asked to present a lecture there during a one-day conference on Polish Jewish history. Felek was lecturing that same day and I think it was love at first sight. Unfortunately for me

Felek is eighty years old and married. After hearing me talk Felek strode over to where I was sitting, gently kissed my hand, then introduced himself with the words, 'You must come to Kraków with me.' I instantly recognized the great honour that had just been bestowed on me. I told Trudi, the organizer of the event there, who replied, 'If Felek asks you to go to Kraków with him you drop everything and go.' So this was how I came to be in Kraków that summer. We caught up on our news, and arm in arm entered the magnificent 500-year-old building of the Jagiellonian University to attend the opening ceremony for the conference. The ceremony was formal: various prominent Jewish historians addressing us with long academic speeches that were impossible for me to follow. At last Felek spoke, injecting humour and life into the sleepy room again. He read from his recently published collection of essays, *What Shall We Tell Miriam?*, which consists of sensitive and humorous recollections of his past life in Kraków and present relationship with Poland and Poles. Included in one of these essays is the story that Felek had read to me months ago back in London when I told him of my quest for Rodinsky:

A man went to Cracow and on his return tells his friend, 'The Jews of Cracow are remarkable people. I saw a Jew who spends all his nights dreaming and all his days planning the revolution. I saw a Jew who spends all his time studying Talmud. I saw a Jew who chases every skirt he sees and I saw a Jew who wants nothing to do with women. I saw a Jew who is full of plans to get rich quick.'

The other man says, 'I don't know why you are astonished. Cracow is a big city and there are many Jews, all sorts of people.'

'No,' says the first, 'it was the same Jew.'

I was sitting in the library of the former *bet midrash* in Kazimierz, the former Jewish quarter of Kraków, staring at the framed image in front of me, young *cheder* boys falling asleep at their books, taken in another time but in the same place where I now sat. Behind me

were three American students talking rapidly in modern Hebrew.
The bookcases in the library were no longer filled with volumes of
Talmud and Mishnah but instead with books on the Holocaust. The
building was modern; designed by a famous Polish architect and
renovated with US funding, it now functions as the Judaica Institute.
This is where we began our studies. Our first session started with
each student introducing themselves and explaining their reasons
for attending the conference. Being typically British, I normally find
these situations intrusive and contrived but this wasn't. There were
students from Poland, the States, Lithuania; a varied group of academics, teenagers, scientists, writers and professors, all with a
common interest in studying Polish Jewish history.

A chubby, pleasant-faced teenager dressed in standard American
summer gear (shorts, T-shirt with something printed on the back
and front and colourful baseball cap) stood up first. 'Hi. My name is
Jacob. I'm from California and in my final year at Brandeis. My
grandparents were from Poland and I'm trying to trace the village
they came from.' The serious-looking student next to him was one
of the two Poles in the group. 'My name is Gwido, I am Polish now
living in America. My mother is Catholic, my father a Jew. She saved
his life by hiding him during the war and they married soon after. I
only learned of my Jewish heritage when I was twenty-five years
old. I have been living in the States for seven years now and converted to Judaism two years ago. I am now working on my Ph.D. in
Polish–Jewish relations.' The introductions continued, each story
being more fascinating to me than the last. There was Lisa from San
Francisco, who had come to Kraków to complete her Ph.D. on
stamps and the Holocaust and to retrieve as much Judaica as she
could collect, from antique stores, flea markets, anywhere she could
purchase it. 'My family makes a point of buying Judaica from
Eastern Europe with the aim of giving these purchases as wedding
gifts. They should be in Jewish homes.' The other Polish student
was a gentle young man called Tomek from Warsaw. 'I am Catholic
but have a growing interest in Jewish life. This began when I was
twelve years old and visited the Jewish cemetery in Poznan and

began to ask questions. Last year I spent the summer in Israel and I am presently studying Hebrew.' Tobie, an angry young fashion victim from Los Angeles, mutters, 'What are you, a Jewologist?' We laugh but this is a new phenomenon, Poles who feel the loss, who see the footsteps of the former Jews embedded into their streets, hear the whispers in their music, taste the remnants in their food.

The last to speak was a fresh-faced 'guy' from Boston. 'My name is Ran. I'm here for my grandparents. Both sets of grandparents are Holocaust survivors and both sets are still alive. My grandfather has given me a map of family possessions he buried in a courtyard behind his home in Łódź during the occupation. I am here to try and retrieve that treasure.' Ran had been informed that the treasure consisted of a large wooden chest filled with family photographs, candlesticks and books: rare handwritten translations of the Torah by Ran's grandfather. The following week Ran travelled to Łódź with Tomek as his guide. They returned with two Yiddish books found by the present occupants of his grandfather's house. He showed them to me. One was in quite good condition, a rabbi's book on *Halacha*, written in Yiddish. Extra pages from other books had been inserted, including handwritten notes, in Hebrew and Polish, resembling one of Rodinsky's constructions. Maybe this format was not as haphazard as first appeared, was actually part of a long rabbinic Eastern European tradition. The books were preserved sandwiched between two pieces of wood and stuck in a wall. The second book he carefully took out of the Jiffy bag and unwrapped from the newspaper binding. Crumbling pages in Yiddish, stuck together with a glue of cobwebs, so fragile that it seemed if you breathed, the letters would fly away and the pages would turn to dust.

The following week, with Tomek's help, Ran hired a car and two Polish radiologists with sophisticated depth-finding devices and returned to the courtyard. The Polish family that now owned the house were eager to help, and when three likely locations were detected the teams all dug. Hours later they all hit something hard. It turned out to be a deep brick-lined hole set in the foundations of the former building. Tomek retrieved some shoes and a shampoo bottle from the 1950s – someone had been there before. Just as they were about to give up, the detector beeped again and they all dug furiously. They found a terracotta tile. When they pulled it out and brushed off the dirt they could see a Star of David with initials etched on either side that corresponded with Ran's family name. Ran was satisfied: for him this was the end of a two-year research project and he felt he could put the family legend to rest. The Poles that were with him were disappointed and eager to continue. The peasant family who lived there invited them in for tea and sausage. From where he was sitting, Ran could see the empty room where his grandmother had lived. He dreamed of coming back in his summer break and living in that room, eating with the peasant family downstairs and working in the Jewish cemetery where his great-grandparents and great-great-grandparents are buried.

Everyone had their own golem to chase. I felt instantly at ease with this group. For the first time I recognized that I was not alone in my obsessive pursuits but part of a worldwide phenomenon in my generation. I added my story to the others; no one here thought my research bizarre or obsessive and Rodinsky became a talking point for all of us, desperate for a story of survival in this land of ghosts. But Rodinsky was not the only reason I had come. I was here to visit my family in Łódź. I was the only foreigner in the group who still had living family members in Poland. My great aunt, Gustawa Lubnika, is now eighty-two years old. She was in Auschwitz and survived because they experimented on her. She still has a hole in her thigh you could put your fist in. She lost her first husband and child in the camp and returned to Łódź after the war hoping to find other family members. She was not successful, but she did meet her second husband who was there for the same purpose. These two survivors married and had another child, who married one of the only practising Jews in Łódź, and they had a daughter who is now fifteen. When she was twelve years old they thought it was safe to tell her she was Jewish.

During the week we were gradually introduced to our speakers.

Running the programme is Professor Polonsky, director of History and Judaic Studies at Brandeis University (California) and editor of *Polin*. I had met him many years before when I was a student. Professor Polonsky was involved in 'Testimony', a collaborative project with the Jewish Student Union and the Oral History department of the British Museum. The aim of the project was to record on videotape the testaments of Holocaust survivors in England and deposit this material in the museum's archives. While studying at Sheffield University I became involved in the project as the camera operator for the North of England. We conducted and documented a series of long interviews, often with survivors who had never before spoken about their experiences. I remember one particularly painful interview when after three hours of talking the man we were interviewing began to sob heavily. But he was still talking and he was not able or willing to stop and we needed to record it, and I had to hold the camera very steady and try not to shake.

Polonsky is an expert on Polish and Russian Jewish history. I find it physically impossible to keep up with the vast amounts of data that fire out of him during lectures. If he was not able to lecture he might spontaneously combust because of all the information stored inside him. He is commonly known as 'the human encyclopaedia'.

Through Polonsky's lectures I gained great insight into the type of life the Rodinsky family might have led in Russia before they came to London. Kushovata (the shtetl where Rodinskys were said to have originated) was situated in an area known as the Pale of Settlement, on the periphery of the Czarist empire, the nearest city being Kiev. Before World War Two this area contained the largest Jewish population in the world. The Jews who lived there were much less integrated than those in the rest of Europe, where a certain amount of assimilation and emancipation was starting to take place. In Kushovata and the surrounding shtetls life remained steeped in traditional rabbinic Judaism and Hasidism. Polonsky told us a particular form of Hasidism was practised in that area, revering an ascetic lifestyle, believing pleasure denied in this world would be granted in the next. I thought of Bella Lipman describing David Rodinsky's post office account book, and the money his mother had saved for him. David Rodinsky did have money but he chose to live like a pauper instead, continuing in the tradition of his ancestors.

Polonsky read us romantic descriptions of Hasidism that seemed to mirror Rodinsky's ideals; he defined Hasidism as 'a ladder whereby man reaches heightened consciousness. It has many rungs and one needs to descend into dark depths before one can rise to luminous heights.' Rodinsky's ancestors would have lived a rural lifestyle for generations, surrounded by Jews who spoke their own language, dressed in their own fashion, ate their own foods, served God in their own way, and ran their own institutions. The life blood of this shtetl existence had always been the written word: Yiddish for daily communication, Hebrew for the holy text, Aramaic the ancient language of the holiest prayers, and Russian for conversing with gentiles. Even the simplest peasant would have been bilingual, and the majority of Kushovata's inhabitants had probably been multilingual. The Rodinskys' interest in languages was therefore not unusual.

I learnt about the rapidly deteriorating position of the Jews in the Pale of Settlement from the 1880s onwards. Haicka Rodinsky,

David's mother, had been born into a period of great political instability, a precarious period for Jewish existence as economic conditions worsened and first trades and then residence became restricted. She must have lived in a constant atmosphere of fear and danger. In 1881, after the assassination of Alexander was blamed on the Jews, the first wave of pogroms began. During the three waves of pogroms, over a quarter of a million Jews were murdered. During the Russian Civil War, peasant anarchists were fighting the Bolsheviks and believed the Bolshevik revolution to be a Jewish plot. It was during one of these pogroms, according to Carol Wayne, that Rodinsky's mother had been raped. Haicka Rodinsky's nervous behaviour seemed entirely logical in the context of her background, as did all the Rodinskys' deep-seated fears of bureaucratic institutions. They came from a tradition and place where it was legitimate to have a natural fear of authority; friends become enemies overnight, and everyone was highly suspicious of each other.

We learned about day-to-day life in the shtetl, which seemed to consist outside working hours mainly of study – for the men, of course. I imagined that if Rodinsky had been born there he would have spent his days debating the Talmud, studying the Hebrew alphabet, and discussing issues of *Halacha*. In fact these were activities he was engaged in for most of his life, but increasingly separated from his community. This was not how it would have been in Kushovata, this was not the Jewish way. If he had been born in Kushovata, he would have studied in the *yeshiva*.

The first myth about *yeshiva* study is that it is a silent process. On entering you are greeted with the intense sound of a thousand simultaneous arguments. Each scholar works with a *havrusa* and the basis of *yeshiva*-style learning is to work hard with your *havrusa* at finding opposing points of view and debating about them, loudly. Who was left in Princelet Street for Rodinsky to study with? I thought immediately of his English to Hebrew Conversational Dictionary and how tragic the imagined conversations and debates written there now seemed. The more we learned the more I recognized his isolation. He continued all the activities of his people and

slowly withered away without their presence. David was left in the
attic, furiously studying like a good *yeshiva* student, but alone.

Polonsky's lectures were hard for me to follow, densely packed
with statistics and facts too detailed for my purposes. More often
than not I would find myself daydreaming, gazing out of the
window of the *bet midrash*, much as I imagined the *yeshiva* boys
would have done half a century ago, desperate to escape from the
drone of their *melamed* and to feel the heat of the sun on their faces
and the air on their pale cheeks. Even if I could have escaped there
was no such opportunity for me outside. The weather had settled
into a constant downpour and we were receiving reports from
around the country of the worst flooding Poland had ever experienced. I worried that our trip around Galicia would be cancelled. I
was very much hoping to cross over the border and into the Ukraine
to go and visit Kushovata.

I drifted back from the sodden view of the market square outside
to Polonsky's quick patter. The other students were furiously taking
notes and leaping up to ask complex questions at every opportunity.
My notebook was full of sketches of the marketplace and the other
students; then, suddenly, I would be fully engaged, writing furiously
as Polonsky read out some fact or poem that I could relate to the
Rodinsky quest. Then it would be me, the quiet Brit, asking him the
questions, bugging him after class for the translation of a poem or a
quote. He introduced me for the first time to some incredible
Yiddish writers and poets. Polonsky, as well as being a scholarly historian, is also a deep romantic. As he read the evocative translations
of the Yiddish poets and writers, his voice would crack and tears
would appear in the corners of his eyes. He described these artists,
whose lives were so tragically cut short, as the prophets of their
time, able somehow to foresee the horrors that lay before them. The
poet who interested me the most was Bialik. Polonsky described
him as 'an orphan in exile, a symbol of the Jewish people in his own
time, a solitary poet, steeped in tradition, learning, mysticism, and
legend'. To me this image conjured up my first notions about David
Rodinsky. The comparison grew stronger as Polonsky told us of

Bialik's agony, his love for orthodox Judaism and the lack of human love in his own life. I was particularly moved by one section of Bialik's poem 'And If The Angel Should Ask':

My Grandfather had a Gemara, rough scrolled pages, crumpled.
And in its belly – two of my Grandfather's white hairs,
Threads of blemished tassels of his small prayer shawl
And marks of drops of tallow and wax.
In this Gemara, in the belly of dead letters
Alone my soul fluttered,
– And it choked? –
No, it fluttered and sang my Angel!
Out of the dead letters welled forth songs of life.
In my Grandfather's bookcase the eternal dead quaked.
Different were these songs: about a small clear cloud,
A golden sunbeam, a shining tear,
About blemished tassels and drops of wax –
But one song it never knew – the song of youth and love
And it yearned to escape, it moaned and found no solace,
It fainted away and was squeezed almost to death.
Once I visited my tattered Gemara –
And suddenly it flew from my soul.
And still it flies and soars in the world,
Soars and wanders and finds no solace.
On the dark nights at the beginning of each month
When the world prays over the imperfect moon,
It clings with its wings to the gate of love
Clings, knocks, secretly weeping,
And prays for love.

Being in Kraków gave me the distance I needed to reassess the information I had gathered so far about the Rodinsky family. From their behaviour I concluded that David and his sister, Brendall, were deeply affected by their mother's terrible experiences during the pogroms. Although David was born into the relative freedom of

England he never seemed to realize what this meant as the family
hadn't managed to assimilate successfully into their new situation.
Many Jews described the process of immigration from Russia as like
leaving a prison and entering a free world. But Haicka, David's
mother, never appeared to have felt this. According to Alvin and
Carol Wayne, she was extremely disturbed when she arrived in
England. 'She would jump if you touched her with a feather.' Carol
said she always wore the traditional long heavy skirts of her home-
land, layers of them at the same time. Her entire wardrobe, hanging
on her for fear she would have to leave quickly. Her children followed suit, looking eccentric in the mild winters and hot summers
of East London. 'He always wore this long dark coat and dirty old
cap,' said Carol Wayne. It appears that Haicka guarded her family
from encounters with authority and the outside world by shutting
them safely inside the attic room. Any attempted contact, particularly by institutions of the state, was ignored and feared. I felt that
the Rodinskys subconsciously recreated in miniature exactly what
they had left, their own self-imposed prison. And from their attic
window, Princelet Street may have looked like a street in Kushovata,
another state within a state, a ghetto without walls, with the sounds
of Yiddish drifting up to them from the street below.

My portrait of him began to shift into focus. I knew he had never
married and that after the death of his mother and sister he lived
alone for nine years, in acute poverty. I suspected he spent the
majority of his time in his room, experimenting with linguistics
and various religious studies. His collection of travel books and
contemporary literature showed he had a thirst for secular knowledge but he also seems to have been immersed in the world of
rabbinical Judaism, as the many religious books and artefacts found
in his room suggest.

Rodinsky's main occupation appeared to have been writing. Just
as his contemporaries had written in hidden rooms, sealed-off attics
and underground bunkers all over Eastern Europe. While studying
in Kraków I heard how archives were assembled in the Warsaw
ghetto in milk cans, then sealed with lead before being buried, in the

vain hope that they would survive as a record of their authors' existence. The line printed boldly in the books I retrieved from the synagogue in Greatorex Street came to mind: FOR FUTURE REFERENCE. In the ghettos, diaries were written on any book that could be found, in as many languages as possible – French, Yiddish, Russian . . . – and in an attic in East London, in a later but parallel time, David Rodinsky sat alone and wrote in Letts diaries, on old newspapers, cigarette packets, in Greek, Hebrew, Chinese, Russian. Rodinsky would have been eighteen years old at the time of the ghetto uprising, slightly older than the average age of the rebel fighters. But he didn't bury his books, he didn't need to, he just locked the door and left a tomb without a body, maybe hoping someone in the future would find it and decode his tale. He shifted constantly in my mind from scholar to lunatic to hero.

I dreamed about him, stuck in a black hole that spirals from the centre of his room, a tight dark tunnel that will not allow him to move either above or below. He existed as a wandering *dybbuk*, waiting for a soul to possess to free him from his state of misery. I think he did attempt to transcend his situation through his obsessive pursuit of languages, imagining that this new knowledge might create a key to another life. But it appeared he could not shake the bondage of his past. His mother's presence and his commitment to his religion seemed to weigh heavily on him. Even after her death he was not free. As Bella Lipman remembered, he tried to break the bonds of his past by going out more and eating Indian food. But he always returned to the room because of his mother; he was duty-bound, as the letter to Carol Wayne's mother showed. The significance of his room suddenly became clear. It was his world (all that remains of it), it was his portrait, his *flesh and blood*. My mind was racing – here in Poland it was all beginning to make sense. David Rodinsky could not be properly understood back in Whitechapel. Perhaps this was the real reason I had felt inspired to come back to Poland. Maybe this was the reason why Rodinsky spent the last days or weeks of his life in a mental asylum. Could he have been sectioned, and taken away to the Longrove psychiatric asylum because of the way he lived? Because the chaos of his room and his obsessive scribblings were so absolutely misunderstood by English social services? What did they know of observing the eleven months of mourning required of orthodox Jews? What did they know of Hasidic traditions, of charity to the poor, of the pursuit of cabbalistic magic? As these new realizations sank in, I felt deeply sad. I sensed that when he left Whitechapel for Epsom (I did not know if this journey was forced or voluntary), he truly felt his strangeness in the world, and retreated; death came quickly.

Ideas were flooding my mind: I was thousands of miles away from the room and had never been more obsessed. I confided in Lili Cole, a gentile New Yorker at the conference who originally became attracted to me by her deep love for all things English. Unlike most Americans, who love England for its antiquity, Lili loved England for the reserved and civilized characters that she fantasized most Brits to be. She had spent a six-month sabbatical in Cambridge and had told me, 'I felt at home for the first time in my life.' She certainly didn't behave like most Americans, and I found her gentle demeanour and quiet voice very soothing after a noisy day of study with the rest of the group. I had told her about the Rodinsky research I was doing and she showed a great interest and was delighted when I invited her to my room to show her the photographs of his artefacts I had brought with me. She knocked on the door, and slowly her petite frame, dressed in a pastel flowered dress (that seemed to be a feeble attempt to disguise her intellect) appeared. Lili has a Ph.D. in Russian Literature, and she speaks a number of languages fluently. She was fascinated by the photographs and became particularly excited when she spotted a page of his diary written in Chinese that she translated as 'My name is David Rodinsky', written over and over again.

We must have talked late into the night about Rodinsky, and throughout my time spent in Kraków Lili was never far away, always eager to hear more. Our parting was a sad one, but it was only when I returned to London that I realized the true impact the Rodinsky story had had on Lili. Waiting on my doorstep was a thin pink

envelope from New York which contained the following poem she
had written, entitled 'Love for Rachel Lichtenstein'.

> You as a child, haunted by dreams of holy men
> scholars, scribes, *tzaddickim*
>
> You who adopted a girl
> from a row of photographs
> in an Auschwitz barrack,
> took her as a sister
> then thought she was you
> yourself as a child headscarfed, round eyes
> looking out impassive,
> from the wall of death
>
> You find a man
> twenty-eight years dead
> explore his unsealed attic
> read his dusty notes
>
> 'My name is David'
> in English, Aramaic, Chinese,
> write him into a book
>
> You excavate his mysteries
> the village in the Ukraine
> where his mother was raped
> his secret, silent sister
> remembered by neighbours
> she shared his attic
> but left no trace
> his death in a madhouse near London
> ten days before you were born
>
> You try to exhume him

bone by bone
as the holy man in Israel
told you to do
you were born to uncover
the secrets of the earth
when he sent you home to England

Home to the attic
where you photograph each paper
the phonograph, the handwritten dictionaries
later you discover a double exposure
her face
over a stack of his notebooks

You cannot find it, the madhouse
only a pile of brick and ash
where it burned to the ground
only a death certificate
in a London courthouse
but no portrait, no close friend, no survivor

You dig and he fades
you call and he answers
from a great distance
in a language of ash, ruins, dust
words, words, words he wrote
and wrote and wrote

In Jerusalem the rebbe told you:
a soul may wander for ten days
before it finds a home
in the body of one newly born

The days are long, wet and difficult; they drift into each other. We
meet former activists of the underground Zionist and communist

movements, leaders of the struggling Jewish community in Poland, bringers of terrible tales I would rather not know. We leave the centre, walk through the rain and take the short tram ride back to the dorm. Sometimes we linger a while in Kazimierz. The majority of the buildings there are very run down, unable to be renovated or sold to Poles as they still belong to Jews. The buildings sit and wait, empty shells harbouring ghosts. There are a few new kosher restaurants in the main square along with a wooden kiosk where you can buy Israeli flags and wooden figurines of Hasidic Jews. Yiddishkite is in vogue in Poland at present. We wander through these deserted streets, knocking on doors with our guidebooks in hand, making inquires, our hollow footsteps ringing out on the stones.

One day, while conducting such a search with Jacob from Boston, we came across an open door at the site of the abandoned Temple Synagogue. We entered the musty, deep pink interior, which was faintly lit by light filtering through the dirty but magnificent stained-glass windows. The place had the same intoxicating smell as Princelet Street, but the interior must once have been much more magnificent. Jacob and I were overjoyed to have come across such a site and were happily recording and exploring the lower floor of the building when a short, white-haired, milky-eyed peasant shuffled over to us from the sleepy shadows in the corner.

He was grinning inanely, pointing at us and asking, 'Juden?' We nodded in silence. He spoke no English but it was clear he wanted to show us around the building, and he wanted money for his pains. He stuck to us like glue, his dusty leather apron giving him away as a worker there and not the caretaker (the synagogue was in the process of being reconstructed). I became increasingly irritated by this man, as he blocked our way as we attempted to go upstairs, holding out his hand for change. 'No way, mate, this is my place.' We ignored him and pushed past, stomping up the wooden stairs, leaving clouds of dust in our wake. The view from the balcony was breathtaking. The Pole shuffled behind, breathing deeply, pulling at my arm, pointing at things randomly, holding out his hand. We left in disgust.

I was an old hand at these kind of trips, having spent many
months years ago, criss-crossing the country with guidebook in
hand, trying to locate former synagogues. I had never been brave
enough then to walk away crossly from the rudeness of some of the
Poles I met, who would treble the price of Jewish artefacts on a
market stall or try to gain a fee for showing you around an old
building that could have been your grandfather's home. I knew
then that anger would have been dangerous, but times are changing
and with Jacob by my side I was feeling braver. Many afternoons
were spent like this, until we gradually had built up a mental map
of the old Jewish quarter in Kraków. Other days, when the rain was
too heavy for us to walk, I would retreat to the library with its old
maps, and books of poetry and Jewish legends. I became particularly fascinated with any stories I could find about the Golem of
Prague.

This fantastical tale developed in the middle of the seventeenth
century, a dark time of massacres and pogroms for the Jews of
Europe. I don't believe there is such a thing as an accidental folk
legend. These stories are not just fanciful fictions; rather, they are
mirror images of the complex historical and cultural experiences of
a people. When I had first set foot in the synagogue in Whitechapel
students had been there making a film loosely based on the life of
David Rodinsky called *The Golem of Princelet Street*. Even though I
felt the film was a weak effort, I do think the idea of comparing
Rodinsky to a golem is very apt. To me David Rodinsky's story seems
to touch on a human need for a contemporary myth of discovery
and survival. Sometimes I question whether Rodinsky ever existed.
Has he been created from our desire to believe in an eternally wandering Jew, one who seems to vanish every time someone attempts
to define him? I want to believe in Rodinsky, a Jew whose belongings
are all intact, a Jewish scholar continuing the centuries-old tradition
of learning, a cabbalistic genius who magically transported himself
to a higher realm, a Jew who achieved the impossible and outwitted
his own fate. By digging and searching I eventually summon him
into my world. How often have I looked at faded photographs of my

own perished family members and attempted the same thing? Rodinsky becomes a modern-day golem and like the Golem of Prague he has been created as both protector and destroyer. And like the Golem of Prague he eventually turns to dust in the forgotten attic of a synagogue.

Many years ago the Baal Sham Tov went regularly to a sacred place in the forest to light a fire and recite a special prayer. After his death his student forgot where the place was exactly but lit the fire and said the prayer. The next generation did not know the place or the prayer but they still lit the fire.

(story told to me by Antony Polonsky)

I shall never forget the morning we left for Galicia. I awoke early, disturbed by shouting outside my window, and hurried out to the balcony. Four floors below lay a body in the rain, a man in his early forties with a swollen yellow face half covered by a grey plastic sheet. His glasses were broken and lying beside his left hand. As I studied his face I realized I had seen him the previous day, appearing from the ochre shadows of the dormitory corridor. I remembered the brief scene distinctly, as I had been curious about his presence there. So far as I knew, the fourth floor was taken up with our young group. I had watched as he bowed his head, avoiding my gaze while hurriedly placing a key in the lock of the room next door to mine. Now I was looking at the same face and desperately wishing someone would close his eyes.

The dining room was alive with the sound of excitable students, all greedy for information on 'the body'. A stool had been found pushed to the edge of the balcony railings, a brief suicide note had been left. The man was not Polish and the police were trying to identify him. When we returned after breakfast the body had gone; only a faint impression remained in the wet grass. His glasses had been removed and in their place was a pair of surgical rubber gloves.

We loaded the bus and began our five-day horror tour of eastern Galicia. Grisly tourists, speeding through the sodden countryside, stopping to pay homage to the deserted sites where our ancestors once lived. Our first stop was Rymanow, to visit a seventeenth-century synagogue. As we approached, Polonsky read us the description of the place from the guidebook:

> If one ruined synagogue could stand as a memorial to the
> Holocaust it could be this tragic ruin in this nonedescript
> village in the south-east corner of Poland. Perched on a hilltop
> at the edge of the town, the synagogue is a highly evocative mass
> of brick and stone which looks as if it fought hard against its
> destruction and lost.

The synagogue had been used for many years after World War Two to store grain. The tin from the roof was later removed by the town's mayor to repair the church. We entered the building through a narrow archway held up precariously by large iron supports. As we stepped inside, two goats scrambled through the foliage into a dark alcove, bleating in terror. We were left to explore, jovially fighting our way through the thick undergrowth like jungle trekkers, falling silent as we noticed the bullet holes that riddled the crumbling columns and frescoes.

The elderly man from the village who escorted us into the ruin told his story. His grandfather was the last rabbi of the synagogue, shot here by Nazis along with the rest of his family. Our guide remains, the sole survivor, and like Rodinsky he has taken upon himself the role of *shames*. He campaigned for years to try to get the roof repaired but to no avail. He welded and fitted a large metal door on the entrance and tried to brick up the windows, but the goats and birds still get in and trees burst up through the floor and rip at the foundations. All he can do now is open up the building for rare visits from groups like ours and for the Hasidim who come here from New York and Israel in order to pray. He tells us this is probably the last year that visitors will be able to come inside the building. We speak quietly so as not to disturb the fragile construction. I am fascinated by him, would like to stay and record his story properly, but there are too many tales to tell. He is the first of many such elderly men we meet in the coming days, a member of the 'caretaker community' which is all that remains of the vast Jewish populations of Poland, Byelorussia and the Ukraine. They have chosen to remain, guarding the decaying remains of their heritage.

In the next town we stand in the rain and listen to our guide's description of the synagogue and *bet midrash* that used to stand proudly in the now-derelict concrete site. Turning clockwise we face a park; underneath the flowerbeds and gravel paths lies a Jewish cemetery. I watch young couples strolling arm in arm and wonder if they know what they are walking on. Our guide tells us that bones are constantly being dug up by dogs. We tread gently – the horror of what lies under my feet never leaves me while I am in Poland.

We are wet, restless and unsure of how to respond to this place. A couple of drunks approach us leering and shouting, paranoia sets in, we are all desperate to leave. We drag ourselves back on to the bus and arrive soon at the next horror spot. Now we stand on a site where hundreds of Jews were shot dead; the remainder were transported to Auschwitz. We walk to the cemetery. The rain is coming down in sheets, the grass inside the cemetery is long, the graves are broken and half buried, and we don't know where we are treading. We hear how Jews were shot here after being forced to smash up the gravestones of their families then pave the roads with them. We huddle together and say Kaddish, the memorial prayer for the dead. And for the first time since I arrived in Poland I feel hot tears rolling uncontrollably down my face.

The following day begins more positively: it is not raining, and we are journeying to see the tomb of a famous rabbi, Eli Melech. He was known for his supernatural powers and belonged to a mystical Hasidic sect that was very popular in Galicia and in the Ukraine, where Rodinsky's family lived. Gabby, the former lawyer now history teacher, who is anything but shy, goes to the front of the bus, takes the microphone, and sings a beautiful melancholic Yiddish tune about the rabbi. A number of the American students enthusiastically join in while I stare from the window of the bus at the wooden houses, their yards teeming with chickens, and the peasant women at work in the fields.

Eli Melech's tomb is littered with thousands of scraps of folded paper covered in urgent requests in many languages. We deposit ours among the cracks of the ancient stones and burning candles, then add our names to those that cover the walls. I can identify twelve different languages here – Rodinsky would have liked this. The mood of the group is light as we tour the cemetery that surrounds Eli Melech's tomb. The sun is shining and the air is filled with the sound of farm animals from the valley below. We walk around the cemetery, translating the Hebrew names on the graves until we learn that what we see is not as it seems. All the headstones had been used as pavement material then brought back here after the war and replaced randomly in the cemetery. The tomb in front of me claims to mark the resting place of Sara; it is quite probable that it does not. Fake histories are everywhere.

We continue to the next town, stopping in the rain to view a bus station that was once a Jewish cemetery. On the way to the next site there is a commotion at the back of the bus: some students are talking excitedly with our tour guide. Apparently we are driving along the border of the Ukraine, and the area of Rodinsky's mother's birthplace, Kushovata. Many other students have family who originated from there. I rush over to join the group talking with the guide: if there is any way we can go there I am going. The guide tells us that many people have got through by bribing the border guards with a hundred and fifty dollars. I become overexcited: the journey to his village would still be approximately three days away by train, but surely the ultimate pilgrimage for me. A small group of us drive the guide mad with questions. Maps are retrieved from the bottom of sodden rucksacks and we study them, tracing the faint lines until we locate the position of these now-vanished villages. Rodinsky's small shtetl can only be found on a pre-World War One map of Russia. But I know where it is: only the length of my finger away from where we are now. Polonsky joins us and advises against attempting to make the journey: the probability of getting through the border is only fifty-fifty. We would need a large amount of cash and to prebook hotels and hire a translator and car. I feel the desire to get closer to the origin of my quest, and our guide promises to make some telephone calls at the next stop.

We stand and wait for him to make the calls in the forecourt of a petrol station. Opposite us is the wreckage of a synagogue now used as a grain store. Our guide returns with disappointing news: border access has tightened up. In April you could sometimes get through by bribing guards; now the only way is with an official invitation and visa which can only be obtained from the Ukrainian embassy in London. I still feel determined to risk it until I hear that even if we had invitations we couldn't go as the border is closed because of flooding.

I'm disappointed and frustrated. I press my nose against the wet window of the bus, trying to look for the eagles, bears, bison and wolves I'm told live in this area of the Carpathian mountains. It is not them I want to see. On the other side of the mountains is the Ukrainian border I yearn so much to cross. This area was once almost entirely Jewish; but it seems so alien from the bustling urban ghettos of East London and New York inhabited by Jewish refugees from these places.

Our next stop is in Lesko, a small town far up in the mountains and the first place in Poland where Jews were not a minority. There are no Jews here now. One synagogue remains that now functions as an art gallery. Most of the Jews here were murdered by the Einsatzgruppen (killing squads who operated behind the lines as the German army invaded Russia). We slide up a mud track and visit the remains of a seventeenth-century Sephardic cemetery, fantastical, set deep inside a dark forest on a steep incline. Everything is wet, green, dripping; we struggle up the hill, slipping in churned-up mud, trip-

ping over ancient fallen stones. Moss and algae cover the tombs, and we clear them to read the inscriptions. There is a sense of discovery here, as if these are ancient ruins in a tropical rain forest, a living resting place full of birdsong and crumbling beauty. We study the graves and say Kaddish.

The next town we visit became a centre for Hasidism in the early part of the twentieth century. Meneche Mendel, a pupil of Eli Melech and himself a famous *tzaddick*, lived here and had a huge following. He lived a strictly ascetic life and was famous for his gifts of prophecy and healing. As I learn more about this particular tradition, the Rodinskys' frugal way of living begins to make sense. In London, Rodinsky appeared eccentric and poverty-stricken; here he would have been considered pious and holy. The Rodinsky family did not successfully make the transition to the new world. Their attic room became a microcosm of the mystical world they had left behind, but in Whitechapel their sentiments were deeply misunderstood.

We return to the bus. Polonsky is on the microphone again, pointing out the site of a bakery and a fire station that were both once synagogues. The rest of the day is spent much as the others, with solemn visits to cemeteries, synagogues and burial sites. We stand in the wet grass, Hebrew letters and bones under our feet, chanting the mournful words of the Kaddish. We become invisible time-travellers, our activities totally alien from the lives of the Poles we see through the rain-smeared windows of our bus.

Our trip is an urgent one; there is an edge of mania to our travels. Not only are the monuments disintegrating, but these years will be the last in which it is possible to meet the extraordinary caretaker community that has chosen to remain to guard these places. In one town we knock on the door of a tiny barber's store. An elderly man comes out and opens up for us the only remaining wooden synagogue in Poland. It is now used for local art classes. The smell inside is rich, an exquisite mixture of damp wood and dust, evoking in me memories of my first visit to Princelet Street. I am fascinated by these men that protect the buildings. Much like David Rodinsky, they appear unable to break the bonds of their past, sacrificing their lives for the life that was there before.

Many of the cemeteries we visited were extraordinarily beautiful: set on hillsides and in forests, the ancient tombs leaning in different directions, appearing like praying Jews in the evening dusk. This romantic vision would often be shattered as we learned we were standing on a mass grave.

As we arrived at each site, most of the Americans would jump in front of the monuments, swapping cameras with each other, to catch on celluloid the moment of 'being there'. Warped tourism, horror snapshots. Others would place carefully collected stones on to tombs, while softly murmuring prayers. Somehow our presence on this blood-saturated earth was necessary because our being there meant that the bones of the people beneath our feet were not entirely forgotten. We knew about them, we went there, stood there, prayed there and learned a little about their lives and deaths from the old men who trekked up the hills to share with us their fading memories.

As we enter Tarnów, Gabby becomes very excited. This is the town where his grandfather grew up. We go to the local museum for a lecture on the Jews of Tarnów, and Gabby madly takes notes, asks a thousand questions. I know how he's feeling: he is close to the source, and the psychic energy is making him buzz. There are no synagogues left in Tarnów; they were all blown up by Nazis, successfully obliterated; most of the Jews were shot in the forest in a large unmarked grave. A few returned after World War Two; the last Jew in Tarnów died two years ago. We see a video of him, sitting in his empty self-constructed prayer room, mournfully singing a song of his childhood in Yiddish before kissing the Torah he holds in his arms. The effect of this act is overwhelming: tears are streaming down everyone's face, we are reaching saturation point. That night I dream all my teeth fall out, crumble in my mouth as I press against them with the back of my tongue. My gums are a bleeding raw mass, to expose them even to the air is extremely painful. I can digest no more.

We walk around the old Jewish ghetto, recognizable by the still-native textile and cheap-clothing factories, much resembling

Fashion and Princelet streets in Whitechapel. I now experience the
surreal nature of being on a guided tour, much like the ones I conduct myself in East London – pointing to the derelict sites where a
vast synagogue had once towered over the heads of the community,
to an abandoned parking lot where the *mikve* once housed the holy
waters for purifying, to the prayer house, the *cheder*, the kosher
butchers, all no longer there. Our guide tells us how in June 1942 the
street where we now stand was a river of Jewish blood. The townspeople have decided to keep the original pavement as a grim
reminder. We keep walking; he points to the site where the great
synagogue was burnt to the ground. It took three days to burn, and
for weeks afterwards small fires would break out among the floating
hot embers. As with all our tours, we finish in the cemetery. Three
thousand Jews were shot dead here. A monument was erected in
their memory by a small committee of three elderly men who look
after the cemetery. The monument is made from the rescued pillar
of the old synagogue. We tramp through the wet grass, weeds up to
our armpits, our limbs covered in nettle stings, and we visit the
grave of the last Jew of Tarnów. I place a stone on his tomb. He is
buried next to his wife as was his wish, but who is left to say Kaddish
for him? He was the last, the responsibility is now ours.

I am feeling drained and depressed by our trip. The only person
who is feeling positive is Gabby. He is terribly excited, his usual
serious demeanour has become animated, and his eyes are
sparkling. In the evening he is travelling to Wojnicz to meet an
archivist who took on the role of collecting the records of the Jews
of the Tarnów area. He finds his grandfather's birth certificate. He
tells me the story over breakfast the next morning. He proudly
shows me the certificate. 'Look, I even have the name of the assistant to the *mohel* at my grandfather's circumcision.' Gabby deserves
this solid piece of evidence – he has been on his quest for ten years.
Last year he visited Theresienstadt to trace his great-grandmother.
He found her name on the records, a brief line in German that
confirmed she had been transported to Treblinka. Fortunately he
has other tales to tell. His father and grandfather are both survivors

from Auschwitz; they probably survived due to the fact that they managed to stay together throughout their three-year imprisonment. They were on a transport of one thousand. There were only sixteen survivors. Like myself, Gabby had also been to Poland before on a lone quest to try to find the house of his grandfather. He had been taken to a house, walked around the circumference, had his picture taken outside, only to find out two years later that it was the wrong house. On this trip Gabby finds the right house. The entire group stops there as we pass through the village. Gabby and his wife stand proudly in front of it. We are all overjoyed; everyone photographs them.

We arrive in Nowy Sącz, a small, bustling tourist town. We enter a small courtyard. To our right stands a small modern synagogue. Mr Muller, a tiny man, opens the door. He affects me deeply before he has uttered a single word: he looks exactly like my late grandfather. He does not want to speak to us in Polish, so our translator is made redundant. The only people who can speak Yiddish are Polonsky and Gabby. Polonsky realizes the importance of this journey for Gabby and allows him the honour of translating the Yiddish for us. Mr Muller was the last remaining Jew in the town and was forced to leave during the anti-Semitic campaign of 1968. He now lives in Switzerland, but since 1983 he has returned here every summer. He is the only survivor of a family of eight who were all resettled by the Nazis in the Warsaw ghetto. 'It was Gehenna, hell on earth.' He built this small synagogue over a number of years with help from local builders. It stands on the site of the former great synagogue of the town. He prays here every day, and sometimes groups like ours come to pray with him.

'Why do you come back, Mr Muller,' we ask.

'I do it because it lies in my blood. As long as God allows me to travel I will return here. This is my life, I live with it.' He describes Nowy Sącz as being one of the former holy cities of Poland, an extremely orthodox place. He still feels connected here, and has good relations with the non-Jewish townspeople, who do not bother him. When we ask how old he is (he looks ancient), he tells us, 'Two

onions and a half' and winks. He walks with us to the cemetery at a
great pace. As he speeds ahead he points. 'This is where I saw a family
shot.' He looks at us, urgently, with huge, red-rimmed penetrating
blue eyes. 'I was witness to that.'

We enter the former synagogue, an empty shell now, and he
stands on the spot where he once sat with his father and brothers.
He shows us a photo album he has collated of Jewish life in Nowy
Sącz. It is a copy; he gave the original to *Yad Vashem*. Inside are
fading sepia images of Mr Muller and his young friends posing in
front of the Maccabbee sports club, of his parents, brothers and sisters, sitting beside their single-storey wooden house, exactly the sort
of place my grandfather would have been born in; of beautiful
laughing girls, names forgotten by Mr Muller now. Street scenes of
Nowy Sącz in the earlier part of the twentieth century, the long
coats and swaying sidelocks of the Hasidim visible everywhere. 'All
gone,' he says. 'Only me now.' We walk together around the walls of
the former ghetto, as he points at the river bank opposite, telling us
horror story after horror story. 'When I come here my heart cries.'
He gestures to the air, looks at us with those mournful Jewish eyes.
'I still cannot believe it could happen.' We are nearly at a running
pace now. He points constantly – 'The rabbi's house was here, there
the *mikve* . . . all gone' – I dread to hear the story that accompanies
his finger, I can absorb no more. He stops, and we move into a
tighter circle around him: he becomes very anxious if anyone from
the group strays, we must hear, he has to tell us, time is running out.
We are in the cemetery, but there is not much to see: the graves are
like amputated stumps, bleeding wounds, smashed to pieces and
abandoned. As he points out the site of a mass grave we hear a loud
sound of metal against metal and then harsh barking as a huge
alsatian dog tries to break from its leash in the garden next door. Mr
Muller speeds ahead, we are all saturated again, he has more to show
us, we must keep up. After saying Kaddish we return to the bus
soaked to the skin, and Mr Muller leaves us, tiny head bent towards
the floor, walking at great speed to his synagogue. He is soon out of
sight.

The bus struggles up a steep hill to reach a small mountainous village. We walk through a beautifully kept cherry orchard, where a pleasant-faced man called Ignancy Bielecki appears from behind the trees, his arms stained deep red up to the elbows with cherry juice. He disappears into a small allotment shed next to a fence and returns with black yarmulkes for the men. He then leads us through the orchard to the Jewish cemetery on the other side. It is the first cemetery we have visited where the grass is freshly mown and the gravestones are upright and in good condition. He knows the history of each tomb and tells us it in intimate detail. The place feels like a secret garden. He takes us to the monument to the Jews that died here, an impressive piece of sculpture constructed from the rescued broken tombstones of the cemetery. When I ask him who built it he replies, 'The cemetery committee.' This turns out to mean himself and a local stonemason. He is tall but bent, he has two silver front teeth and a lovely smiling face. He is probably about seventy years old. I feel I could trust him with my life. His wife shyly follows us around with a large basket of cherries, offering them to everyone. He is the caretaker of the cemetery and the cherry orchard belongs to him. His allotment shed is positioned on the fence between the two and it is as natural for him to tend to the cemetery, cutting the grass, repainting the letters on the headstones, as it is for him to tend to his cherries. He is Polish Catholic. He tells us his story. 'I grew up here. I have never lived anywhere else. My brother died in the Battle of Britain, two others as soldiers in the East, the rest of my family were taken to Auschwitz because of their communist activities. They never

returned, I am the sole survivor. This place is very special to me. Where the cherry orchard now stands was the field where my mother used to pasture her cows. I used to come here as a child to look after them and I spent many hours in the cemetery. When my brothers and mother were arrested I slipped out the back window and came immediately here. I hid underground, underneath an ancient tomb, and lived on the milk from the wandering cows that still came here. In this way I survived the war. This place gave me my life and now I dedicate my life to it.' We are speechless, but he takes us to a small wooden table outside his shed and removes the baskets of cherries from it, goes back into the shed and returns with a large leather-bound book. His shaking hands gently open the pages and he reads to us. We hear about the many visitors from many countries who come here to see the cemetery. He is very proud of the book and asks each one of us to sign it. We do it gladly and then each one of us shakes his hand. I leave with tears in my eyes. This man and his story have moved me more than anything we have seen or heard so far.

Our next visit is to Dąbrowa Tarnowska, a village high up in the mountains. We are all squeezed into the front room of a private house. A man sits in front of us, talking disjointedly in Polish. Polonsky tries to translate; the man leaves him no time to do this, he talks over him. We receive abstract scraps of information: 'Searching through Red Cross, didn't get through ... wrote every week ... lost in Soviet Union ... letters sent back ... mother had piles of them ... it would be better if all this were not true.' The man stands and shows us a thick, ugly scar that runs along the top of his skull. 'You can follow the history of these campaigns by the scars on my body.' He passes around unidentifiable crumpled photographs; I think he's telling us he was a lawyer and Egyptologist. He then stands up, shouting now, he is asking us to put pressure on the authorities to save the village's synagogue; he says it was the most beautiful synagogue in this region of Poland. It is not possible to go inside this year, too dangerous. 'This is our last cry for preserving it.' He is the last Jew in the town. He describes a lively Jewish life here before the war: Jewish dance clubs, sports clubs, many synagogues, a casino even. He passes around a photo album showing the interior that we will never be able to enter. We feast our eyes on the frescoes. He walks with us to the home of the last orthodox Jew in Dąbrowa Tarnowska, who died last year. We enter a narrow corridor and walk up a dark stairwell to a small attic room.

It takes a few moments for my eyes to adjust to the dim light and to register where we are standing. I stop breathing, turn very slowly, trying to seal the image in front of me in my mind. My heart misses a beat. I inhale deeply: the intoxicating mixture of candle wax and ancient text. In front of me is a small wooden table covered with a deep green cloth. On it are placed a number of home-made candlesticks and a menorah, constructed from old exhaust pipes. Beside them is a black cap, resting next to numerous books, in many languages. In a corner of the room, beside the tiled stove, is a wooden bench piled knee-deep in books. A crudely hand-embroidered velvet curtain hangs in the other corner, sucking the light into its dusty folds. A small bed rests opposite covered, like every other surface, by books. Maybe Rodinsky truly was the eternally wandering Jew and throughout the centuries there were thousands of abandoned rooms like this, always with the green tablecloth, the towering piles of books, the alchemist's tools.

I am deeply involved in my fantasy, urgently taking photographs of every corner, anxious we will be quickly ushered out of here. I want to stay here: nothing is catalogued, there is much to do. My concentration is slowly broken as I hear the guide tell the story of this room. I move closer, hanging on his every word. The man that built and lived in this room was called Roth. He never married, and lived here with his sister. He survived the war by escaping to the Soviet Union, and then returned to his birthplace and never left it. He loved Judaism; he was a scholar who spoke many languages, and was the last practising Jew in the town. He never had a *minyan*; he chose to stay here alone and continue his tradition of study and learning. He was well-educated. He stayed on here to guard the cemetery and would journey out there every day to pull up weeds. He pushed and pushed to get the authorities to erect a fence around the cemetery. After years of campaigning they did.

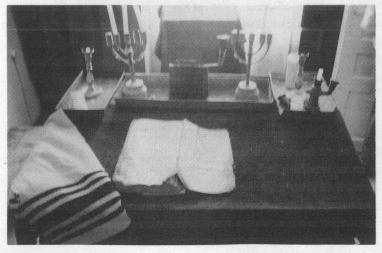

When he died the local people decided, in his honour, to leave his room exactly as he had left it. His dying wish was to be buried next to his sister. His wish was granted. Our tour guide reads us a section from his obituary. 'He was the last religious Jew living in Dąbrowa Tarnowska; he was simple and humble. He lived his whole life in the shtetl. Many came from many countries to visit him. A few years ago there were hundreds and thousands of Jews like him. He was the last shtetl Jew in Poland, he was undoubtedly one of the *lamed vavniks*.' Later I ask Polonsky what is a *lamed vavnik*? He tells me, 'The myth is a pre-Hasidic myth about the thirty-six righteous men who always live in the world. Their good deeds stop the world from being destroyed. Their power rests on the fact that no one knows who they are or where they live. They do their work in secret and are not rewarded. When they die another is born.'

My head is spinning. This is the story I most favour. I imagine both Roth and Rodinsky as *lamed vavnicks*, their activities running simultaneously, in parallel time. They were part of an ancient tradition, humble men who constructed rooms, the last survivors, duty-bound to stay, quietly practising their own magic, holding the world together.

Roth was well known and respected in the town, and when he died the townsfolk made a collection for his tombstone. His funeral was on Thursday 14 December 1995 around five o'clock. From the moment of death, Jewish custom dictates that there should be a watcher over the body and someone to prepare the body for burial. There was no one left from his family or community. Fortunately a distant cousin had been visiting him from the United States before his death. She stayed on to perform this task and managed to gather together a *minyan* from Kraków. In black yarmulkes, on a day of heavy snow and dark clouds, they accompanied Samuel Roth to his grave. They buried his religious books with him as was his request. He was buried in a simple wooden coffin without nails.

We take the short walk to visit him in his final resting place. Our guide tells us how Roth knew every grave here and the story behind it. As we stand in the centre of a ring of large oak trees, she relays to us what he told her. 'On this spot he saw religious Jews, led here by Nazis. They brought a bottle of vodka with them, they drank, danced and shouted *L'Chaim* as they were shot.' We tramp through the long grass to the back of the cemetery where Roth is buried. His gravestone is black marble with letters in gold leaf. It is kept clean and weed-free by the townspeople. We say Kaddish for him and everyone falls silent. Suddenly through his tears Polonsky speaks. 'The Hebrew name for cemetery is *bet olam*, which means eternal house. It is true, the cemeteries are the most alive places for the Jews in Poland.' Everyone is crying by the time we return to the bus.

In a state of numbness we journey on to the centre of the Nazi killing machine. For the first time on the trip the bus is silent; we are all full of dread. We spend three days in the town of Oświęcim in the appropriately named Hotel Glob: a communist nightmarish construction with a cancerous concrete exterior, filled with polyester-covered brown furniture. Our bedrooms look out to the railway tracks. One of them leads to the nearby camp, and trains thunder past all night long. I share my room with Rachel Nuremberg, a tiny, fragile young woman from New York training to be a rabbi. We put on the television very loud to drown out the noise of the trains and drink whiskey to dull our fitful sleep.

On arriving at the Auschwitz museum I discover a new archive has been opened up since my last visit in 1990. It is possible to fill out forms searching for family members. I scratch out the familiar names of relatives untraced, the same names I have entered into databases in New York, Israel and London. I add the names of the Rodinsky family to my quest in the vain hope I may recover some further information. We are in a room full of suitcases, I cannot ignore them. There are names on the cases: with my nose pressed against the glass I search for a name I might know. I turn to my left: everyone is silently doing the same thing. I can see my faint reflection in the glass, superimposed on to towering piles of shoes.

We sit quietly at the breakfast table. I feel as though I have swallowed a pint of lead. Today we are going to be guided around Birkenau by two survivors. They sit at the table opposite us, and we eye them nervously. There is laughter, how odd. Ran, the young American who discovered the buried treasure in the courtyard in Łódź, is laughing with Professor Polonsky; now he is going over to the two survivors and talking rapidly. They throw their arms in the air then grab Ran in an enthusiastic embrace. 'Of course we knew him, the butcher with the big nose, we played football together!' They are talking about Ran's grandfather. They all came from the same town, Shulim Karsnietski, so now there are three known survivors. Ran is in ecstasy and phones immediately to Boston to tell his family.

The day is a long one. We start by visiting the SS watchtower of Auschwitz-Birkenau. I can see the railway tracks beneath us and fields and fields of standing chimneys where the barracks once stood. One of the men from breakfast is standing in front of us. He has a broken car aerial in his hand, and is pointing to squares on a map, showing us where he escaped. The other survivor who accompanies us has less romantic tales to tell. He was in the Warsaw ghetto and escaped from the first transport and remained in hiding until 1943, when he was betrayed by a friend and taken to Auschwitz. His first memories: 'I was repeatedly beaten on arrival, tattooed and given wooden clogs to wear, I was put straight to work. I was responsible for burning corpses after they had been gassed. . . . We were suffocating and crying in the stench and smoke of our dead relatives.' The rest of the details of his testament are too horrific to relay. Little Jacob can take no more. 'How can you live with yourself?' he asks.

'You can get used to anything.'

With heavy steps we walk across this valley of bones to the sombre marble memorial to the murdered victims of Auschwitz. We have organized a small service, and various people stand up and read passages of Torah, poems by Primo Levi, psalms in Hebrew. We concentrate on the words of the speakers. Gabby, normally so rational and in control, can no longer contain his grief and begins to sob heavily. Tears soon afflict us all. Everyone has learnt the Kaddish for this moment. Those of us that do not know it by heart have written it down. Those that cannot read the language have transliterated the solemn prayer. We begin in unison. 'Yitgadel v'yitkadash sh'mei rabba . . .' It is hard for all of us to finish but we do; this is all we can do. It is all we have been able to do to give us and the souls we have visited some comfort. At this precise moment I realized for the first time why I had become involved in the quest for Rodinsky. The rabbi in Jerusalem had almost hinted at it and now it seemed so obvious I could not believe I had not thought of it before. I had discovered Rodinsky's place of death but I did not know where he was buried. I had traced all known relatives and realized that no one had been to his grave and said Kaddish for him. This was what I now had to do. This was the purpose of my quest.

Our visit to Auschwitz ended the six-week programme based in Kraków. The following day, after many tearful goodbyes, I left the group to begin an official trip with the Polish Cultural Institute. I had miraculously obtained a scholarship for this in London with the help of Felek Scharf. After organizing my trip to Kraków, Felek suggested I meet the director of the Polish Cultural Institute in London. 'I think you shall like one another.' He made a phone call and Dr Hannah Mausch, the director, called the next day inviting me to come to her office in Portland Place. I was unsure what the exact pretext of the meeting would be but I arrived promptly the following Monday at ten o'clock. I was kept waiting for a long time in reception, but eventually I was led up a magnificent marble stairwell, flanked by richly carved mahogany banisters, to Dr Mausch's office on the second floor. Her assistant ushered me into a huge wood-panelled room, full of plush furniture and crystal chandeliers. Two women sat around a large oak table in the centre of the room. The younger of the two, smartly dressed and probably in her early forties, stood up as I approached and introduced herself as Dr Mausch. The older woman remained seated and barely looked up as I entered. Both women were drinking brandy and smoking cigarettes. It was still early morning. The atmosphere was thick with tension – something was very obviously not right – and the younger woman gestured for me to join them and made a mumbled apology about 'all this', pointing to the half-empty cognac bottle.

I sat down gingerly, unsure what I had walked into, and Dr Mausch asked me to cheer them up by telling them about myself and why I wanted to visit Poland. I took out my portfolio and began to describe my work over the past ten years. How I had been tracing my Polish Jewish background through my art work and described to them the mosaic I had made in Israel and how I hoped to find a permanent resting place for this in Poland as a memorial to my family. As I spoke I realized tears were falling down the cheeks of the older woman and she grabbed my arm firmly and told me that what I was doing was incredibly important. She then got up sharply and left the room. Dr Mausch then explained to me what was going on. The elderly woman, Mrs Goldstein, was a Jewish survivor from Auschwitz. She had lost all her immediate family during the war and had only survived with the help of a Polish Catholic woman whom she called mother.

She had been trying to locate this woman for the past fifty years through the Red Cross and various other organizations. Dr Mausch had been helping her with her search for the past three years and that morning they had finally had confirmation from Warsaw about the woman's location. She had died in Poland in 1967, and Mrs Goldstein was in extreme shock. She returned and repeated the story to me in her own words along with graphic descriptions of her wartime experiences. The three of us sat around the table, drinking brandy, smoking cigarettes, crying, laughing and talking for the next four hours. As this incredible meeting drew to an end, Dr Mausch left the room and returned with a one-page form written in Polish. It was a visitor's proposal form for an official trip to Poland to visit anywhere, any institution I desired. She wanted me to fill in the form, and with her recommendation it was likely I might receive a scholarship. We filled in the form together and before I knew it I had

a trip organized and paid for, visiting museums and galleries of my
choice in Poland.

I knew little of what to expect from this trip but had received an
impressive itinerary from the Polish Cultural Institute before I left
London. I arrived in Warsaw exhausted from my experiences at the
Jewish sites, and began the next day with a visit to the curator of the
Museum of Contemporary Art. It did not start very well. When the
very important lady realized I was not the director of the National
Gallery or some such institution, she seemed most put out. 'So who
exactly do you represent then?' This was a hard question. What was
I to tell her? I was here chasing a disappearing Jewish scholar from
East London and through a strange string of coincidences I had
been granted a scholarship for this visit? I thought of an answer. I
had come to Poland loaded with catalogues for the exhibition I had
recently been involved in, and on behalf of the curators I was trying
to find an appropriate venue for it in Poland. I took the catalogue
out of my bag; it looked quite official. 'I am here as a representative
for this new show, "Rubies and Rebels: Jewish Female Identity in
Contemporary British Art".' I might as well have handed her a burning hot coal – she literally threw the catalogue on the floor. 'I am
completely uninterested in the type of exhibition that feebly
attempts to ghettoize ethnic groups. I'm absolutely not interested in
showing Jewish artists as a . . .'

I was speechless. This supposedly liberal-minded curator of the
most contemporary art gallery in modern Poland's capital city obviously had a problem with the concept of a Jewish art show. I was not
about to leave the subject now. I started to show her images from the
catalogues and to describe the artists, their work and their connection to their Judaism. I was too intrigued to be shocked. I had learnt
so much about Polish anti-Semitism in the last few weeks but had
not expected to experience it personally. But suddenly the woman
lost her defiant manner and instead sat in silence, looking at the
floor. When she eventually raised her head, her eyes were filled with
tears. 'I am going to tell you something that I have not yet told
anyone, even my husband. . . . My mother died two months ago

and on her deathbed she told me she was a Jew. I had no previous knowledge about this. I am forty-eight years old. I do not know what to do.' The woman was obviously struggling with her own prejudices and eventually admitted that she was curious to find out more about Judaism. Fortunately, I was able to help. Thanks to the people I had recently met in Kraków, I gave her a long list of contacts. We had an emotional parting. I was pleased to be able to give something back as I was being treated like a royal visitor during my trip and felt like an impostor. All week I visited the directors of various institutions and galleries. But I was impatient for the one meeting that really mattered to me, with the director of the Jewish Historical Institute in Warsaw. I hoped that the institute might have some information on Kushovata, the shtetl in the Ukraine from which Rodinsky originated.

I arrived at the institute and met with the director, Mrs Bergman. She was friendly and helpful, and when I told her of my project she introduced me to the chief archivist, who disappeared into the long rows of boxed material to search for information on Kushovata. He returned fifteen minutes later, unsuccessful, but there was plenty of other interesting material to scour through, and I settled down in a corner and began to search through large files on the Łódź ghetto, where my Aunt Guta had been for three years before being transported to Auschwitz. The archivist had brought me a selection of original photographs. They were so tiny; to examine them I needed a magnifying glass. The images were sad and familiar, ghetto Jews in long coats, hundreds of anonymous faces that could all fit Rodinsky's description.

The library was empty except for me and the archivist. We worked together in silence. Mrs Bergman came back into the room with two visitors she was showing around. I noticed from their accents that they were British; I had not heard another British voice in over two months. I continued to glance through the files in front of me but could not help overhearing their conversation. The couple had come to the institute with the usual request, to search for a lost family member in the files. It turned out that they already had all the

information the archivist could supply them with, and they continued to chat away with Mrs Bergman. Suddenly my ears pricked up
as I heard the British man discussing his work in England: 'I am
involved in setting up a safe house for Judaica in London and docu-
menting synagogues and cemeteries . . .' I could contain myself no
longer and told him about the disused synagogue in Whitechapel
and the need to conserve and document the artefacts from it. It
turned out that the man knew all about the synagogue next to the
old Kosher Luncheon Club. His friend Sam Melnick had told him
about it and he was already involved with Evelyn Friedlander in
trying to house the artefacts.

I asked him to tell me about his work on Jewish cemeteries. He
told me he specialized in the history of London Jewish cemeteries
and tombstones and was available for family members who were
trying to trace the graves of lost relatives. I had come all the way to
Warsaw and found the one person from London who might be able
to help me trace Rodinsky's grave. I had to restrain myself from
jumping up and kissing him. I told him about my quest. At the
mention of Rodinsky and Princelet Street he nearly leaped out of his
chair and his eyes filled with tears. 'This is *Besheret*, I have a huge
connection with that building, I was very involved in the early days.
I was one of the first people into Rodinsky's room.'

I knew this man's name before he even told me. 'Then you are
David Jacobs; I have been trying to track you down for months.'
David and his wife were speechless. I began to explain that
Rosemary Weinstein from the Museum of London had given me
David's name about six months previously, but that she did not
have a current number for him. Bill Fishman had also mentioned his
name, as had Evelyn Friedlander.

The conversation that followed was emotional and frantic as
we talked over one another, gradually working out all the connections and mutual contacts we had. David and his wife were as
moved as I was about our strange meeting and we continued to
talk for hours more over lunch in a nearby café. They told me they
had both been on a ten-day tour around Poland organized by their

local synagogue. Every moment of their time had been tightly planned and that afternoon they had decided to break away from the group and come to the institute to conduct some personal research. David was convinced it was God's will that he should get involved in helping me trace Rodinsky's grave. His first thought was that he would be buried in Waltham Abbey cemetery. We arranged to meet on my return.

VISITORS

Iain Sinclair

For hours he paced up and down in his chamber in a
restless perturbation of the spirit and then fell into a
strange delirium in which he seemed to suffer the most
indescribable horrors. He spoke, as if with an invisible
guest, in despairing, often incomprehensible tones and for
hours fought a desperate battle with all kinds of imagined
demons; finally he cried out, 'I confess that I cannot
command thee, and I confess that I am consumed by Fire-
Fire-Fire!'

Gustav Meyrink, *The Angel of the West Window*

It was a strange time, a time between times. I didn't belong there
any more, not as a labourer or as a book dealer scuffling the
Sunday market. I wasn't a writer. I wasn't anything. Whitechapel
was under a dustsheet. I had taken a couple of months away from
the stalls to work on a novel. This forced narrative, part exercise in
false memory, part mediumistic rant, seemed to have fixed the
future. Nothing moved or breathed. I kept seeing chapters that had
broken free from the stream of fiction, out on the streets. People I'd
never met rebuked me for banishing them from the story. I imagined – it was half a line in the book – that for one instant, on an early
autumn evening, walking back up Brick Lane towards Hackney, the
smooth curvature of space–time quivered; for one step on to a raised
kerbstone I was in the Eighties. 1888. Not back, but there *now*. That
it was possible, looking down from a porthole window, high in the
wall of the brewery, to shadow this person I would become.

Place was unchanging, but time was optional, in flow. Rodinsky's
room was a necessary metaphor, a symbol of transition. The room
was the only way I could see of getting *inside* the story that had to be

told. Nothing equalled that view from the small kitchen, now heaped with rubbish, north towards Hanbury Street. The occluded gardens, the great unseen spaces of Whitechapel; the vines and tendrils and green creepers overwhelming the weaving sheds and huts and out-works that had grown up between the tenements and the mute Georgian survivors. Rodinsky's room was the module through which an important narrative of immigrant life, hardship and schol-arship, would be recovered. I wasn't qualified to hunt down the human story, that would be the task of someone even crazier than I was, someone capable of handling bureaucratic obfuscation, work-ing the files, spending days chasing dead ends on a hot telephone; travelling like a spy, winning the sympathy of fragile family connec-tions. Someone who belonged here by birthright. Someone who could read the history of the room as an analogue of their own undisclosed heritage.

It was the room, the set, that obsessed me. Millet's *Angelus* calen-dar like a secondary Surrealist window, a window on the inside of the inside. A window that opened, in cartoon form, on to a land-scape of peasant piety. What possible significance could this image have for David Rodinsky? Salvador Dali, in *Le Mythe tragique de L'Angélus de Millet*, was happy to comb the dim painting for trans-gressive fetishes and talismans: the pitchfork that becomes a crutch. But Rodinsky's Millet, found in large and small versions, was one item from a catalogue of astonishingly disparate objects. The note-books and papers of the secret scholar, the old 78s, the cigarette packets, the bottles, the chunky tweed jackets, so hairy that they appeared to be still growing. It was difficult to believe all this belonged to one person. The man himself, as far as I was concerned, had to be taken on trust. He was as remote as a character from Leo Perutz's Prague stories *By Night under the Stone Bridge*, or from Gustav Meyrink's *The Golem*. My attitude towards the room at the top of this forgotten building was unforgivably predatory. Cheesy romanticism was only the latest outrage in a long chain of exploi-tation. I wanted to bring outsiders here, writers and painters whose work I admired, or simply those with an interest in the hidden attics and subterranea of the city. I would construct a picture from bounced light. By seeing how the room affected other people, I would perhaps discover what it meant to me.

The poet and performance artist Brian Catling, who had worked with me in the brewery, was one of the first. He lived at this period in a small flat just to the south of Fieldgate Street, in the shadow of Tower House, the vast, red brick, twin-towered poverty barracks that had been photographed (as 'The Monster Doss House') for the first edition of Jack London's *People of the Abyss* in 1903. A small remnant of hardened drinkers and outcasts with diseases too contagious or obscurely medieval to be housed in the London Hospital squatted the nightmare corridors, the cabin-like chambers that were supposed to make former merchant mariners feel at home. Memory cells built to contain more than six hundred souls. Rank mattresses, cardboard suitcases, tattered paperbacks with a cancelled stamp from the Seaman's Library in Cable Street. These charity cases, tolerated vagrants, were waiting to be found out. They were an anachronism. Twenty or thirty Rodinskys, retired from the sea, or expelled from their pits by the tide of development.

The Polish landlord of the Queen's Head pub, a powerful man with a mysterious past, a service revolver under the counter, acted as a benevolent patron. He pulled their yellow fangs and kept them, like deformed pebbles, in a confectioner's jar; rewarding the bloody-mouthed tremblers with a knock-out shot of Polish spirits. A biscuit tin would occasionally be produced in which faded newspaper cuttings, more dust than ink, told of the nights when Joseph Stalin and Maxim Litvinov lodged in Tower House.

There was a connection – or so I felt when I met Catling for a session in the Queen's Head – between the expressionist architecture of the doss house, now boarded up, forbidden, and the attic room above the Princelet Street synagogue. Both sets had to be visited under sufferance. With candles or torches, in late autumn or early winter, when hot breath chilled to ectoplasm. You felt that a later visitor would be able to thaw out foolish conversations left floating in the air. I tried to make something of this supposed relationship,

Rodinsky's garret and the deserted dormitories of Tower House, in a story called 'The Solemn Mystery of the Disappearing Room'.

The missing element was fire. The shriek of Gustav Meyrink's possessed visionary, imprisoned in the darkness of the Tower of London, from *The Angel of the West Window*. The fire of divine inspiration, conjured from its contrary – horror, dampness, silence – is translated into the flames of martyrdom. From Rodinsky's room it was possible to look across Princelet Street to the west, to the site of the first Yiddish theatre, at number 3, where on 18 January 1887 a 'false cry of fire' (as Bill Fishman has it) set off a panic in which seventeen people died, crushed on the stairs as they struggled to escape. Established Jewry took care to distance itself from the consequences of what they saw as vulgar, tribal hysteria: vermin of the ghetto who had not yet learned to behave like Englishmen.

Fire, I felt, contained 'the essence of voices'. The shape of the word, the hiss of expelled air, set off a chain of conditioned reflexes, a loss of control. It was a primitive fear. Fire was the shock of enlightenment and the invisible element that was missing from the dusty dryness, the heaped papers of Rodinsky's room. Catling and I said little, talked in whispers. We projected on to the room all the cobwebby lumber of years fascinated by the labyrinthine mysteries of Prague, the fictions of Arthur Machen, Algernon Blackwood, H.P. Lovecraft and William Hope Hodgson. Untrustworthy geometry, walls that moved. Beds that shrank in the night. Dream chambers that could never be discovered by daylight. Picking through the unsorted detritus of a lost life, it was too easy to summon the phantoms of the English Gothic, the world of the penny dreadfuls and 'bloods', Sweeney Todd and Spring-Heel'd Jack. Jack was the pulp version of a fire demon. He could leap over buildings, leaving a sulphurous perfume behind him. He was a revenger.

The antiquarian and occultist A.E. Waite, in his essay *The Quest for Bloods*, enthuses over these blind rooms in tumbledown houses; houses that exist only to persuade some innocent to describe them. Palsied, top-heavy, mud-and-wattle ruins overseeing the Fleet ditch. Brothels that ghost through Clerkenwell, making a second visit impossible. The byways and the 'purlieus' beyond the limestone-and-mortar boundary of the city of business. 'The terror of old houses which totter over reeking quays and of that which is done on their roofs . . . the dead alive and the weird or wicked burials.' The city requires its fictional underclass. Dens where collectors of rags and bones, books they are incapable of reading, will spontaneously combust. Dickens's Mr Krook in *Bleak House* has wandered by accident from the yellow serial of the street into a proper work of literature.

Away from the insinuating junk which served to divert the story of David Rodinsky, his life, his researches, his premature but unremarkable death, into illegitimate mystification, the high room offered a tight passageway that led out to a narrow ledge above the street. Our shoulders brushed the walls. The passage was blocked with bottles and tied bundles of newspapers. Here were the only cuttings I found that referred to the Holocaust. Emerging from this secret, half-disguised space, we were returned to the light. To the sun, setting over icy Bishopsgate, behind the white bulk of Christ Church. This perch, I was sure, had never been occupied by Rodinsky. He belonged inside. With the weight of books and memories, the clothes, the pans, the furniture offered up for curation by future scholars and busybodies.

Shortly after my first visit with Catling, and long before we had formed any proper notion of the life of the supposed hermit of Princelet Street, Catling staged a durational performance, called *Saline Apparitions*, under the dome of the Central School of Art. I sat in this gallery, my back to the wall, for hours. But, again, time was optional. Drift was the preferred mode, minimal interventions at the perimeter of boredom. Catling tapped and washed and moved, and did those things performance artists do, that would have them arrested if they set foot on the street, or moved outside a privileged environment where spectators have been processed to appreciate a slow theatre of psychic disintegration. Through a skin tube the sculptor produced posthumous sounds. He whistled through a flute stuffed with locusts.

I was mesmerized: the space around a single red-granite pillar was exactly the set I had imagined for a scene in my Whitechapel novel. Catling had become the Victorian surgeon Sir William Gull (to whom he bore, when he chose to signal it, an uncanny resemblance). Gull was brought before a committee of senior masons to answer charges of medical malpractice, in a place that I had described but never previously seen.

Catling is barefoot, padding around the room in a greasy soutane. A peasant Father Brown conducting an inquisition on his own heresies. After the event he made a few notes: 'He brings: salt, needles, sulphur, a heavy cast iron dish, water, simple animals, oil lamps, a towel, lenses, a cast iron horn, bread, the shabby robe of a priest, glass and butter. . . . The operator lost in time tunes his identity . . . he begins to draw energy and direction from the filling reservoir of his other mind.

I receive a letter which Catling signs as 'J'. It tells how, after the performance, the locusts were released from their flute. He address the letter to 'Rodinski' (a name which he then deletes).

```
Above the well of Jacob

Dear ~~Rodinski~~

I set the locust free, balanced in a privet
bush in the park in Red Lion square, some of
them were too damaged to stand, half dead,
salt burnt from the taste on my lips, legs and
antenna snapped off, sentanced to dust green
diesel fumes. I don't think even the birds
would eat them, no point taking them bact to
Walthamstow the chameleon and geckos would
spit.
I am covered in bruises and odd muscles in far
corners ache like fuck but thats o.k. it gives
me a taste of the locusts. I think even in
```

```
this state they carry the message like damaged
resistors or a kind of splintered wedge to
keep the door open.
Anyway its done and I'm off to try and wash
the cankerous stench of rancid butter and sul-
phur out of the collar and cuffs of the bor-
rowed cassock, it has to be back to hang in
the vestery of St. Georges clean before the
sunday service.
```

By the late Eighties, therefore, Rodinsky had been pressed into the cast list of *samizdat* literature. He was a 'figure', part-fabulous, part-documented; someone whose identity was in danger of being colonized by the imaginations of the lowlife artists who were beginning to creep into the Spitalfields fringes. This was the first stage in the room's progress towards museum status. The man would be quietly marginalized as the set was restored and given a respectable context.

Rodinsky's room lacked sound. In those interim years it was a camera obscura. A beam of light, breaking through a knothole in the shutters, printed the outline of an eye on the dust of the table. If we clumped awkwardly around the set, picking up books, fiddling with drawers, there was the nautical creak of our weight on the boards. Otherwise, nothing. Truancy. Reverse sound. A complexity of objects drinking the available air. Heavy furniture and stiff cloth as baffles muting the distant street, killing the process of time.

Soon after composing his Rodinsky letter, Catling moved into Heneage Street, on the east side of Brick Lane. This was territory which by reputation, in the years before and after the First War, fringed on a zone of Jewish prostitution. Catling's flat, a long narrow room, had once been part of a synagogue. It was here that Mr Shames, son-in-law of Meyer Reback of Princelet Street, saw Rodinsky for the last time. The 'pasty-faced chappie who always looked undernourished' had undergone a miraculous transformation. He was now a linguist, carrying on a conversation in the Arabic that Mr Shames had picked up during his war service.

Rodinsky, autodidact and secret scholar, fades from oral history, and lends himself, as a guide and inspiration, to a new set of incomers, impoverished bohemians eager to make contact with ghosts of the previous. The legend of the man informs a number of student films and guerrilla videos. He drifts through poems and obscure novels. Each psychic theft disguises the difficulties and the occlusions of a life spent in the shadows. Each performance, each coded appearance in film or fiction, stripped a layer of meaning from the Princelet Street garret. Each visitor left behind some small rearrangement, some revision to the narrative. The more the mystery of Rodinsky was discussed and debated, the dimmer became the outline of the human presence.

After the years when entering the room felt like a violation, the *Mary Celeste* years, Princelet Street enjoyed a period of accessibility. Dominic Dyson, who had been appointed as a co-ordinator by a registered charity, the Spitalfields Centre for the Study of Minorities, acknowledged the energies of the students, artists, and local inhabitants who were fascinated by the building's atmosphere. Plays were performed, films were shot, parties were thrown, installations appeared in the basement, the old kitchens. The space was almost public. But this openness came with a price, damage was inflicted on the fabric of the building by careless film crews. Artefacts were liberated by casual visitors. Rodinsky was a gothic thrill or he was nothing. The scholar was made to work for his continued non-existence.

Now I was creeping back on a regular basis, the room had become a reservoir of stalled time, to be checked and invigilated. One day soon, I was convinced, it would be gone, dusty venom neutralized by respectful curation. I did a short reading in the synagogue, on a cold winter's morning, for a film Paul Tickell was making for BBC2's *The Late Show*. The *bimah* was still in place. The study area, on the left as you stepped in from the street, was an office of sorts, heaped with a treasure trove of boxes and papers. Dominic was often to be seen, hammering away on an old typewriter, rummaging through the files.

It was another film, made by Bob Bentley in Christ Church,

Spitalfields, that led to the meeting that, as far as I was concerned, defined this interim period. Bentley had laid down the tracks for a shot that would feature the saxophonist and composer John Harle tooting away at his *Terror and Magnificence* in the setting of Hawksmoor's church, which was now established, post-Ackroyd, as a cathedral of baroque speculation. Harle, in the notes published with the CD, writes that 'the darkness beneath the architecture and the very fabric of the stones pushed the idea towards a text'. The language here harks back to Ackroyd, towards privileged notions of place. The church was, in its proportions, a score to be unravelled; an overweening Pythagorean geometry to be tapped and sounded.

Rodinsky's room would have to be visited, as a parallel mystery, a subtext or counter-theme to the post-human rhetoric of Hawksmoor. Harle pursued a Manichean dualism: 'Light and darkness. Good and evil. Sacred and profane. The double think of the medieval mind.' The vision he had of Spitalfields was haunting but unpeopled. Rodinsky's story, despite the prompts of the upright piano and the old gramophone, was too tricky to exploit. There was no text to act as a guide, no voice.

But this time, as Bentley and I arrived in Princelet Street, we were met by someone who was already in possession of the room. I wasn't taking an outsider into a place of potential fascination, but meeting a young woman who was already there. Rachel Lichtenstein, workmanlike in leather jacket and jeans, had brushed aside the cultural baggage of the old men, the references, the analogues, the faltering attempts to register a coherent narrative. She was launched on her own quest and it was soon very obvious that the journey was more autobiography than biography. That was the joy of it: the enthusiasm, the refusal to recognize difficulty or to be sidetracked by petty mystification. I had an immediate sense that we, daytripping thieves of energy, were now redundant. The room might as well have been sealed with the symbol of the Holy Ghost, its door painted with blood. Rodinsky had found his witness. There would be no let-up, no prevarication, until the story was told. The narrative momentum came from the threat to the stability of the

Princelet Street synagogue, not only from the coming development
of the area, the new Spitalfields, as a satellite of the City, but also
from the pilot fish of development: conservationists, explainers,
justifying sentimentalists. Fabulists with a compulsion to take a
unique episode and to make it universal. Rodinsky's room needed
someone who could kick down doors with enough charm to make
the custodians thank her for it. Rachel Lichtenstein was that person.

Dominic Dyson moved on. Andrew Byrne of the Spitalfields
Historic Buildings Trust was now the presiding spirit, the person
who might choose, if it suited him, to answer the bell on the street
door. Rachel kept the key that Dyson had given her. Her researches
continued with no interference from Byrne. On the contrary, Rachel
found him a sympathetic, if slightly mysterious, benefactor. Meeting
on the stairs, he was ready for conversation. Now, if I wanted to
show somebody Rodinsky's room, I did it through Rachel. The
building itself had drifted into limbo: no longer would we encounter
film crews hoovering up atmosphere, primitive exhibitions or
riotous wedding receptions. The door was locked. Brown paint
lapped over tired wood, disguising the synagogue's fabulous history. The paint represented the building's blood, sepia ink made
from the crushed shells of insects who had devoured libraries of
odd volumes, diaries, maps, prayer-books.

Inertia had a professional basis. Number 19 Princelet Street
aspired to the condition of a steel engraving, a tactfully composed
black-and-white photograph. The heritage cabal had a genuine love
for, and knowledge of, bricks and mortar. Some of them had been in
the area for twenty or thirty years; they had established themselves
before Rachel was born. They had fought their own battles, become
squatters to protect the inviolability of cornices and consoles. Dan
Cruickshank deplores the loss of a doorcase, 'a definite monster . . .
that once enlivened a mid-18th-century house in Greatorex Street',
where Rachel Lichtenstein storms over the destruction of the Jewish
luncheon club and the sacrileges committed against the relics in the
synagogue.

Discretion (the handmaid of invisibility) is what the Spitalfields Historic Buildings Trust wished on itself. To proceed by stealth. To protect an imaginary (though well-documented) inheritance against the mindless vandalism (as they saw it) of socialist planners and city sharks. The building withdrew. It opted out of the street, the new energies fretting it from east and west, the buzz of the leather-ware shops, the incursions of the loft-prospectors. Keep your head down, seemed to be the message. If Andrew Byrne knew something, and it appeared that he did, he wasn't talking. If Rachel arranged to take the occasional visitor up the stone steps, and on to Rodinsky's room, then Byrne hovered at her shoulder. With his flopping aristocratic hair and his cancelled smile he was like a quotation from *The Waste Land*. HURRY UP PLEASE ITS TIME. Get on, get it done, get out.

It was an odd place, therefore, to bring Jah Wobble. The musician, prolific composer/performer/producer and serial London walker couldn't be disguised as a timid architecture buff with a passion for authentic Georgian panelling. Wobble was burly, busy, motor-mouthed. His grey eyes burnt. He was a tall geezer in a beret. A fast intelligence on the grab. Bethnal Green by way of everywhere. Up for it. With a lively past, interesting connections and great independence of spirit. Peter Ackroyd would have him pegged as one of his 'Cockney Visionaries', congering behind William Blake, Thomas De Quincey and J.W. Turner. The garret shrunk around Wobble as he entertained Rachel with his pitch: his own family, Irish Catholics, coming from so many different places in such numbers, and so rapidly, they never stayed anywhere long enough to be classified as immigrants. He yarned about his days as a guard on the underground, sepia afternoons mini-cabbing second-division hoodlums across the river, his travels and his beliefs.

We'd been talking, very vaguely, about a collaboration. And Wobble, like John Harle and a number of others, toyed with the story of David Rodinsky. Street music, Jewish songs, liturgy, North African female vocalists. The cabbalist who disappears. Wobble thought it might make a performance piece. Steven Berkoff as the voice. The elements were all in place. Wobble was leaning against the

wormeaten joanna. For one terrible moment I had a vision of Lionel
Bart, a fiddler on the roof, and a chorus of chimney-sweeps, rabbis,
dockers, nannies and unicorns led across the cobbles by Dick Van
Dyke. But Wobble is no fool. His energy is ferocious. Like Rachel he's
in pursuit of the evidence, images and sounds that will confirm his
identity.

The Rodinsky notion drifted. I didn't see Wobble for months,
then met him one autumnal afternoon, out with his wife, pushing
a smart pram along the Regent's Canal by the Cat and Mutton
Bridge. Wobble's latest CD, *Umbra Sumus*, came with a small Marc
Atkins portfolio of photographs, which included a cover design
based on the sundial from the synagogue on the corner of Fournier
Street and Brick Lane. This was the building always used as a
symbol of cultural adaptability: the Huguenot chapel taken over by
the Methodists, before becoming the Spitalfields Great Synagogue
and, most recently, a mosque. Wobble, it appeared, had found the
metaphor he needed – without fuss, almost by accident, a casually
apposite response to the spirit of place that made room for
Rodinsky's story without damaging its integrity. (I thought of the
series of paintings Sir William Rothenstein completed after what
Peter Marcan in his survey of *Artists and the East End* calls 'an
accidental visit to a Spitalfields synagogue'. The oil painting *Kissing
the Law*, of 1906, shows what lies behind Wobble's sundial. The
robes and rituals and human presences that the preserved synagogue so ruthlessly excludes. These figures have to fade in order for
our attention to move to the design of the pillars and the way the
light polishes the brass globe beneath the branching candle-
holder.)

I asked Wobble what had stayed with him from that first visit.

'I remember going upstairs. It was very dark in there, quite a
spooky feeling. And suddenly you're in this room. Deep in the void
that's beyond time and space. Is it a big room? Is it a small room?
You can't quite make up your mind. You can see where the ostensi-
ble boundaries of the room are, but it goes on forever. There's also a
Mary Celeste sense. A room that's been left behind is a mystery.

Although a lot of people have been in there over the years, it still has a sense of the unexplained. Something happened.

'I think, as an artist, you always get into detective work. You want to find out about a person. You want to ascertain what the person who lived there for so long was all about. And, being on a bit of a mystic kick myself, you begin to think: this feller had been a buffoon for years, and supposedly a bit backward, and then suddenly he can speak Arabic and speak Hebrew, and he's got some knowledge of philosophy. And that was interesting. That East End thing of the old Jewish people, the real hoarders who had terrible lives and lived through miseries and torments. There was a tradition of old Jewish people at the library, in Bancroft Road, wearing 1920s brogues and clothes, and who were hoarding bus tickets. I remember those little bus tickets fascinated me.'

'Do you see Rodinsky as a *frummer*, a black-coat scholar, or as a seeker whose journey carried him beyond the constrictions of religious orthodoxy?' I asked.

'With Rodinsky, to be honest, I'm thinking to myself, "Is this the room where this feller encountered the Great Being, the Truth that is unchanging behind all the state of flux?" I'm thinking, "Yes, it feels possible." There's a certain stillness here. Something of the hermit's cave, I suppose. A feeling of renunciation. This is somebody who has given up on the bollocks. And who has connected with the Truth, the Great Truth. You could almost smell that some kind of alchemical process had taken place here and this person had crossed over into another area. One of the signs of that is when somebody gains knowledge in a very quick way, there's a smell in the air. What should take about ten lifetimes to get together has been achieved in a few weeks. Some spiritual catalyst has come forth and suddenly this person is transported backwards, through all those thousands of years, in one instant of time.

'I'm forming a story from the objects in that room, because I've got a neurotic need to identify with people. It's very human, a small mean reaction. I'm just projecting my needs and values on to this situation. You're waiting for the geezer, his ghost, to come through the wall and say, "Oh, no, it wasn't like that at all. It was all a sham. I'm just a magician, a joke." But that duality is fascinating. It's as if Rodinsky represents a magical part of the psyche. He's a trickster.

'In his room you are at a meeting point between light and dark, madness and sanity. The atmosphere that day with Rachel, when you brought me here, was of a junction point in the stream of time. Nothing would happen unless it was meant to happen. Unless Rachel was meant to be the one who had to go forward and complete it. Find a grave. And then it would be right, a proper gravestone, some kind of ceremony. The room would be properly sealed.'

The curious thing now was that the intensity of Rachel's investigation, the information she was acquiring, the elderly witnesses she had confronted with their memories of the room and its occupants, seemed to depressurize the garret at the top of the synagogue. The public space of the synagogue, the long room built out over the old garden, was unchanged. It was still cold, dignified, reserved. Still capable of inducing a temporary sense of awe, a slowing of the blood. Sitting quietly on a bench in the privilege of that light made the visitor feel that he or she was capable of something else, an unlooked-for leap of faith or sympathy. Don't move. Don't say it. Stay *stumm*. This illusion of a better life, it will pass. Fade with the magic of place. There's nothing left to exploit. Atmosphere. If only you could bottle it.

When I came here with Kathy Acker, and again with Michael Moorcock, it was strategic. Now the book existed. Rachel existed, and she had reassembled the lineaments of Rodinsky. A second Rodinsky. Another life on the pattern of the first. Rachel had lived through her own trials and doubts, the book was writing itself. An unstoppable momentum; the joyous, terrifying rush of having to work to keep pace with what's there, the revealed story. Author as scribe. It's a wonder when it happens, draining the writer as she struggles to live with the promptings of her own inspiration, the voices from elsewhere.

Organizing the Polish material had been a major difficulty, but that was done. The meeting with David Jacobs turned the story back to Rodinsky, the final chapter. Rachel always believed, she had the confidence, there would be a conclusion. She saw herself gathering together all those who had known the man, all who had participated in her telling of the story, and bringing them to the grave.

One morning, as she spoke to me on the phone, keeping me up to date with the latest frantic developments, I realized where the grave would be found. Rachel's need for a fitting coda made it inevitable. The books I admire are written backwards from one specific location. I could see the field, hear the comfortingly familiar sounds beyond the hedges and the pylons at the limits of that field. It was the end of a book that Kathy Acker and I had once talked about, but never come close to writing. We didn't take it very far because I wasn't sure how it would work, what the form would be. It was a detective story of sorts, beginning when an American woman leads a Londoner through the cloisters of Westminster Abbey and out into a garden that is only open on that particular day. The obvious explanation is that the woman is a ghost and that the man has been hired to tell her story, which she revises as she goes along, to the point where his existence, his presence in the narrative, is threatened.

Acker, meeting me now in Spitalfields, was late. She had great difficulty finding the wine bar, manoeuvring her bike around the City checkpoints. I had some vague notion that, if Rodinsky's room meant enough to them, a few writers might be persuaded to come up with some short response. My part in the Princelet Street book would fade into a chorus of echoes and reverberations. Obviously, I wouldn't ask them to do it, nothing as grim as a deadline or another open-ended and underpaid commission.

Andrew Byrne was lurking with intent. Kathy in her customized leathers, hefting a glossy crash helmet, walked through the synagogue while I did my best to bullet-point the Rodinsky story. But Kathy had stories of her own. We didn't spend long upstairs. We weren't welcome. A virulent wallpaper, narrow green and gold bands, was peeling from the wall. The table was scrubbed and bare.

It struck me that as Rachel's investigation neared its end, as she found out more and more about the man and his family, the ones who had lived so long in this room, so the room itself was impoverished, de-energized. Kathy thought that she'd let the idea float. She had other problems: a basement flat in Islington she didn't like, difficulties finding English publishers, the urge to go back, once again, to California. A new job, a resumption of the old life.

Moorcock was another exile; the great Londoner, memory conduit, had shifted himself, along with his books and furniture, to a small town thirty miles outside Austin, Texas. Hampstead Garden Suburb with a broken thermostat. The heat out there this summer made him fear for his sanity. If the air-conditioning failed he would melt into a puddle in front of his word-processor. He lived in dark blue long-johns, scaring the daylights out of his wife's friends when he wandered through the kitchen. The garden looked good in photographs, green and lush behind a pleasant white house with a deck that solicited rocking-chair and mint juleps, the evening pipe. But if you set foot on that David Lynch lawn, giant red ants would eat you alive, kamikaze mosquitoes would puncture every unprotected centimetre of skin. Moorcock lived through the Net, the telephone. Airmailed English newspapers and outdated magazines (he may well have been the last human to have read a copy of *Punch*). On bad days, when the inspiration wasn't coming, he found himself composing deranged, but imaginary, letters to the *Guardian*, while listening to tapes of Radio 4 programmes that would have his eyes rolling backwards in boredom if he'd caught them at home. Home. Notting Hill. Holborn. Fleet Street. The post-war years, the bomb sites, when his first jobs had taken him around the still-active warehouses, wharfs and rivergates, the small businesses of Wapping.

Moorcock's vision of London was entirely fabulous, unwarped recollections of events that shifted from life to fiction, chunks of books revised for cross-genre mutation, epics of lost literature customized into comic strips. He had a project in which he was compiling an encyclopaedia for a city that existed only in his imagination: towers from Lisbon would be grafted on to the canal alongside Kensal Rise cemetery, rookeries would be re-established behind dull contemporary façades, synagogues burnt to the ground in Poland would emerge as lending libraries in Limehouse.

An alternate, parallel London: Moorcock was dressed like a time-traveller in layers of tweed and gaberdine, silvered, fly-catcher beard and moustache, hawk-winded hair topped off with a vast cap. The kind of Celtic disguise John Wayne pulled over his eyes after going toe-to-toe with Victor McLagen in *The Quiet Man*. Every time we paused in our travels, the perspiring monologuist would lose this item, secrete it in a fathomless pocket. If he dropped the cap on the pavement it would soon fill with coins. The man had a large presence. He created a whirlwind of minor difficulties as he settled himself in a restaurant, or cleared a path with an expensive walking-stick tipped with the cap from a Ralph Lauren scent bottle. Coming back, returning to this place that he had never, in spirit, left, Moorcock found himself allergic to everything: smoke, margarine, green peppers slipped into an otherwise benign curry. He was on a regimen of pills that had his mood spiralling like a weather system coming in from the Florida Keys. Launched on a Jack Trevor Story monologue, tears would moisten his eyes, until the narrative capsized into low comedy. He had to operate in the intervals between steroid-induced rage and fugues of pain and physical discomfort. In the trough he would savage old comrades who had failed to stay the course; then, swinging back up, he discovered qualities in writers who were not so much forgotten as unborn. To call them anonymous would be to flatter them. Fame and obscurity were both fraudulent snares. He had perfect recall of a sentence in Pett Ridge nobody noticed on first publication and he'd completely forgotten the name of the person who had invited him to dinner.

What was he doing here? What had I got him into? It leaked as we walked through Spitalfields. It oozed and seeped and dripped, inch by inch, through all Moorcock's protective layers. He couldn't tell where this water was coming from: sweat or rain or melting stones. He said that his legs had gone, they'd lock like well-oiled shotguns before he crossed Bishopsgate. But he swam down Artillery Lane, up

Brushfield Street, in and out of the Magpie bookshop, without breaking stride.

I think that Princelet Street, the synagogue and Rodinsky's room, became part of an all-enveloping dream of rain and moderate discomfort and stealthy movement. Asthmatic rhapsodies: he was talking without pause. I wouldn't call his argument discursive because that would suggest that it travelled in a particular direction, was burdened with a beginning and an end. He soaked up enough water to carry him through three Texas droughts.

We rang the bell, were admitted, allowed up the stairs, ushered out. We carried on towards the Jago Gallery, Arnold Circus, talked of Arthur Morrison. Moorcock had no special sense of Princelet Street. 'It's a haunted place,' he said, 'but not badly haunted.' Our visit was in pursuit of a story. In order for buildings to survive, he believed that they required 'a good clean narrative'. The synagogue reminded him of his own Jewishness. 'I'm South London. Gypsy, Jewish, Anglo-Saxon. Well mixed up. My Jewish story goes back to Disraeli. Which means there's a bastard in the family. I used to go to 10 Downing Street and my uncle would pause on the stairs and point to Disraeli's portrait. Nice to be able to claim descent from a writer. I'm writing a book on the Holocaust because I think I actually caused it. There's that whole notion of guilt, survival guilt.'

He was fine now. He was hurting but the cloudburst and the distance, the alleyways, pubs, broken anecdotes, shorthand sketches, were effortlessly absorbed. Through Columbia Road, Queensbridge Road, over the canal. He'd capped a sentence but not yet navigated the architecture of a paragraph. I don't know if the story of Rodinsky had touched him. He'd brought something to the room. And I felt rather as if I had grabbed Charles Dickens by the elbow and pitched him a likely location for some future novel. Moorcock could make what he liked of it. All or nothing. That was his affair. But it was the finish for me. I abandoned any notion of collecting Rodinsky stories. Anthologies were a plague on the market.

As Rachel followed Rodinsky's trail away from Princelet Street, so his strange mappings on the friable copy of the *London A–Z* began to make sense. They were a scrambled dreaming, actual journeys achieved in a state of reverie, heat-paths that Lichtenstein was elected to complete. Much of the push was to the north and east, a direction that I had always assumed led to the asylum in which his sister was incarcerated. This may have been wishful thinking on my part, any excuse to carry me down the line of zero longitude from millennial Greenwich to Waltham Abbey, where my new project, a walk around the M25, would begin.

Whatever else she had achieved (the perfect quest, the epic search that ended with a question mark), I guessed that as Rachel neared her conclusion a new spirit had come over the synagogue. The period of quiet, of secrecy, husbanded privilege – a building talking only to itself – drew to a close. As did any notion of Rodinsky's singularity. It was clear to me, and the impression was confirmed by a conversation with one of the tour guides, Alan Dein, an oral historian I chanced on in the synagogue, that this story, the recluse in the attic, was only one of many similar tales. Now elderly Jewish people, some of whom attended the Stepney luncheon club, many of whom relied on charitable deliveries of food, were invisible. Fearful of street life they no longer understood, they kept to their flats, out of sight, out of mind.

I signed up for a walking tour guided by Andrew Byrne. 'Georgian Street Life', he called this ambulant lecture, performed in June 1998 as part of the Spitalfields Festival. It didn't take a genius to guess that our short ramble, dodging the showers, would conclude in Princelet Street. I hoped that listening to Byrne might offer some insight into the future of the synagogue. The Spitalfields Historic Buildings Trust were the landlords but what did they actually *do*? Was it their sole purpose to freeze time, to wrap precious fragments of another age in clingfilm?

I knew that Byrne had a real feeling for Georgian Spitalfields, a passion, in its own way, as obsessive as Rachel's. It was easy to get the impression that he lived in some barricaded corner of the old synagogue. There was a rather wonderful photograph by Stephen Humphreys ('Andrew Byrne . . . hardly at work, 1998') which depicted the conservationist at his desk, surrounded by Rodinsky-like accumulations of books, hunched over a typewriter. Meditating on nothing. On the passage of light. Being there. Absorbed by the drift of potential narratives. Byrne, I fantasized, was the most recent hermit of Princelet Street. His fierce possessiveness made him the self-elected caretaker. The cycle was complete. The building returned to its Huguenot beginnings. The immigrant was now a member of the established orders, a person whose interest came without liturgical baggage, unburdened by metaphysical speculation. The shape and design, the architectural detail, was everything. Byrne, like the vanished cabbalist, was clinging to a defeated poetic, a fable that would be swept aside in the mindless rush of development, speculation and, worst of all, explanation. To know everything is to lose everything. A story brought to its finish is a story abandoned.

So the small crocodile shuffled under its umbrellas from Artillery Lane to Christ Church, to the rectory, to Princelet Street. It was all very English, apologetic, hushed; small, neat children with polished shoes being told by distracted parents how exciting and relevant all this was. Byrne delivered his spiel with some discomfort, refusing to be distracted by punters who wanted information on the parts of Spitalfields that remained unrepentantly non-Georgian, the poverty hutches and shelters for vagrants, bristling with plaster madonnas and last year's surveillance systems.

Byrne's golden crop was astray in the weather. He looked as if he'd just stepped out from a cold shower. He was the classics master deputed to show a slightly suspect clutch of nouveau parents around the cloisters. Sports jacket and open-necked shirt. The walkers were expensive. They could take out your eye with the ferrule of a black umbrella. Or step on a sleeping wino to get a closer shufty at the unspeakable imminence of a 'truly Greek' finial. These coiffured Huguenot wannabes were essentially trawling for pedigree. They'd laid out heavy equity for properties in Elder Street or Fournier Street and they wanted the photograph, the certificate saying '100 per cent kosher Georgian'. (Yes, I know, there were other folk with more innocent agendas on the tour – but this was the most vocal element, the question askers.)

We found ourselves at the finish, sheltering from the rain, inside the synagogue, huddled in groups or wandering off to inspect the list of donations, while Byrne delivered his version of the story of Princelet Street. The Rodinskys were not mentioned. This was a narrative of the building, a building which did not connect with its neighbours. We were not told that families had lived and slept, sixteen to a room, in the next house; that, in fact, the Rodinskys were comparative plutocrats, with only three of them (frequently, when Bessie was institutionalized, two) sharing a set of close-ceilinged but perfectly habitable rooms. They were reclusive by choice, living their secret lives as so many others, the orthodox remnant, still do.

We learnt that number 19 Princelet Street was the 'oldest purpose-built Ashkenazi synagogue in London'. We heard much about the speculative builder, Samuel Worrall; about the fortunes of the Huguenot family who first occupied the property. 'One hundred and sixty years after the house was built in 1718/19, the synagogue was built in the back garden.... It has survived remarkably intact. They did it up about a hundred years ago and then the congregation moved on and the place closed down. They left their prayer-books and benches.'

Byrne waved towards the heaps of unsorted furniture at the south end of the synagogue, the residue of film shoots, parties; stoicism blunted by apathy in the face of seemingly hopeless quantities of rubbish.

'The synagogue,' he concluded, 'is, in a sense, a community centre. The *shul* was in those three front rooms ... you only ever came to *your* synagogue ... on the death of a member of your family you would make a donation. We want to restore this building as a Museum of Immigration. I won't go into the long story of that.'

There were questions. Visitors pored over the remarkable photographs of Spital Square, printed from large negatives: haunting, elegant, estranged from time. Images dignified by the pain of loss. The mindlessness of destruction linking these empty hallways, grandiloquent staircases with the genealogy of destroyed European

cities, bomb-damaged cathedrals, rubbled public buildings, smoul-
dering terraces. Figures of workmen, chimney-sweeps or draymen
with curious flat hats, stood frozen, positioned in aesthetically sat-
isfying triangles in the street, to satisfy the long exposure. Something
blurred and fast, a dog or wolf-thing, challenges this false serenity,
stalking across the frame. They are all waiting for the hot white blast
that will print them into the cobblestones.

This was a rare chance to find out what was happening to the synagogue. Were there any plans to disturb the long sleep? I asked what
I felt were a couple of innocuous questions. 'What is the status of the
building now? What is going to happen to it?'

Byrne coloured. I thought he would lose it. He blustered. 'Don't
you *know*?'

'No, I don't. I don't know. Only what I hear through Rachel.'

I'd blundered into an area that was painful. I felt that I'd made
some terrible clumsy intrusion. I was sorry for Andrew who evidently believed he was the victim of a cunningly laid trap.

'We're working on ways of rescuing it from limbo. I won't say
more.'

A few weeks after this exchange, I heard from Rachel. Byrne was
out. He was kicking the walls in rage. But the situation was not as
extreme as Rachel imagined. Byrne would lose his sole occupancy
and share the space with a vortex of energy, in the form of Susie
Symes. Symes, a terrifyingly effective bureaucrat, ex-Treasury, well-
connected, was taking on the case on behalf of the Spitalfields
Centre. Very soon we were called in for a grilling. Who had visited
here? Who gave permission? What contracts had been signed?
Filming, in future, in however modest a form, would be absolutely
forbidden. The trustees wouldn't hear of it.

This somewhat fraught meeting was rescued by Michael
Moorcock. Symes heard that Moorcock was in town. Would I come
to Princelet Street and conduct a recorded conversation with him?
Fine, of course. (I was slightly surprised, remembering our first conversation, when Symes's partner rang me to ask if it would be all
right if this Moorcock chat was filmed.)

The Spitalfields Historic Building Trust staged a Twenty-first Anniversary Exhibition. Symes, splendidly visible in a pink jacket, and Byrne, happier and more forthcoming than I'd seen him before, were both in evidence; working very different circuits. Photographs were hung around the walls of the synagogue. Susie Symes had done an incredible job, much of it by her own physical labour, in tidying the cellar, targeting areas for repair, chucking out bags of certified rubbish, junk left by builders, squatters, media vermin.

The exhibition was a classic of Spitalfields Trust invisibility. It would run for a couple of weeks, open for a few hours in the afternoon. A very small neat notice pinned to the street door. Ring the bell for admittance. No publicity. A discreet event, tactfully invigilated. It was there if you knew it was there. A number of the converted made themselves available for a sermon of celebration. The last rites of the years of limbo. After Susie Symes, nothing would be the same. There would be no skulking in obscurity. No single story would achieve domination. 'You novelists,' she chided Moorcock and myself, 'you can only see the romance.' She was right. Now Number 19 would have to justify its existence in a street which was rapidly being dragged out from behind its scaffolding and gauze wraps, revealed as a burnt-orange and chocolate-cream nest of loft apartments and investment opportunities. Unless the synagogue could pitch a good yarn it would be condemned as an antiquarian pamphlet, a brief stop on the heritage trail.

I was shocked, on coming home one evening after hearing of Andrew Byrne's expulsion, to see him on the local television news. I had never been able to picture him anywhere outside Spitalfields, but here he was, bright, on the button, in a patch of woodland, just north of the M25, in Theobald's Park. He was talking about pulling down Wren's Temple Bar, the last of London's gates, so that it could be reassembled on the banks of the Thames as part of the new St Paul's makeover. Millions of pounds would be required to return this grandiose folly to a place it had never been. Private plunder revamped as public spectacle. The National Lottery application would rival the sum Susie Symes was looking for to launch her

Centre for the Study of (not 'by') Minorities. Temple Bar had slumbered for years, quietly crumbling behind its protective fencing, on land that was once part of a Jacobean palace (now divided between the Abbey National 'Centre of Excellence' and the Tesco Country Club). A bridge across the M25 led to a narrow road, frequently decorated by burnt-out vehicles; tolerated countryside, private housing protected by surveillance cameras, horses, and the well-hedged fields of the Western Jewish Cemetery. This was the very place I had been haunting for months, the start of my walk around London's orbital motorway. Were the heritage boys moving out of the inner city and into tarmac? Seeing Byrne here, as a wild-haired prophet, I understood that anything was possible.

DAVID IN FOCUS

Rachel Lichtenstein

I returned from Warsaw to London for less than twenty-four hours, just enough time to pack a bag and catch a plane to Ben-Gurion Airport. I was going to Jerusalem to attend Jennifer's wedding; she was a rabbi's daughter from New York, with whom I had shared a studio in Arad. Jennifer was marrying Estaban, a passionate Argentinian she had met during her stay in Israel. The wedding was a fantastically noisy affair. The Argentinians leaped on to tables as the bride and groom entered, clapping and cheering while waving brightly coloured maracas before lifting the bride and groom high up on chairs and twirling them around at great speed to the sound of khlezmer music. The Israelis, dressed in brightly patterned clothes, danced joyously in circles around the pair, before feasting from tables heaving with food. The New Yorkers fitted perfectly into the scene, adding noisy chatter and Hebrew song to the backdrop of Jerusalem's walled city. The day after the wedding I returned to Tel Aviv to collect Adam, the man I was going to marry, and we journeyed together to the desert, spending an idyllic week at the Ein Gedi kibbutz next to the Dead Sea. I had planned this trip very consciously, aware that the wedding, the brilliant sunshine, the peaceful desert setting and Adam's soothing company would all help to wash away for a time my dark memories of Poland.

I had intended to contact David Jacobs as soon as I arrived back in London but did not. I felt reclusive and inexplicably tired. As the days went on, I felt worse and worse: all I wanted to do was sleep and cry. I visited my doctor and discovered I was pregnant. Adam and I were delighted.

When I had first seen Adam I had presumed he was Jewish. His hair is jet black, his eyes dark brown and heavily lashed, his skin porcelain white. He has a typical Ashkenazi look. On our first meeting I had told him of my experiences in Israel and he had broken into song in perfect Hebrew and then told me that his father is a Muslim from Pakistan and his mother an Irish Catholic. He had grown up, with his three brothers and a sister, in a Jewish neighbourhood in Leeds called Alwoodley. Due to his family's many friends and connections within the Jewish community in which they lived, Adam and his siblings had been the first Muslims in history (as far as I know) to be members of Habonim, a Zionist Jewish Youth organization. His two elder brothers had spent a considerable amount of time in Israel in kibbutzim, and Adam and his twin often attended synagogue. Somehow, Adam and I are a perfect match.

I had met Adam soon after the Slaughterhouse show, and after my visit to the cabbalist in Jerusalem. Just a few weeks before I had decided not to complete an orthodox conversion. This decision was a very difficult one to make. I had felt duty-bound to continue to be a link in the chain that had existed for four thousand years before my birth. The deaths of so many members of my family appeared futile if I did not continue in the faith for which they had died. The weight of this responsibility had always hung heavily upon me, so I tried, tried very hard to become orthodox.

Through study for the conversion, my admiration and respect for the orthodox religion and way of life only deepened. But returning from Israel to London, to my secular friends and lifestyle, I realized that that the giant leap to an orthodox life was not a realistic possibility for me. I would not be a hypocrite. I would only complete the conversion if I was prepared to live as an orthodox Jew for the rest of my life . . . and I slowly began to realize I could not do this. Maybe, if

I had stayed in Israel, lived within an orthodox community, cut myself off from my family and former friends it might have been possible. But back in London, I was too deeply connected to the secular life I had always lived. It was incredibly painful for me to upset my parents by not being able to eat in their home, to offend my friends by no longer being able to go swimming with them. So many activities that seemed ordinary would become impossible. I found myself alone in my beliefs and practices, misunderstood by the people around me. I could understand how difficult it must have been for David Rodinsky, continuing with his religious observance and intense studies, thought of as mad by his non-orthodox doctors and social workers. But I also empathized with his attraction to the secular world around him, his thirst to know of other cultures, learn other languages, taste other foods. In the end, for me, this temptation was too much. I believe that if I had stayed in Israel, I would have completed the conversion and lived an orthodox life. But I chose a different path, came back to London, the city of a thousand cultures, and eventually it was this world that I embraced. As David Rodinsky could not break the bonds of his upbringing, neither could I break beyond the bounds of mine.

The pregnancy gave me the opportunity to write up the discoveries of the Rodinsky quest so far. It wasn't physically easy for me as I was suffering from water retention and my hands had swollen so much that in order to continue writing I had to place my fingers in buckets of ice. I was also incredibly sick and could barely move my head without vomiting. It was only a couple of months after returning from Poland that I was finally able to make arrangements to visit David and Hannah Jacobs. They invited me over to their home in north Finchley for Shabbat lunch.

Inside their modest-looking suburban house was an Aladdin's cave; it was bursting at the seams with artefacts salvaged from disused synagogues, bought during excursions to East End markets or saved from skips outside buildings about to be torn down. All of this was being collected to go in the London 'safe house' that they planned. David gave me a tour of the house, showing me his favourite things from his private collection; among them was a wooden board that would have hung in the Great Garden Street synagogue, with the names of former members hand-painted in gold leaf. Arranged in a heavy walnut frame were family photographs going back four generations, and next to them a picture of David with his daughter Leah when she was a young baby, standing beside a rare headstone in a Sephardic cemetery in Whitechapel. Shelves lined the walls of the house, packed with Jewish books.

After the *kiddush* we sat down for lunch. It was hard for my eyes not to wander towards the certificates on the dining-room walls, the objects on the mantelpiece, the thousands of books that surrounded us. Nevertheless, I was very anxious to hear what further thoughts David Jacobs had as to the whereabouts of Rodinsky's grave.

The Jacobs seemed equally excited to see me again, and told me how our meeting in the empty basement library of the Jewish Historical Institute in Warsaw had become their favourite dinner party story. I spoke with them about the pregnancy, Adam, my recent trip to Israel. Considering I had only met them once before, I felt remarkably relaxed in their company.

In addition to being an expert on Jewish cemeteries, David also works as the co-ordinator and adviser for the Reform Synagogues of Britain. Back in the Eighties David was very involved with the Princelet Street synagogue (although he told me he had not in fact been the first person into the room; that had probably been Douglas Blane of the Spitalfields Historic Buildings Trust). He expected he still had a file of old cuttings somewhere, so he dashed upstairs, returning soon with a large folder of clippings for me to browse through. Much of it was new to me: things I had not seen at the Bishopsgate library or anywhere else.

There was a letter from the *Jewish Chronicle* of 24 June 1988, entitled 'A Mystery Solved':

As a boy in the late 1930s David Rodinsky was 'boarded out' with my mother and father, who were Jewish Board of Guardians foster parents.

Many years later, around 1967, I came across him again in the course of my work as a JWB social worker, and by then he was living at the synagogue.

More recently the room was 'discovered' with his books and personal effects left untouched as though he had just walked out. Rabbi Hugo Gryn asked me if I could shed some light on his background, and I searched for the JWB file which I knew went back to about 1930, but unfortunately it had been destroyed.

Incidentally, he did not disappear; he died of a stroke when he was in his mid-forties.

Michael Jimack
Research and Information Officer
Federation of Jewish Family Services

This was a mystery solved, or one part of it anyway. Of course, by now I knew that David Rodinsky had died at the age of forty-four. But I had not known he had been fostered out as a child. It made perfect sense: at some stage his mother had been unable to cope either emotionally or financially, and David had gone to a foster home. I do not think this had been a happy time for him. I remembered the letter he had written to Carol Wayne's mother when he spoke of his 'lost years, from five to sixteen when I was torn away from my home'. Carol had had no more idea what this meant than I did at the time, but it now seemed very clear. Eleven years away from his mother, most of his childhood. But this long time apart seems to have done little to sever his attachment to her and the room. So as far as I can work out he returned there as soon as possible, and I do not believe he would ever willingly have left it.

Apart from locating the grave, his final departure was the other piece of the puzzle I was trying to fit with what I knew of him. How did David Rodinsky get from his attic room in Princelet Street to a psychiatric asylum in Epsom? Before going to visit the Jacobs I had spent another few days going through Rodinsky's artefacts again, in the vain hope of finding another clue. It was been many months since I had thoroughly searched through the boxes above the synagogue, and I was now armed with a considerably larger amount of information. I knew where and when he had died. I knew his age, a little about his mother and sister, I had met a few relatives and other people who had known him. I had read about the lives of his ancestors and visited their graves. I had walked the streets he had highlighted in his hand-drawn additions to a 1960s *London A–Z*.

I began the painstaking and difficult task of unwrapping his artefacts from their acid-free tissue covers. This process was difficult in the sense that the more I knew about him, the more 'real' he became to me, and the more uncomfortable I felt about browsing through his personal belongings. He was obviously a very private man. Iain Sinclair had told me the room was 'a trap'. Maybe, but I felt Rodinsky had chosen me to tell his story, and I wanted to ensure it was told as accurately as possible.

It was a strange time, as I desperately sought information about a man who had died before my own birth while feeling the first gentle flutterings of the new life inside me. It was a time of transition, time to put Rodinsky properly to rest and to focus on what was to come.

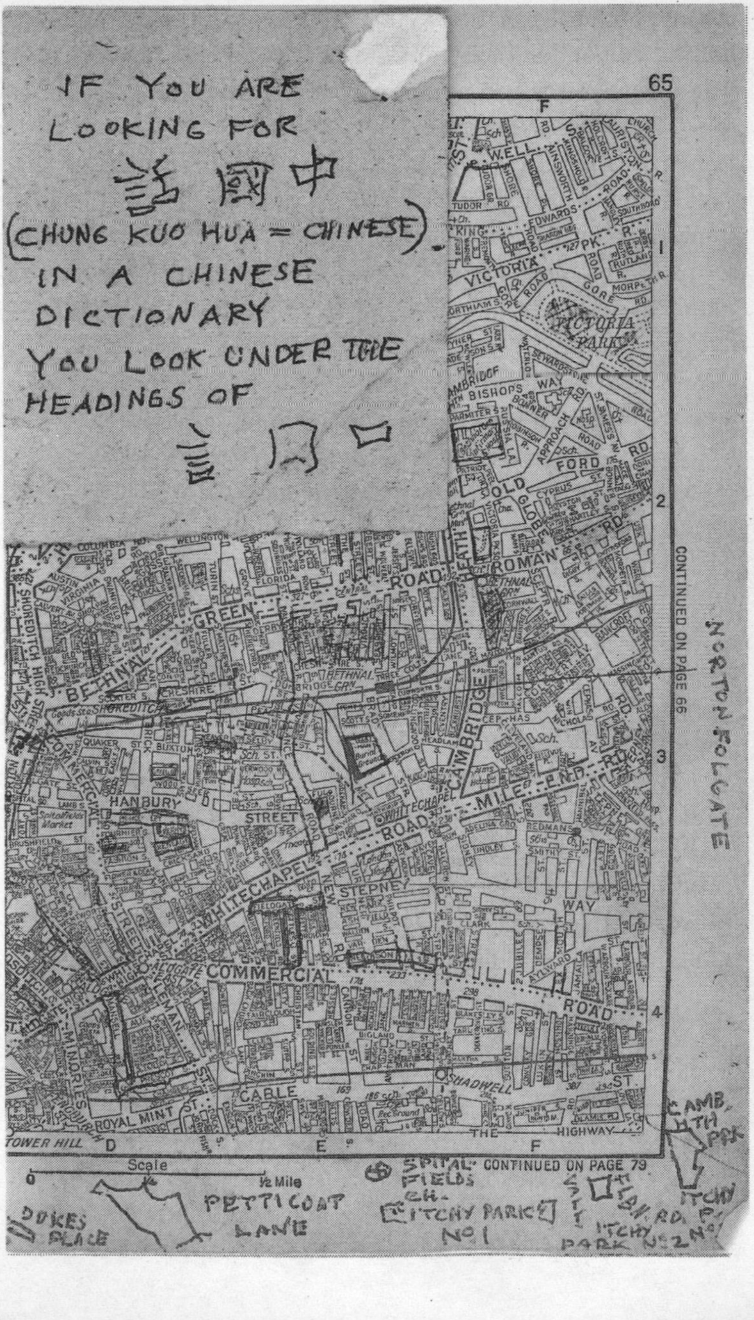

IF YOU ARE
LOOKING FOR
話國中
(CHUNG KUO HUA = CHINESE)
IN A CHINESE
DICTIONARY
YOU LOOK UNDER THE
HEADINGS OF
言 冂 口
65
VICTORIA PARK
BETHNAL GREEN ROAD
ROMAN RD
CAMBRIDGE
MILE END RD
WHITECHAPEL ROAD
HANBURY STREET
STEPNEY WAY
COMMERCIAL ROAD
CABLE ST
ROYAL MINT ST
MINORIES
TOWER HILL
THE HIGHWAY
CONTINUED ON PAGE 66
CONTINUED ON PAGE 79
Scale
½ Mile
NORTON FOLGATE
SPITAL FIELDS CH.
ITCHY PARK No 1
PETTICOAT LANE
DUKES PLACE
CAMB. HTH PRK
ITCHY PARK No 2

I discovered notebooks I had not seen before, as if placed there for
me. The scribblings inside quickly contradicted any previous mis-
givings I may have had about his mental capabilities, or lack of
them. David Rodinsky suddenly unmasked.

His notebooks were so dense, with such a wide variety of languages, that I think it would be impossible to decipher them unless
one were an extremely competent linguist. While flicking through
one of them I came across a coherent and fascinating chapter (I
believe Rodinsky was himself trying to write a book) in English:

> All that can be said is that Assyrian is entirely a dead language but
> its study is fascinating and important for those interested in the
> biblical study of semitic philology. It gives an insight into the
> structure of semitic grammar in general and is the missing link
> between the semitic languages – Arabic, Aramaic (Syriac)
> Ethiopic and Hebrew (and of course Assyrian and Accadian) and
> the Sino-Tibetan languages – Anamese, Burmese, Chinese, Malay,
> Siamese and Tibetan as well as to the non-classified language –
> Japanese – which cannot be grouped into any specific group of
> languages, which adds to the fascination of its study. But anyone
> learning it, even if he knows any other semitic language must
> remember that it is a language which cannot be mastered as any
> other – if attempting to do so from the point of the other semitic
> languages it will only lead to bafflement – as its peculiar grammar
> alone requires more patience and closer study than any one of its
> related languages and its script requires more patience than the
> Chinese script! It is a form of writing that one can never be too
> sure of. But patience can overcome all of this and it will thus
> prove to be a very interesting and fascinating study.

After reading this and many other sections of his notebooks I was
left in awe of him. Unfortunately I did not have the ability to
decipher his material. All I had was the determination to try to
uncover the mystery of his disappearance and the facts of his life.

As with the last notebook, a letter suddenly appeared to me. A letter that proved to be a significant clue to his disappearance from the room and his subsequent arrival in Epsom. Tucked behind his green leather wallet, in a place I was sure I had looked a thousand times before, was a letter from St Clement's Hospital, Bow Road, London E3, from the Social Services Department, dated 8 April 1968. Over the top of the headed notepaper, in large, red capital letters, were written the words DIABOLICAL CONCENTRATION CAMP, A. MORTE. As I gently unfolded the fragile piece of paper, acrid dust lifted off it on to my skin, making me itch violently. The letter was addressed to 'Mr D. Rodinsky' but the address was not 19 Princelet Street. The letter had been sent to the Jewish shelter, 63 Mansell Street, London E1, and it read as follows:

Dear Mr Rodinsky
Thank you for your letter of the 5th of April.
　　There is no cause for concern about your rent at 19 Princelet Street, as the Ministry of Social Security will continue to pay this along with the cost of your stay at Mansell Street. If you run into any difficulty about obtaining this money, please contact the Ministry of Social Security to get in touch with us.
　　The keys to your flat have been retained at the hospital so that the Public Health department can have access for the purpose of cleaning and redecoration. The keys will be returned to you as soon as possible.

I imagined the scenario. Some time in 1968 David had been taken ill and ended up at the Bow hospital. They had thought him unfit to look after himself and transferred him to the Jewish shelter. While there he had received this letter. I could almost feel his fury. They had taken away the one thing he had left in the world. His home, which contained, as he said himself in a letter to Carol Wayne's mother, 'all that is dear to me'. The insult: 'The keys will be returned to you as soon as possible.' I sensed his rage, that 'they' might decide his room needed cleaning out and redecorating. I imagine that if he felt this was going to happen he might well just disappear, too furious to return for fear what they might have disposed of.

David Jacobs showed me one other interesting article that I had
not seen before. This was another letter printed in the *Jewish
Chronicle*, dated 18 November 1993, and entitled 'Happy memories of
the *shul* in Princelet Street':

My grandfather, Myer Reback, was *shammas* at Princelet Street
for 50 years.
   He lived with his wife and family in a flat upstairs of the
synagogue.
   My parents, uncles, and aunts were married in the synagogue,
my cousins and I were barmitzvah there.
   During the fire bomb attack on the East End in 1941, three
incendiary bombs fell on the main synagogue, and it was one of
my aunts, with great courage, who doused them with sand, and
so saved the building from burning down.
   Up to practically the last day of his life, my grandfather used
to go out at six in the morning in all weathers to press-gang
enough people to hold a morning service.
   I am sure many people must remember *shammas* Reback
from Princelet Street. He was a piece of Jewish East End history.

Monte Dann
Herts

I wrote to Monte Dann but the letter was returned to sender a few
weeks later. His letter had confused me again. I had thought David
Rodinsky was the *shames* at Princelet Street. I was sure that was
what Mr Katz had told me. I knew I now had to try to get hold of a
relative of Myer Reback.

David Jacobs and I talked about the possible whereabouts of
Rodinsky's grave. David suggested I start with the records office in
Epsom, asking them if they knew where inmates of the Longrove
would have been buried. David still favoured the idea that Rodinsky
was buried in Waltham Abbey cemetery.

I would not follow this up for some months yet. There is much
superstition about visiting cemeteries whilst pregnant. I decided to
wait until after the birth of my baby.

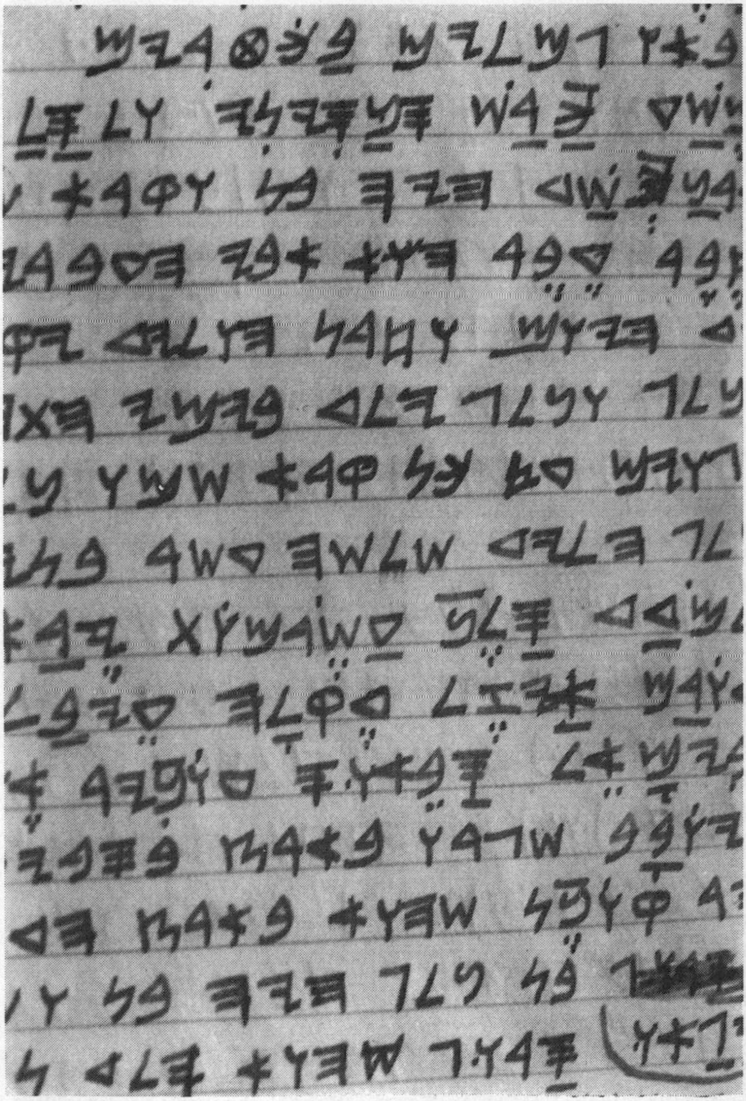

My son David was six weeks old. I had recovered from the birth and was anxious to restart my investigations into the whereabouts of Rodinsky's grave. But my quest was temporarily put on hold by new and extraordinary information I received from my friend Alan Dein. Alan and I met many years ago through our mutual mentor, Professor Bill Fishman. Still only thirty-four, Alan is the only other person I know aged under seventy who conducts walking tours of the Jewish East End. He moved to east London about ten years ago, 'determined to be reunited with the streets my great-grandparents had encountered years ago as Yiddish-speaking immigrants. My family couldn't understand why I was moving to the East End they had left for suburbia, but I was inspired by the entire history of the place.' Alan is a professional oral historian and has recorded many fascinating interviews with the remaining Jewish population in the area. He recently produced a programme for Radio 4 entitled 'After You've Gone' during which he interviewed elderly Jews from the Beaumont Day Centre in Stepney and Kosher Meals on Wheels recipients in East London. The programme begins with a frail voice saying, 'The old Jewish East End is forgotten now. . . . We are the last and let's face it we're in our eighties, some of us in our nineties . . . it's not a life here any more, it's what you call a burial ground. It's just waiting to go.' After finishing the programme and gaining access to the homes of elderly Jews living alone in blocks like Bella Lipman's, Alan told me, 'There are many Rodinskys still in Whitechapel.'

Like myself, Alan has a passionate love for the Princelet Street synagogue. In the mid-Eighties he was working for the Jewish Museum in Finchley with David Jacobs, and was involved in transporting some of the material from Rodinsky's room to the Museum of London. He told me about a remarkable find by a colleague of his, Viki White. 'Underneath Rodinsky's pillow, inside a crumpled brown envelope, she found a short handwritten note and half a gold locket. It was a love note, to a woman. I don't think it was ever sent. I don't remember the full story. You could try speaking to Viki. I think she was the person who discovered it.' I had never seen this locket or heard any stories of a love interest and was very curious to find out more. Alan gave me Viki White's number in Edinburgh. It must have been the tenth time I'd called in a week when the phone was picked up by an older-sounding man with a thick Scottish accent, who turned out to be Viki's father. He said, 'You are very lucky to catch us, we are just packing the last box out of the house into the car. Viki is moving to Aberdeen today. If you had called five minutes later we would be gone.' Viki vaguely remembered the locket but had no idea what had happened to it. It was a number of personal diaries that had made the biggest impression on her. 'They were full of mad rantings, it really seemed as if he had lost his grip on reality.' I had not seen these diaries, which according to Viki documented his lonely last months in the attic. The image of Rodinsky's room still haunted Viki. 'I shall never forget it, everything was just as he had left it except it was covered in years of dust. The imprint of his head was still on the pillow. It was very strange.'

But it was what Alan had to tell me that was far more interesting. 'I was doing a walking tour last week and we passed by 19 Princelet Street. I was telling the story when an elderly woman in the group interrupted me, saying her brother had lived in number 21 for most

of his life.' Alan has become involved in collating an archive of oral
testaments of former synagogue members and people who lived in
Princelet Street (for use when 19 Princelet Street eventually becomes
a functioning museum) and he asked the woman for her brother's
number, hoping to interview him. Her brother, called Sidney Lynn,
agreed to the interview and told Alan he had lived at number 21 for
over fifty years before moving to the small village in Hampshire
where he now lives. Alan asked him on my behalf if he knew David
Rodinsky. 'Of course, he was my best friend as a kid. Ginger Rodinsky
we called him. We used to play cricket in the street together.'

Maybe Sidney could relay some happier tales from Rodinsky's life.
The discovery of this elderly man gave me hope that my thoughts
about Rodinsky's early life had been wrong. I had imagined him
trapped in his attic room, his mother terrified to let him out of her
sight. I was desperate to meet Sidney, but Alan suggested that he
should go alone for the first visit, impressing upon me the need for
Sidney to tell *his* story before I bombarded him with questions about
Rodinsky. I reluctantly agreed, and Alan promised to ask Sidney to
expand on his story of Ginger Rodinsky. This is part of the interview:

Sydney Lynn: I was born 23rd May 1920 in the London Hospital,
Whitechapel. My mother was from Lublin, and she left in the
1880s with the first wave of refugees from the pogroms. Her first
home was in Fournier Street, which was full of furriers then.
She moved to 21 Princelet Street around 1903, and this is where I
grew up. It was a slum in those days, but in spite of that there
were some very important buildings in the street. There was a
shoe factory named Jackson and Joseph's just a few yards from
where I lived, it was modern for the time and employed lots of
people locally in the 1930s. All the houses in the street were
tenements then, the conditions were terrible. There were often
up to ten families to a house, not like now, full of yuppies and
pop stars, with just two to a house, in my day it was more like
forty. Next door to the left of us was the Princelet Street
synagogue and next door to us the other side was one of my

mother's customers (she was a printer of cap linings), named
Rabin, they were cap makers, a big industry at the time.

When I lived in Princelet Street the building functioned like
this: the front door was always open, the front room was the
workshop and people used to walk in and see the printers. The
floor was made of rough wood planks and you would walk
through the narrow wooden passage and there were three doors
off it. One was the workshop, the other the living room and
kitchen combined, my mother did all the cooking there, and
there was a little bedroom between the two, which was where I
slept with my brothers. There were many other families in the
house, somewhere between seven and ten, on each floor at least
two families. People were squashed in together in almost
inconceivable poverty. Looking back at it now through the eyes
of a man of seventy-eight years, I can see now we were very
poor. There was only one toilet for all the people that lived in
that part of the house. We had absolutely no privacy, that was an
unknown concept for the future: your life was everybody's life.

Alan Dein: Can you tell me about your mother?

Sidney Lynn: She was an exceptional person, a survivor, she
did not dwell on nostalgia or look back. She never spoke about
life in Lublin, she looked forward, that is how she survived, she
was a fighter. She went into a house on fire in Hanbury Street
once and rescued a couple of kids, that was the sort of woman she
was. It is very hard not to be emotional when I think of these
things. Now I hear properties in Princelet Street are being sold for
such ridiculous sums it makes me laugh, the idea of one family in
that building, inconceivable for us. The premises were in such a
bad state when I lived there, I remember going to the council to
get a certificate for repair work and they laughed at me and told
me it was not possible as the building was condemned. But we
never knew the kind of grinding poverty where you did not have
a roof over your head or shoes on your feet, I remember seeing
these kinds of things in Whitechapel but we never stooped that
low, we were petty bourgeois in comparison. It was this grinding

poverty that I was always aware of that made me turn my back on religion at the age of sixteen and become a communist. My inspiration was the battle of Cable Street. Everywhere people were talking politics in East London, about Stalin and Russia, and these conversations would take place most often outside the synagogue in Princelet Street. In 1938 and 1939 you could not get away from politics anywhere; it was in the air, particularly in Spitalfields, the air was saturated with it. I can't convey it by talking about it sixty years later, not really.

My mother was horrified when she found out I had become a communist. She heard from Mr Reback, our neighbour. He was the *shames* at the synagogue next door. He saw me speaking at Bloom's corner, at the corner of Old Montague Street and Brick Lane, that was the site of the original Bloom's before it moved to Aldgate. We used to put our platforms there on Sunday mornings and spout, sometimes we had a van and a microphone and then we'd get a real audience. My mother fully expected me to be either a violinist or a rabbi; all I wanted was to be a professional revolutionary, that was my number one ambition. I was often arrested by the police as a youngster for my communist activities and I was forced to leave the *yeshiva* in Thrawl Street. To find a Jewish communist in a *yeshiva* was shocking in those days.

Alan Dein: Can you tell me about the synagogue next door?

Sidney Lynn: I was bar mitzvahed there. It was an amazing place, the atmosphere was different to anywhere else locally. It was special, the women were upstairs, the men downstairs, the noise was fantastic. I wore a bowler hat for my bar mitzvah, which I thought was hilarious at the time.

The synagogue had rows of wooden seats running right down the side and facing the ark and a large wooden *bimah* which was in the centre of the floor. There was a beautiful chandelier hanging from the ceiling and, by the standards we were used to, it had quite a big hall. There was a very elaborate purple velvet curtain covering the ark where the *sefer* Torahs, holy scrolls, were kept. They were bedecked with silver and Hebrew inscriptions made by craftsmen. The atmosphere and artefacts there were incongruous. It did not seem to have any relationship with the poor people that came to pray there, who were nearly all tailors, honest poor Jews. That was the impression of the place to me. It was a place of worship.

My father died in December 1930 and I would go next door to the synagogue every morning for the eleven months to say Kaddish for him. The *shames*, Mr Reback, and his family lived upstairs and they were the same stairs you would go up to reach the women's department, and the fact that it had a separate women's department meant it was quite big by the standards of Spitalfields generally. And the wood was polished, highly polished, it was very well looked after and the Hebrew inscriptions on the balcony were kept clean and painted in gold leaf. It was a place that demanded respect, you would hold your breath as you entered. It did create that aura of respect.

Alan Dein: Do you only remember the one family that lived there?

Sidney Lynn: Yes. Just the Rebacks. They lived in luxury compared to the rest of us, that was their status. He was the *shames* and was treated with great regard. But I never knew the inside of their flat because I never went up there. But definitely, it was just them. I knew everyone in the street.

Alan Dein: But what about David Rodinsky who lived at the top?

Sidney Lynn: No, that's not right. Rodinsky was my friend who lived on the other part of Princelet Street, over Brick Lane, it used to be called Boot Street. And that is where Ginger Rodinsky lived. I remember him, I can picture him now. I understand his room was found abandoned and that he was some kind of reclusive type of person – my daughter Vivian told me, she read it in the *East London Observer*. It said he lived the life of a religious recluse. I found this very hard to reconcile with the boy I knew, but I did not know his family, never met them. I only knew him. I knew he was religious, but we all were in those days anyway. I think his family were in the tailoring, something to do with tailoring. I knew him very well, all my growing up, when we were both youngsters, before I went to the *yeshiva*. When my daughter told me about his fate I was quite shocked 'cause he was a lovely lad. Quite good-looking, Ginger, lively, a good bowler, I remember that because I was a lousy batsman and he bowled fast and breaks as well. Which was very unusual, a spin bowler would usually be slow and rely upon spin. Now he, he was a fast bowler that managed to get breaks to swerve in, and if Ginger was facing me he would always get me out. We played cricket constantly in the centre of the street. When traffic came by you stopped – traffic could be a horse dragging a cart behind or occasionally a motorized vehicle. Just outside my house and the synagogue there was a short stretch where the cobblestones turned to asphalt and we used to use that. Me and Ginger built a wicket, made of wood. We also played football and all sorts of other games, always outside in the street, and we used to play in Wilkes Street, round the back of Truman's brewery. There was a lamp-post there that we used for our wicket and we'd play on the pavement. We were chased away by the police from time to time, but it didn't matter, it was part of the fun, and when you thought it was safe you came back. I'm talking about when I was ten or eleven, the early 1930s. Ginger was the same age as me. Ginger Rodinsky was part of the gang of boys in the street that I was part of, there were others, Mossy Kaufman from Fournier Street and Woffy Sokoloff who lived in number 25. I lost touch with Ginger when I went to the *yeshiva*. People moved away, I don't know what happened to him.

Alan Dein: It is interesting. I think he was still around when you had your printing business in the 1950s in Princelet Street. He was living in the top room of 19 Princelet Street. Right at the top in the attic.

Sidney Lynn: I don't think so, the only people that lived there then were the Rebacks, they had the whole house. There was a

family, they had two daughters, Bella and Rachel and a son
Simon. They came from the same area as my mother – no other
family lived there. I would have known, my mother was great
friends with the Rebacks. I don't remember anyone else. I'm
sure he didn't live there, I think he lived down the other end.
But I did not know him as a teenager at all. Ginger had gone out
of my life as I had gone out of his. So I'm only talking about
childhood memories and I remember him very clearly, he was
bright ginger that was the most memorable thing, with freckles,
and blue-eyed, he didn't look particularly Jewish at all. He was
boisterous and lively. What else can I tell you? He wasn't
particularly tall and he wasn't particularly short. He wasn't
chunky, he had no marked physical features I can remember or
describe him by. He was ordinary, very.

As soon as I finished transcribing the interview I called Carol and
Alvin Wayne. Carol confirmed what I had suspected. Her own bright
auburn hair had aroused my suspicions. 'Yes,' she told me. 'I did
have a brother with red hair. He was called Mossy, but everyone
called him Ginger. Ginger Rodinsky.' No wonder Sidney had been
surprised at the descriptions of Rodinsky's reclusive life and abandoned room. Mossy, Carol (formerly known as Ethel Rodinsky) and
their family lived at the opposite end of Princelet Street, near my
grandparents' watchmaking shop.

Sidney Lynn had lived next door to the Princelet Street synagogue for over fifty years. His family were great friends with the
Rebacks (who lived on the floor below the Rodinskys) and his best
friend was a cousin of David Rodinsky. In his own words he was 'a
tenacious child who knew everybody in the street'. He can still reel
off lists from memory: 'There was Isenfish Israel, the job buyer, next
to him Jackson and Joseph's the boot manufacturers, then the synagogue, with Rabin the cap maker's one side and us the other. Further
down the street on our side I remember Joshua Heller the furrier,
Yelin Lionel opticians, Goldberg's greengrocery and Lichtenstein's
jewellers.' Unlike most of his childhood friends who moved out of

the area in the Thirties and Forties, Sidney Lynn was in business at 21 Princelet Street until the late 1950s. I had potentially found my best eye-witness yet. But Sidney Lynn had never heard of David Rodinsky, never knew he existed.

David Rodinsky was not part of the Princelet Street gang of young boys. He did not belong to the Communist Party or the Brady Club. From the letter from Michael Jimack and the letter to Carol Wayne's mother I now knew he had spent many years away from Princelet Street, which might account for Sidney's lack of knowledge about him, but they were definitely neighbours for at least thirty years. I can imagine David watching Sidney and his pals playing cricket in the street right outside his window. I don't think he would have joined in. When I called Carol Wayne about identifying Ginger Rodinsky she told me she had found another letter that David had written to her mother a few years before his death. It confirmed my suspicions that David Rodinsky was far from enjoying his solitary life in the attic of the old synagogue. Carol sent me a copy of the letter.

> 19 Princelet Street
> Brick Lane
> London E1
> 21/9/61

Dear Betsy,
Thank you very much for your New Year card for which I am sending you one, please find it enclosed. In the name of *rachmones*, do you have an unfurnished room for me? I am all alone here by myself. They told Brendall about this and she has had several fits. If you don't like my cap I will not wear it if you let me have a room.

Yours Faithfully
D. Rodinsky

David Rodinsky had been deeply misunderstood by the media back in the 1980s. There was nothing romantic about the room. I now

believe that his life, particularly the latter part of it, was grim and
lonely. For the first time I truly realized quite how isolated and
reclusive David Rodinsky must have been. I recalled the imaginary
conversations in his handwritten English to Hebrew dictionary. Here
is the English he chooses to translate:

Are you leaving already?
Must you go now?
Is it really absolutely necessary for you to go?
You've only just come.
It's early yet, stay a little longer.
You seem to be in a hurry.

I am very busy today.
I have a lot to do.
I have important business.
I have a long way to go.
I have many roads to take.
I have an important interview to attend.
I'm afraid I'm late.
It's time for departure.
I won't disturb you any longer.

When will we see you?

Very soon.
Well, as soon as I possibly can.

You'll be back after the interview of course?

I'll let you know.
I'll come eventually.

It's a pity you have to leave so soon, we were getting on quite
nicely (or not too bad).

I called Iain Sinclair to tell him of the new information I had discovered. He was not surprised to learn that the lively young boy
who played cricket in the street had turned out to be someone other
than David Rodinsky. I told Sinclair about the other articles that
David Jacobs had given me and he told me to look again in
Downriver, in which he had published the letter from Mr Jimack,
along with a response from a Mr Ian Shames:

Stoke Newington

4.7.88

Dear Mr Jimack

Having read your letter about David Rodinsky, I am prompted
to write to you, which is now a matter of history.

I am the last surviving son-in-law of the late Myer Reback,
who was the *shamash* of the Princelet Street synagogue, & I
married his daughter (now deceased) in 1937.

I was no stranger to the Rodinsky family and knew them
well. They occupied a two-room flat above the living rooms of
the late Mr and Mrs Myer Reback, & I made a few visits to
them.

There was the mother a widow, & she had two children, a girl
named Bessie, who unfortunately was mentally backward,
spending most of her life at Clayberry Mental hospital. Her
visits to Princelet Street were rare & there was David the son,
who was always pasty-faced & the flat was always like a
'hagdesh'. The mother was not overbright, she was toothless, &
always walked about with a blanket over her shoulders. Please
forgive me, but I gave her the name of 'Gandhi' & by that name
she is still mentioned by the Reback family today. Her life was
full of worry for the future, & the Reback family helped her in
various ways, under her poor circumstances; all in all, the
mother & son lived like hermits on the top-floor flat above the
synagogue. Now about David: he was not bright in his youth,
his complexion was very sallow, something about him in his

speech was rather hesitant in conversation. My daughter Lorna
(who is now 49) knew him quite well & remembers him, as she
spent many hours at her grandfather & grandmother's flat when
she was quite young.

In 1939, I was called up to serve in the RAMC through the
military hospital reserve, & having seen service in the Middle
East, India & Burma, I returned to England (a trained nurse) in
1946, & my connection with the synagogue was history. It was in
1948, while working at the German hospital in Dalston as a male
nurse, I attended a bar mitzvah at the Heneage Street
synagogue, & to my surprise I met David, he was there for the
kiddush!

He recognized me immediately, in the few years of my
absence he had grown taller, more manly, & very coherent. He
still lived at no.19 Princelet Street, & to my surprise he was quite
fluent speaking Arabic. This came about when I told him of the
many places I had visited, & could converse with him in Arabic,
as I had seen service in the Suez Canal & Cairo. This was my last
meeting with him, & this ends my story.

I decided to try to track down Mr Shames and Mr Jimack. I wrote
to the addresses on the original letters, knowing there was a large
possibility that they had moved on since 1988. I also now realized
that the living members of the Reback family would be the only
people alive who might be able to fill in for me the missing gaps in
the story. I thought back to Mr Katz's description of Rodinsky: 'Of
course I knew him, he was the *shames* there, his daughter comes
once a year to light a *Yahrzeit* for him at the synagogue.' He had not
been describing David Rodinsky (I expect, like Sidney Lynn, he
had never even seen him) but Myer Reback, the *shames* and great
community figure who had lived for over fifty years in the flat
below the Rodinskys. I expect it was the Rebacks who rented the
flat to the Rodinskys and it seems they helped the family considerably. Sidney Lynn's interview had also made me recognize who
Bella Lipman was. Stupidly, when I had gone to interview Bella, I

had been so excited by the prospect of her being Rodinsky's
daughter that when she had denied this I had failed to ask whose
daughter she really was. She was of course Myer Reback's daughter.
The rest of the Reback children must have left the synagogue, leaving Bella and her husband who stayed on as the true caretakers of
the building many years even after David Rodinsky had left. Bella
was the key; she had all the answers to all the remaining questions. I rushed out to interview her, kicking myself I had not
realized this before. I felt guilty, for I had neglected Bella over the
past few months because of my pregnancy and the birth of David.

Concrete cancer had eaten away more of the façade of the terrifying
block of flats where Bella lived. I nervously entered the stairwell,
afraid of a repeat of my previous visit when I had been threatened
in the lift. I made my way up to Bella's flat and knocked on the
door. There was no answer. Knowing that Bella was terrified of
callers (as a result of the horrific attack she had suffered which had
left her blind in one eye) I called my name through the letter-box.
As I did so I got a shock. The patterned carpet had gone, revealing
bare floorboards covered in plaster and cigarette butts. I rushed to
the kitchen window and peered in. Her rows of pills had disappeared, the fridge, everything, all gone. All that remained of Bella
Lipman was her faded net curtains. I felt sick. I hoped she had
moved on to better premises but I feared the worst. I knocked at the
flat next door, and eventually a pair of terrified brown eyes
appeared at the window. I was not sure if the woman understood
what I was asking – she kept shaking her head, then closed the curtains and ran to the back room of the flat, shouting something to
other household members in a frightened voice, speaking a language I did not understand.

I had to find out what had happened to Bella Lipman. I started
walking up towards Brick Lane to see if Mr Katz knew. To reach his
shop from Bella's flat I walked past the site of the former Kosher
Luncheon Club and Great Garden Street synagogue. The art guerrillas had moved on. The building had been boarded up and new

flats had replaced the dome of the synagogue above the luncheon club. A large sign sat beside the entrance:

Partners in Regeneration
Bethnal Green City Challenge are building on this site a
Business Development Centre
providing a satellite for business links in East London

The building was covered in scaffolding; builders were crawling all over it, ripping out the old synagogue windows, throwing them into a skip full of splintered wood and marble crumbs.

As I turned off Greatorex Street into Brick Lane I could not hear myself think; the noise was tremendous. I had not been down the Lane for a few weeks, since the birth of David, and the place was already unrecognizable. All the old buildings were shrouded in green netting and scaffolding. Cappuccino bars had opened up on every corner and the air was thick with builders' dust and the sound of concrete being drilled. But Mr Katz was in his shop. He was delighted to see me and to hear about David's arrival in the world. I asked if he had seen Bella, and he told me he had not seen her for many months and doubted whether she was still alive as she had missed her father's anniversary, a day when she always journeyed to Princelet Street to light a *Yahrzeit* for him. He then told me his sad news. The developers were forcing him out. He could no longer afford the rent. In a few months he would have to leave. 'Fifty-seven years,' he lamented. 'Fifty-seven years.'

When Mr Katz has gone there will only be one other obviously functioning Jewish business in Brick Lane: Elfes stone masons. I visited there after seeing Mr Katz, and as I walked into the plushly furnished showroom it was clear that A. Elfes Memorials was doing very well. Three young men in expensive suits sat behind their desks, busily making funeral arrangements on the phone. I had time to wander around the showroom and look at the various marble designs, along with a board of 'Suggested Quotations for Memorials':

Shalom
Always in our hearts
Always in our thoughts
Life is eternal, love is forever
His precious memory will never fade
He lived respected and died regretted
May his dear soul rest in eternal peace

One of the men finished on the telephone and immediately rushed over to me. I told him I was just looking, but I think he was convinced I had a relative who could be a potential customer. 'All our marble is imported from Carrara in Italy,' he told me, while pointing at a large colour poster of a sculptor standing with chisel in hand in a quarry bathed in sunlight. 'Each stone includes a hundred free letters, in lead of course; gold is extra.'

In a daze I left the shop and made the short walk to Princelet Street. Every derelict house in the street had been renovated, the doors covered in bright new gloss and shining brass accessories. It was strange to stand outside number 21 now, after hearing Sidney Lynn's testimony that 'up to ten families, forty people, had lived in each house.' I watched as a smartly dressed couple came out of the house. She was talking on her mobile; he politely opened a door of their silver jeep for her before driving off into the choking dust.

It was time for Rodinsky and for me to move out of this place. We no longer belonged. There was just one thing left for me to do for him, and I had to start straight away.

As David Jacobs had suggested, I tried the Epsom records office first. When I eventually got through to someone I was told only what I already knew. All the records from the Longrove had been destroyed in the fire, and they could not help. I tried the Federation of Synagogues Burial Society next. I told the man the details from Rodinsky's death certificate and he went off to check the records. He returned a few minutes later and told me he had definitely not been buried in a Federation cemetery. I told him I was worried he might not have had a Jewish burial. He said if this was the case, it was possible to make arrangements to exhume the body and replace it in a Jewish grave and cemetery, for an approximate cost of one thousand pounds. He suggested I might try the United Synagogues Burial Society. I called immediately and spoke to a very helpful man who enthusiastically took down all the details. I asked if Waltham Abbey was one of their cemeteries. 'It is, and we have all the records for that cemetery here on database.' I asked him to check there first and waited while he searched. It did not take long. 'Yes, lady, David Rodinsky was buried here . . . WA2 . . .' I was so overwhelmed I forgot to write down what he was telling me. I asked him to repeat

what he had just said. 'Of course. He was buried here in the paupers'
section, on the fifth of March 1969, the site of the grave is WA25, row
T for Tommy, no. 708.' David Jacobs's prediction back in Warsaw had
been correct. I asked him if it was likely there would be a headstone
for him. 'Being in the paupers' section, I expect not.' He told me it
was possible to have a stone setting and a service, that they could
arrange this with a United Synagogues orthodox rabbi, and he gave
me a list of the stone masons in London that could be used for
United Synagogues cemeteries. One of them was A. Elfes Ltd., situated at the Whitechapel end of Brick Lane.

I called Carol and Alvin first to tell them the news. They were very
grateful and took down the details so they could visit themselves.
Then I called David Jacobs. He was delighted and offered to drive
me to visit the grave and say Kaddish. David suggested we visit on
Sunday in two weeks' time. He told me, 'This is the perfect time to
visit the grave: you are no longer pregnant and it is the traditional
time of year to visit the grounds, being the month of *Ellul* before
Tishri, just before *Rosh Hashanah.* The Sunday we have chosen is
one of the days of awe before the high holy days, a time of inner
reflection and contemplation, prayer and meditation. These are the
days of *Teshuvah,* a return to God, when it is customary to visit the
graves of relatives and teachers, to remember the sanctity of their
lives and to gain inspiration for the coming year.' It seemed
Rodinsky had chosen this time for my discovery.

I had time before the visit to complete a few more tasks and end
the quest. I needed to hurry – another David now needed my time
and attention. I arranged childcare for little David and went into a
flurry of activity. My first task was to try to trace any living members
of the Reback family, as they were the only people who would have
known the Rodinskys on a day-to-day basis. I was also very concerned about Bella Lipman. I spent hours on the phone to various
sections of the council to try to find out what had happened to her.
They confirmed that she had moved out of Dobsons House but
refused to divulge any further information.

'Please,' I said. 'I just want to know if she is all right.'

'I cannot help you.'

'Please. Can you at least tell me, is she dead or alive?'

'I cannot. Sorry.'

I went to visit Alan Dein to see if he had any other ideas. He suggested I go to the local history library in Bancroft Road and look for the obituary for Myer Reback, Bella's father in the *Jewish Chronicle*. We went immediately together and Alan located it fairly rapidly. The obituary, dated 5 January 1962, read as follows:

MR MYER REBACK
Mr Myer Reback, a founder-member of the
Princelet Street Synagogue, E1
and its reader for over fifty years, died last week.
My beloved father, Myer, passed away. His memory will remain
forever. Deeply mourned by his daughter, Bella.

The rest of Bella's family had all left similar memorial messages, underneath which were their 1962 addresses. I knew it was unlikely that any of them would still be living there, but it was my only hope. I wrote a total of eight letters and waited. At 8.30 a.m. two days later I got the first phone call. It was from Lorna, Bella's niece, the granddaughter of Myer Reback and the daughter of Ian Shames, who in his 1988 letter had written that she remembered Rodinsky. In her phone call she said, 'Amazing how it got to me: I married and moved away years ago, but we loosely keep in touch with the people who live in our old family house and they kindly passed your letter on. I wanted to call you straight away to tell you that Aunt Bella is OK. She has moved into a home, she had a stroke, and it was too difficult for her to look after herself any more. She is with her sister, so she's happy.' I was so relieved, and I asked her if I might go and visit Bella. 'I don't think so you see, because, oh, well in our family you just can't mention age, and she'd kill me if she knew I'd told you where she is. She just wants to be left alone really.' I could understand this and respected it. I had pestered Bella enough. I was just glad to know she was all right.

I asked Lorna if her father was still alive, but he had passed away a few years ago. 'He was such an intelligent man, spoke many languages himself. I remember him coming back from India when I was a child. We were all at the synagogue in Princelet Street and he had a diamond in his hand. He said to us "I'll prove to you this is a real diamond" and he took it to the window of the front room above the synagogue, which was where my grandparents lived, and scratched out his name, Isaac Shames, his real name was Isaac, you see; he anglicized it to Ian. He scratched the name on to the glass and it's still possible to see the faint trace there.' I asked Lorna if she remembered the Rodinskys. 'Not really,' she said. 'I was only a young child you see, my father would have known more about them, or Aunty Bella. I do remember going downstairs to the basement to collect the pickles or herrings that were stored in large jars down there, as we did not have a fridge then, and I would be terrified about passing him on the stairs. I was scared of him really. He was shy probably, and always dressed dark and was very very religious. I did not have much to do with him. To me it felt like the curse of Frankenstein if you passed him on the stairs. Silly really, but I was just a kid.'

The following day I received another early-morning call that was even more unexpected. It was from Douglas Blane, whom I had been trying to get hold of for months. He confirmed that he had been the first person to open up Rodinsky's locked room; it had been Bella Lipman, 'who had been acting as the caretaker at the time', who had taken him up there after the Spitalfields Historic Buildings Trust had acquired the building in 1980. He said Bella had told him she believed David Rodinsky had just walked out one day, that she did not know what had happened to him: he just disappeared and never came back. Douglas's impression of the room differed little from that given by the romantic newspaper reports that had come out at the time. 'The room was orderly, definitely not the room of some drunken lunatic. Everything was left as if he expected to return, the clothes in the wardrobe, pyjamas on the bed, porridge on the stove. It was like a time warp, so still, covered in a thick layer of dust and cobwebs. It looked like a scholar's garret, I was deeply impressed by the wide array of notebooks and fascinating and complex papers scattered on his desk. I imagined a highly intelligent individual must have lived there.'

Each day a remarkable piece of new information seemed to come my way. A few days after Douglas Blane's call, the phone rang very early, even before the baby had woken up. It was Michael Jimack, the man Ian Shames had written to. He told me that the letter I had sent to the Jewish Welfare Board had been passed on to his old address and that the people there had passed it on to him. As he had written in his letter, he remembered David Rodinsky from when he was a child. 'It was 1938, I was eight years old and David was thirteen. He had come to live with us in Dagenham for about eighteen months. As far as I remember he was fostered out as his mother just could not cope – he was from a very deprived background. I remember his sister coming to visit him; she seemed much older and I suspect she had learning difficulties. The mother came quite often as well. She seemed like a very old lady to me; I was scared of her, she had no teeth and she appeared to be below average intelligence.' Mr Jimack told me the Jewish Board of Guardians had a system at the time of fostering out deprived children. An investigating officer would go to the house and if the officer thought it appropriate, the board would get involved and try to find a family for the children. I imagined how terrifying this whole process had probably been for the Rodinskys: David's 'lost years', as he called them. Mr Jimack had some memories of David at the time when David stayed with them. 'I was very young and I thought he had funny ways. He presented himself as being very eccentric. I would definitely say he was intelligent, but odd with it. He was very orthodox, used to *davven* all the time, and was always writing and reading.' It did not sound as if he changed much over time.

Mr Jimack had also come across Rodinsky many years later as in the Sixties he had been a Jewish Welfare Board social worker. 'He was not my client, I remember a colleague of mine talking of him. He was his social worker, a man called Michael Scheider.'

I became very excited, talking over him. 'Do you know where I can find him?'

He told me that Michael Scheider was now a very senior person in one of the largest Jewish charities in the United States and that he lived in New York. I could contact him through the American Joint Distribution Committee. I thanked him profusely, since this Michael Scheider might be the one person left on earth who could answer my questions about how Rodinsky got from Princelet Street to the Longrove. Mr Jimack and I continued to talk about what might have happened. It did not surprise him that he had been at the Longrove: 'There were a number of Jewish clients from East London there. It was mainly a place for the long-term mentally ill.' I asked him if he thought Rodinsky would have gone voluntarily or been sectioned. 'I don't think he would have gone voluntarily. It was a terrible place, all locked wards.' He told me the social workers did not have the power to section, and that if he had no living relatives the social workers would have worked with the doctors to do this if they thought it necessary. I told Jimack about the letter I had found from St Clement's Hospital in Bow, addressed to the Jewish shelter. He said the Jewish shelter was used as a temporary base for the homeless. It was all starting to fit into place. I imagined that Rodinsky had been forced to see a doctor as his health had deteriorated so much. The doctor had probably sent him for a stay in St Clement's Hospital, and social services must have been informed.

It seems they inspected his flat at Princelet Street, decided it was unfit for human habitation and sent him on to the Jewish shelter, telling him, as their letter said, that his flat would be cleaned and redecorated. This was the letter he had scrawled over in angry red letters, DIABOLICAL CONCENTRATION CAMP, A. MORTE. Maybe someone had seen this addition, found his notebooks, decided he was mad. I imagined if David Rodinsky had truly thought his room was going to be redecorated without his consent he might not have even wanted to return there. He might have given up, gone quietly wherever he was taken. The doctors at St Clement's, his social worker and the workers at the temporary shelter might have met together and decided his fate for him – to be locked in the ward of a vast Victorian building in the English countryside. I imagined my predictions were correct, but I needed to contact Michael Scheider to confirm it all. 'Call him,' Mr Jimack said, 'He'll remember. You never forget a client.'

I looked up the American Joint Distribution Committee on the Internet and found an impressive website. There was a list of Executive VPs. I searched down the list and found Michael Scheider and sent him an email straight away. The next day I had heard nothing, so I wrote a letter and sent it by express post. Still nothing. I called twice and left messages with his secretary. 'He's a very busy man,' she said. I asked her to tell him I had just three questions to ask him, and that I would only take a few minutes of his time. Apparently it was the lure of the 'three questions' that finally got him to call.

He said he had not received my letter. I quickly garbled my request, and he told me he was very sorry, he was not in fact Rodinsky's social worker, and he had never heard of him. I gave him more information, hoping to jog his memory. 'No, definitely not, you never forget a client.' He suggested I contact Jewish Care. He told me that they keep archives, a filing system of case cards, filled out every time a social worker paid a visit to a client. I could apply for access to the archives and perhaps would find what I needed. He told me to speak to the chief executive. I called immediately, and was told that all case records were destroyed after five years. By this time, I was beside myself with frustration. I explained that all I needed to know was how Rodinsky had got from St Clement's to the Jewish temporary shelter, and then to the Longrove.

'That's easy,' the executive said. 'I can tell you right now. I also was a Jewish Welfare Board social worker in the Sixties. He was most likely placed in St Clement's through his social worker for a limited stay. He would have only gone to the temporary shelter if he had been homeless.' I told him about the letter, and how his room was going to be redecorated. 'That makes sense, he could not have stayed long-term at St Clement's and he could not return home. If the doctors at St Clement's and his social worker felt his mental condition had deteriorated, they probably would have sectioned him and found him a permanent place at the Longrove.'

I asked him what were the criteria for sectioning someone at that time. 'If,' he said, 'the psychiatrists felt the individual was a physical danger to himself or the community he would have been sectioned.' It did not surprise him that David Rodinsky had gone to the Longrove. 'It was the mental institution that had Whitechapel as its catchment area. There were many Jewish inmates there, not because there was anything particularly Jewish about the hospital but just because there were so many Jews living in Whitechapel at the time.' He told me he was a regular visitor at the Longrove in the Sixties. 'It was a sad place. People were generally hospitalized for life. It was the epitome of the Victorian mental asylum, stuck in the middle of the countryside, taking the mad as far away from their point of origin as possible.' I told him my theory, that I did not think Rodinsky was mad, only greatly misunderstood – the culture he came from was untranslatable. He agreed with me. 'The Longrove was the kind of place that was full of cabbalistic geniuses and religious scholars wrapped up in the world of metaphysics. In that period there were many mistakes made. Many of the nurses were Asian, many of the doctors from Middle Europe, there were very serious communication problems.'

Jewish Care had helped immensely. I could have spent many more months trying to track down Rodinsky's social worker to ask if he remembered whether David had gone to the Longrove voluntarily, but I did not feel this was necessary. I was now sure I knew the answer.

There was only one thing left to do, and finally the day arrived. I left Adam and David and went to meet David Jacobs. He drove me on the M25 to the Essex–London border, and not long after that we took a sharp turn off the motorway and behind a high green hedge was Waltham Abbey cemetery, an endless field of shining white marble whose silence was spoilt by the continuous roar of traffic. The cemetery was busy, full of busloads of elderly Jews who had come to pay their respects to the dead before the high holy days. We headed for the main office to look at a map of the grounds. WA25 row T was next to the Stillbirths section at the far right of the cemetery. It did not take us long to walk there and with David's help it did not take long to locate the grave.

It was much as I had expected. There was no headstone, just a shallow gravel plot with a broken concrete border and a small tin plaque that read 'David Rodinsky, March 5th 1969.' David stood with me in silence. Finally I opened my prayer-book and together we read the Kaddish, traditionally read by the son of the deceased but as there was no son to perform this task I took it upon myself. Before leaving, we both placed a stone on his grave and I read the prayer for the deceased.

O God, full of mercy, Who dwells on high, grant proper rest on the wings of the divine presence – in the lofty levels of the holy and pure ones, who shine like the glow of the firmament – for the soul of David Rodinsky who went on to His world, because, without making a vow, I will contribute to charity in the remembrance of his soul. May his resting place be in the garden of Eden – therefore may the Master of mercy shelter him in the shelter of His wings for eternity; and may He bind his soul in the Bond of Life. HASHEM is his heritage, and may he rest in peace on his resting place. Now let us respond: Amen.

AFTERWORD

Rachel Lichtenstein

In the weeks after the book was published stories began to flood in through letters, telephone calls and people I met.

At least six different people told me that *they* had been the first into Rodinsky's room. That was the pull of the room: it made everyone feel unique on entering it for the first time. But I had to do something about one of the calls in particular. After my brief appearance on Radio 4's *Midweek* programme, my mother took a message from a Mr Pattison. He told her, 'I was the first into Rodinsky's room and I have photographs to prove it.' I spoke with him the following day and we arranged to meet in his studio in Gants Hill.

The studio was tucked between a taxi rank and a nursery in a small side street off the Gants Hill roundabout. Mike was waiting outside the building and greeted me with a firm handshake and a pat on the back, telling me that a friend had caught the end of the broadcast and called him immediately. He was a tall man with bright white hair, probably about the same age as my father. As we walked up the stairwell towards his studio he told me he was a commercial fashion photographer for the *Sunday Telegraph*. He was certainly different from other photographers I had met and so was his studio, large, spotlessly clean, brightly lit, with a separate dressing room for the models who frequented it. A friend, a weary photojournalist just back from Sudan, was sitting next to a table in the corner, sipping coffee and talking fast. 'You see Mike's the best photographer I know, he's got these amazing set of prints from the East End, noone's ever seen them. They're the only photographs I've ever seen that I'm actually jealous of, I mean I wish I took 'em. So that's why I had to call you, so you could do something with them. He's never shown them, never published them.' Mike winked at me while rubbing his hands together. My heart sank. I felt they had been misled by the amount of publicity the book had received and that perhaps they thought that anything concerning Rodinsky's room would now be commercially valuable. Expecting little, I asked to see the prints. 'Let's have coffee first' said Mike. Although I was feeling hopeless I agreed, asking him to tell me a little about himself. His story woke me up more than the coffee.

He said that as I could probably tell, he was not Jewish. But he had grown up in Stamford Hill and was the only gentile in his school. He learnt about Jewish life and people and felt a connection with them. He became a fashion photographer but in his spare time he started to walk around the Jewish East End. He had been doing it for the last fifteen years, and it had become his passion. During that time he had taken hundreds of rolls of film; most of the places he'd shot didn't exist any longer, like the wooden house that used to be behind Elfes Stone Masons on Osborn Street, and he had taken portraits, he said, of the man who used to live in an underground burrow in the Brady Street cemetery.

I was intrigued. I had lived behind that cemetery for a number of years but had never heard of this caretaker. But Mike showed me a photograph of him and told me about his life. He appeared at first to be the caretaker of the whole cemetery but in fact his only job, according to Mike, was to look after one tomb that belonged to the Rothschild family. The marble on this tomb could be seen glowing in the dark from my old bedroom window and the stone was weed-

free, unlike the other tombs which were covered in moss and algae.
This man made the cemetery his home, living underneath one of the
tombs with his dog. Mike Pattison showed me the photograph
which was haunting; a man living in a bare stone crypt, making
Rodinsky's lodgings look like a palace.

He showed me other images: intimate portraits of tramps; wonderful photographs of the last remnants of the Jewish community, in
synagogues, at the Kosher Luncheon Club, walking the streets. His
friend was right, I was almost jealous too. Mike stopped flicking
through the images and looked at me with his eyes sparkling. He told
me that this was the picture I really want to see, but he wanted to tell
me the story of it first. It must have been in the summer of 1980, he
couldn't remember exactly when he was wandering down Princelet
Street, as he often did, and he saw 'this bloke with a key in the door
of number 19.' That caught his attention, because he had walked
past the building a hundred times and never managed to get inside.
Mike is, as he put it, the curious type and not shy, so he tapped the
keyholder on the shoulder and asked if he could come in, explaining
that he was a photographer, and the man agreed, telling him over

and over again not to touch anything. He was a worker for the Spitalfields Historic Buildings Trust, Pattison remembers him saying, and telling him that this Trust had recently acquired the building.

The place they entered was a mess. After looking around the neglected, deserted synagogue they climbed the dark narrow stairs to the attic room using matches to light their way. The man told Mike Pattison he had been given a key to the room by the woman who lived in the flat downstairs. He had tried again and again to open the door but it wasn't budging. The lock was so old and rusted it had obviously not been open for years. Mike tried for a while, then the man from the Trust tried again for at least ten minutes, and then suddenly the key just turned in the lock, as smooth as anything. He managed to open the door just a tiny way on its stiff hinges before he jumped back with a sharp gasp of breath, asking Mike 'did you feel that?' Mike remembers him turning pale and saying something had gone right through him, like a gust of wind or a burst of light. They went into that room very cautiously and Mike Pattison said when they got inside, well, he thought, I must know the rest. Here is his extraordinary photograph of the room, unaltered, unprettified. It is clear from this image that later photographers could not resist arranging the objects slightly to make a more conventional still life composition.

* * * *

The letters I received in response to the book were both moving and informative, particularly those from people who had lived in Princelet Street and the surrounding area or had been long standing members of the Princelet Street *shul*. Not one of them had ever had direct contact with David Rodinsky. This simply confirmed his isolation, which was already so apparent after Sidney Lynn's testimony, who said 'I lived next door to no. 19 for over fifty years and never knew of David Rodinsky's existence.'

Here are a few extracts from some of these letters. Mr Martin Genis wrote:

I was born on 24th December 1936, sharing a birthday but not the year with Lorna Shames. My parents and I moved from Hanbury Street to Princelet Street in 1938. My grandparents lived at no. 20 Princelet Street directly opposite the synagogue and we took the flat on the first floor. My grandmother died about a year after the war started and it made sense to combine the two floors and live in them as one family. My grandfather, mother and I (my father was away in the army) spent most of our time on the top floor. In those days a lot of time was spent looking out of windows, talking to neighbours and watching the world go by. The view directly opposite our windows was of the top floor of the synagogue premises and the slightly higher attic. A very strangely dressed lady known as 'the parachute' occupied it. The name was given to her by my mother presumably because she lived in the sky . . . She could often be seen walking around the external tarmac area of the roof which lay in the front of the exterior setback wall of the attic. I never saw any other person in that dwelling and was never given any reason to suspect that she had a son or daughter living with her. There were of course many visitors to the synagogue: family, friends, maintenance people, worshippers etc. Some would be very regular and it now seems that these would have included David

and his sister. It may be a trick of memory, but I can see in my
minds eye a regular 'visitor' who could well have been David,
given the descriptions in your book.

Martin Genis recalled incidents from the streets of Whitechapel,
including tantalizing glimpses of Rodinsky's mother:

Lorna is reported in your book as saying that the Reback family
never had a refrigerator. This was true but we did. As far as I
know we were the only family in the street, maybe the area to
have one. Consequently, at one time or other and particularly
during the summer months, we were the custodians of meat
purchased in the week which was not required for cooking until
the Sabbath. Various pots and saucepans were delivered, each pot
identified with the proprietor's name, and the owner would call
for it on a Friday. A ring on the bell, a look out the window, and I
would lower a key on a string to the ground. The caller would
then come upstairs and claim their pot, departing with a 'thank
you for my chicken.' On one such occasion 'the parachute' came
to our house. She acted very strangely and seemed frightened.
She looked in the fridge, found her pot, and left hurriedly. That
was the only time I remember having close contact with her.
After my Bar Mitzvah, and given the number of synagogues in
the area, I was often stopped and asked to make up a *minyan*. I
am certain that on one occasion I was stopped by Rodinsky's
mother acting as a *minyan* gatherer. She may well have been
asked to officiate in that position at other times.

Judith Dell also wrote to me, as though the story had filled in some
gaps in her sense of her own family's history:

I became very quickly immersed in your story which spoke to
me as I too have travelled to Whitechapel, Israel and Poland to
seek out my roots and pay respects to my ancestors. Your book
has spoken to me in such a vivid and nourishing way and

completed some of my own family history. I shall explain. My grandfather was the Chazan and Reader of Princelet Street Synagogue for thirteen years from 1893 to 1906. He was also the authorised practitioner of circumcision, operating from his home in Commercial Road. There are few records of my grandfather's time in Princelet Street so I was especially interested in the story of David's Rodinsky's mother as she would have been the same age as my grandfather and they undoubtedly would have known each other.

Writing the book had been for the most part a solitary pursuit. Letters like these began to connect me with peoples' living memories or fantasies of Rodinsky and Whitechapel. Then, as the story went public, I had to as well. I was unprepared for the impact the story would have on others and the amount of public readings Iain Sinclair and I would be asked to do.

The first reading was at Waterstone's in Camden. Iain and I arrived early and in the basement of the bookshop found most of the seats in the room already taken. My throat was so dry I could barely speak. Fortunately I was working with an old hand at such events who coaxed me through it. Iain introduced the event and one after the other we read from the book and told our stories. The sea of people in front of us looked young, fashionable and bright. But there was one man, sitting in the front row, who struck me for three reasons: he was smiling at me the whole time, he was considerably older than everyone else there, and he had an unmistakably Jewish face. I found his presence strangely comforting, as though I knew him but could not place him.

The questions that followed were lively and challenging. In particular I remember a young man asking me whether I felt that the reclusive David Rodinsky would have wanted his life to become such public property. The critic Lisa Jardine had already written in the *Observer Review* that the book made her feel 'deeply uneasy' for this very reason. 'Many of the moves Lichtenstein makes, including the marking of the grave and the request for prayers to be said for him, suggest her personal atonement for the appropriations she has made in the name of art.' My defence in response to the questioner in the bookshop was simple. I told him that before I came across the story David Rodinsky was already public property. When the room had first been opened a number of false legends had built up around the man and his disappearance. I felt that Rodinsky chose me, in some way, to publicly displace these myths with the truth about his life and sad death.

As the reading ended and people began to disperse I felt a light tap on my shoulder. I turned to meet the smiling man from the font row. He shook my hand firmly and introduced himself as Monty Richardson and asked if I was any relation to Gedaliah Lichtenstein. He told me how he had been walking past the book shop on his way to the Jewish museum where he worked and seen the name Lichtenstein in the window. I told him I was Gedaliah's granddaughter. His grip on my hand tightened. 'Your grandfather was a great friend of mine. We used to meet once a week at Toynbee Hall for the Friends of Yiddish Group. Even after Gedaliah moved to Westcliff he would travel up to East London, right up until he was in his late seventies.' We talked for some time about my grandfather and his other friends. I asked him if he had known the poet Avram Stencl and his friend Kreditor who had taught my father his Bar Mitzvah portion. 'Yes, yes' he nodded, still smiling, 'I knew them all well.' We swapped addresses and I invited him to David Rodinsky's consecration service which was taking place in a few weeks' time. Just before he let go of my hand he said, 'Your grandfather would have been very proud of you.' I hope he has some idea of what that meant to me.

Something strange happened at every reading. At Hampstead Waterstone's Iain had a chilling experience when a frail, elderly man approached him afterwards, whispering into his ear, 'I AM DAVID RODINSKY.' I saw Iain turn visibly pale before bursting into laughter as the man explained that he was the actor David Graham who had played David Rodinsky in Brett Turnbull's film, *The Golem of Princelet Street* (I had walked onto the set of the film during my first visit to Princelet Street in 1991).

One of the most unusual readings was at a small independent bookshop in a shopping centre somewhere in Edgware. Iain and I travelled for miles out of our territory into the region beyond the North circular where the majority of the descendants of the Whitechapel Jews of my grandfather's generation now lived. The place seemed utterly deserted when we arrived, so we were surprised to see a good crowd of people sitting patiently in the back of the shop. The atmosphere was warm and friendly and I imagined that eighty percent of the audience were Jewish. After the event a lady came up to me; she had been sitting in the front row. She told me that her ex-husband had asked her to come along and to make sure that David Rodinsky's story was not being mythologized. She explained that he was out of the country and that otherwise he would have come himself as he was very anxious to talk to me. His name was Ivan Reback – the grandson of the *shames* from the Princelet Street synagogue. The ex-Mrs Reback herself remembered David Rodinsky from the times in the fifties when they would visit the synagogue. In her opinion, 'he was not learned at all, he was a dirty tramp who lived from picking things out of dustbins. We would run into him on the stairs going up to the Reback's flat and you felt whenever you passed by he was a dark presence.'

I spoke to Ivan Reback soon afterwards and he added his own description of David Rodinsky to his former wife's. 'He was quite thin, of medium height, walked with a stoop, with his head first and the body following after. We all shared the same toilet and sink and that was where we would meet, on the dull-lit stairs. The little brown sink belonged to my grandparents, David and his mother. In my opinion he was probably mentally ill but we didn't talk much. He was definitely a recluse, he never wanted to leave the synagogue. My uncle Isaac used to call the mother 'Ghandi'. I doubt whether Bill Fishman's description of him giving out money to the poor is correct, you see that was most likely my grandfather, the *shames*, Myer Reback. He would walk all the way from Princelet Street to Stamford Hill looking for men to make up a *minyan*. Sometimes he'd hand out a sixpence to a poor man as long as he'd come to *shul*. It became difficult to find people as everyone began moving out of the area. So I think it was my grandfather and not your Rodinsky who Mr Fishman had seen handing out money to the poor on the streets surrounding the synagogue.'

I telephoned Bill Fishman about this but he laughed gently at Reback's theory. 'I saw David Rodinsky on a number of occasions giving money to people on the streets. I am most definitely not confusing him with the *shames* of the synagogue who I also knew. Mr Reback had a short, closely shaven white beard and David Rodinsky looked nothing like him. I know what I saw.' And so the different Rodinskys lived on in memory.

For me the three readings I will never forget were at Joseph's bookstore on the Finchley Road, Eastside Books on Whitechapel High Street and at the Clerkenwell Literary Festival. The proprietor of Joseph's is a great friend of Felek Scharf's and his bookshop is just a short walk from Felek's home in Hampstead Garden Suburb. It is the only independent non-religious Jewish bookshop in London. Whenever I am in North London I visit the shop and have bought many of my reference books there. So I was delighted when Michael Joseph asked if Iain and I would like to read. We organized an exhibition of my work to coincide with the reading as Michael had recently acquired the old Jewish dairy building next door to the bookshop and was in the process of turning it into a gallery and cafe. We agreed that I would show 'Kirsch Family', the giant mosaic I had made in Israel, which was still searching for an appropriate home.

There was standing room only in the former dairy as people crowded round the mosaic, trying to find floor space that was not taken up by the huge piece. It has to be admitted that nearly half of the audience were members of my family and it was wonderful to see everyone together at an event that wasn't a wedding, Bar Mitzvah or funeral. I was especially honoured to see my uncle Eliah, a survivor from Auschwitz, whose mother holds his baby sister in her arms in the Kirsch family photograph. The other guest of honour was Mrs Fanny Simon, introduced to me through her nephew Anthony Rudolf (another friend of Felek's, an author, translator and publisher who I had the pleasure of meeting after he wrote an intelligent and sensitive review of *Rodinsky's Room* for the *Times Literary Supplement*). She was born on 2 February 1911 in the same attic room that the Rodinsky family had inhabited a decade later. Both Eliah and Mrs Simon were welcomed with heartfelt rounds of applause as they were introduced. There were many tears during the course of the reading, and I was concerned that too many painful memories would be bought to the surface through Rodinsky's story for some of the older people in the audience. I became very worried when one elderly man left the room in a great hurry. It turned out that far from being moved by the story he had left the reading in disgust, muttering under his breath, 'total rubbish, I knew David Rodinsky well, used to work with him in a shoe factory in Princelet Street, there was absolutely nothing remarkable about him whatsoever.' I wish I'd had a chance to talk to the man before he left. David Rodinsky had indeed worked in a shoe factory and I'm sure in this man's eyes it was perfectly true: there was nothing at all remarkable about David Rodinsky. We each see people in a different light, as I had discovered during my search for David, but I would have loved to have spoken with this old ex-shoe factory worker.

The reading at Eastside bookshop was magical. The shop is in the centre of Whitechapel, where the heart of the story lies. It was a swelteringly humid night in June and the tiny bookshop was packed, with people spilling out onto the pavement trying to catch a breath of air. I was so hot and nervous I thought I might faint but I had Iain Sinclair on one side and Professor Bill Fishman on the other. I took the opportunity to thank Bill for his support throughout the writing of the book and took the greatest pleasure in hearing the rapturous applause from my listeners, most of whom seemed to know him and to have read his books.

I was honoured with the presence of my other hero at the Clerkenwell Literary Festival. The organizers asked if I would like to invite a guest speaker along and I asked Felek Scharf, who graciously agreed to come. The event was held in a former gold bullion safe house, around the corner from Hatton Garden. The brick arched spaces had been turned into artists' studios and bars. When Iain and I arrived Felek was already seated alone on the tiny stage, looking uncomfortable as young, fashion conscious people poured in and took the seats in front of him.

He took my arm, whispering into my ear, 'Rachel, this is not my audience, what do I have to say that would interest these people?' I knew what he meant but assured him everything would be fine. I had seen Felek speak on a number of different occasions and had never met a single person who had not been moved by his words. Felek then read from his essay, *What Shall We Tell Miriam?*, to a spellbound audience of over two hundred people, about his life as a young Jewish man in Kraków. For over forty minutes you could not hear another sound apart from Felek's deep, resonant voice hypnotizing the room with his stories of a lost world. The reaction to his reading was tremendous, and it surprised Felek a great deal. He held my hand after the event and said, his face beaming, 'well what do you know Rachel, they do want to hear.'

The angriest reaction to *Rodinsky's Room* came during a reading we gave at Toynbee Hall in Whitechapel, in the exact same room in which my grandfather had spent so much time at the weekly meetings for the Friends of Yiddish Group. An elderly Jewish man stood up whilst I was speaking and slated the book, complaining about my lack of knowledge of the Jewish East End. I told him I felt his complaint to be valid. It is of course difficult to imagine a time before your own birth, but this was not in any case my intention in writing the book. I was delighted when his irritation later led him to write his own memoirs. We kept up a correspondence and he sent me the first draft of his story, which has enriched my picture of the old Jewish East End.

The last reading I gave was at a literary festival in Devon. It took hours to reach Dartington Hall, a magnificent collection of mediaeval buildings around a central courtyard set in extensive grounds. I was suitably impressed but also tired and a little nervous. It was my first talk without Iain and far from my stomping ground. I thought it unlikely I would make a connection here with the upper-class, middle-aged, genteel country audience. I gave a slide presentation in the old barn and after the talk emerged into the bright sunlit court-yard of the old stone house and sat at my cloth covered table, waiting to sign books. The table next door was surrounded by punters trying to get the much sought after signature of Catherine Cookson's biog-rapher. A few people came and bought books from me and one of them was a man called Nicholas Johnson who had lived for many years in Fournier Street (next to Princelet Street) and who in the mid-eighties had the bookstall next to Iain Sinclair's in Camden Passage. Nicholas lived in Spitalfields from 1981 to 1987 and told me that during the eighties, at the end of any street there, you could be in another time zone, another country. He said that it was strange to walk around then as there were hardly any women or children to be seen. He remembered having tea with Gilbert and George and how gay the street was. Hardly any of those people had moved away, they had either died from AIDS or were still there. The Jewish character he remembered most from the street was Solly the furrier. Nicholas said he could still picture his face in exact detail, he must have been in his late sixties then, and he thought that Solly had lost some of his family in Treblinka. I think this must have been the same Solly that Sidney Lynn remembered, one of his 'gang of boys'.

Nicholas shared with me his stories of the Princelet Street syna-gogue and Rodinsky's room. He knew the synagogue well as he had given his own performances there with another artist, Tutte Lemkow. Over the coming weeks Nicholas and I built up a corre-spondence. Included in this material was Tutte Lemkow's obituary in *The Times*, where I learnt he was born in Oslo and had quickly made his mark in musical entertainment. After his arrival in England he reached the peak of his achievement playing the fiddler in opening scenes of the movie version of *Fiddler on the Roof*. So I had finally met someone who had known the solitary fiddler. The first time I saw him I must have been about twelve, sitting in front of the television in my parents house, mesmerized by the haunting figure dancing on the tin roof of a house in Anatevka. I remember my father telling me and my sister that my grandfather came from somewhere like that and I remember desperately wanting to play the violin. Like many Jews of my generation, *Fiddler on the Roof* was my first glimpse into the world of the Eastern European *shtetl*. Nicholas told me how Tutte had suffered a nervous breakdown after acting in a film, he could not remember the title, a scene concerning the Holocaust. The memories that surfaced about his own family members who had perished proved too much for him to bear. Tutte told Nicholas how he managed to escape the fate of the rest of his family by fleeing Norway on skis. He then disguised himself as a German guard and left by train. His disguise must have been good: another German soldier on a train had offered him his last cigarette. Tutte did not smoke but he took the packet and kept it for the rest of his life, often showing it to people.

Nicholas had when he was a child lived in the house opposite Tutte's in Belgravia, and their paths crossed again twenty years later. After Tutte's breakdown he was found delirious, speaking Norwegian, a language he had not used for forty years. The first public performance he gave after this was at the synagogue. There were no rehearsals, no publicity, only the frequent meetings as a friendship evolved between the younger and older man. It may have been, Nicholas thought, the idea of performing in the synagogue that restored Lemkow's confidence. Nicholas remembered it vividly: 'The performance took place on a freezing night in December 1985. We covered the floor in pine branches and were handing out cups of hot mulled wine. The air was filled with the smell of crushed pine and cinnamon. I read poems in front of the ark and Tutte sat on the balcony playing the balalaika. He never went anywhere without his balalaika, its black case covered in stickers and labels. He became rather drunk and wild and would not stop playing the same tune again and again. This was one of the last times I saw him.'

Like myself, Nicholas was drawn to such characters. I felt a strange connection between Tutte and Rodinsky, as I did with another tragic figure from Spitalfields called James 'Banjo' Cross. Nicholas told me about him and about how they met. 'The heavy lorries full of produce from the continent were driving past my window to the fruit and vegetable market at the top of the street all through the night. Often unable to sleep, I would get up and walk around the outskirts of the market, talking with the tramps who lit fires around its edges. I met there an alcoholic called Banjo who became my friend. He lived at the crypt and I sometimes saw him asleep, or awake and crying, on cardboard on the street side. I think I broke a taboo once by inviting him into the house I rented, and primarily I listened to his stream of consciousness and watched out for him on the streets. The last time I saw him, September 1986, he looked very cold and hungry, foraging around saltfish piles thrown out from the Petticoat Lane Deli. Half a year later he was murdered under a railway bridge by three boys of twelve years old, who had somehow seen the banned film *A Clockwork Orange*.' Nicholas gave me a poem he had written in memory of Banjo:

You smashed his skull to the harmonica
of taxis as it were summer and butterflies falling from his brain
the abstract pulse of an addict
jolting a handful of grass, did you see?
When sleep in moonlight gathered wounds,
earth turned over for the soul of a man
who saw the depravity of children
and had to believe it; the soil gauging
his generosity, wit and pride, when hyacinth
juts early, blue in death, branch and bell
spine revisited body, which a stained glass window
showered upon, closed by the hooves of horses
no the horses do not sleep the shadows do not bury

Nicholas Johnson, *Spitalfields*, in memory of
James Cross, murdered March 1987.

Nicholas went to Banjo's funeral and told me there were over one hundred and fifty people there, 'a wide cross-section of the

community; tramps, policemen, artists, well-dressed women.' He
promised to send some photographs, saying 'I have a wonderful
image of Banjo with a friend of his sitting in the synagogue during
the second reading I gave there.' It seems appropriate to include this
image of Banjo, sitting with an unnamed vagrant, in the abandoned
synagogue below Rodinsky's room.

Nicholas also told me that he, Lemkow and Banjo had all been
aware of the existence of Rodinsky's room. 'In January 1986 the keys
to the synagogue were lent to me. I went up to the top floor with
Kate, whom I later married. She took photographs of the stark
room. We stood for a long time in the doorway before finally going
in, touching an object on the table, looking at his bed, and going out
with a sense of shame. Unease. The sense of having to give back a
key and never going back to that room again. It had been tampered

with a great deal by then.' The photos were more intense still-life studies than the wider shots of the room taken by Danny Gralton and Mike Pattison. I was deeply moved by her image of Rodinsky's bed and thought it interesting that this was the only photograph of the room taken by a woman, focusing on his bed like a tomb.

The readings finished and there was just one, very important task left – the consecration service for David Rodinsky's new headstone. From the moment I had first seen his unkempt grave I had wanted to erect a more fitting memorial to him. I visited Elfes Stone Masons in Brick Lane and looked longingly at the beautiful marble stones there, hoping one day I would have the means to purchase one. This seemed like a fantasy until I met Michael Morris from Artangel. I had worked with Artangel many years earlier, running the education programme for their best known commission, the sculptor Rachel Whitread's *House*. On 23 October 1993 she unveiled one of the most controversial public artworks ever seen in Britain. She filled the interior of an empty Victorian house in East London with concrete, before peeling back the brickwork to leave a huge, sombre monument to memory and ordinary lives. Every day for a month I led workshops with East End schoolchildren based on *House*. They were

inspired, and made their own constructions and wrote passionate letters to the council begging them to allow the sculpture to remain standing. Even though Whiteread won the Turner Prize that year, Tower Hamlets Council decided to destroy her work. On 11 January 1994 the bulldozers flattened *House*, to much public protest. That was the same year I met Iain Sinclair and he wrote about *House* and my work *Ner Htamid* (shown in Mr Katz's string shop) in *Lights Out for the Territory*.

In 1998 Artangel embarked on a new series of commissions called *Inner City* which 'encouraged writers and artists to excavate a range of urban places and contemplate the changing nature of city environments and the counterpoint between narrative and place, between language and location.' Michael Morris contacted me about a potential commission and from our first meeting showed a deep interest in Rodinsky's story and my research. I wondered if his interest had some personal resonance.

Artangel's offices are in Clerkenwell, just a short walk from my parents' jewellery shop in Hatton Garden. During our discussions Michael expressed an interest in learning more about 'the Garden' so my father organized a small tour for him. We went, all three, me heavily pregnant at that time, up many flights of stairs to visit the diamond dealers in their attic workshops, hidden from the street below. We went to see Mr Feinstein, an orthodox Jew who escaped Hungary in the thirties and has been dealing in the Garden ever since. He told us some of Hatton Garden's history while his sons, all working in the business and all far more orthodox than himself, sat at the jewellery benches behind him, passing tiny stones with tweezers to potential customers while talking rapidly in Yiddish. Mr Feinstein asked Michael Morris if he was Jewish. He replied yes, he was, but went on to explain that he had gone to boarding school at a young age, with no Jewish community around him, and knew little about his heritage. 'You should learn', Mr Feinstein said. 'It is important to know who you are.'

Over a number of months we devised an artists' guidebook called *Rodinsky's Whitechapel*. The book is designed to take the reader on a personal tour inside the geography of the Rodinsky story. The map inside the front cover marks out a circular route that crosses paths with my own walks, my family history and the remnants of the Jewish East End. The final stop on the tour is Elfes Stone Masons.

Iain Sinclair added to the project by taking Rodinsky's A–Z and following the trails marked out in red biro on some of its pages. These walks were filmed and shown on strategically placed video monitors in Whitechapel during the month of June 1999. Iain also published a small book, *Dark Lanthorns* (published by Goldmark Press), that documents these journeys. Throughout this time I felt there was a role reversal between Iain and myself. After I had found the grave the intensity of my quest cooled. Iain had always been the more detached figure in the Rodinsky story, observing, commenting on my hot pursuit. I felt as soon as he picked up Rodinsky's A–Z that things changed. Suddenly Iain was the one possessed, stalking every step Rodinsky had ever taken, becoming very excited as he learned that the obscure route he had just walked in Dagenham had probably been through the place in which David Rodinsky had been fostered as a child. I knew the only way to release us both and lay the story and the man to rest was with a consecration service and a proper memorial stone.

Early in our discussions I suggested to Michael Morris that we should put Rodinsky's headstone in the budget for our project. We both laughed at the time, aware that it would be the only piece of permanent work Artangel had ever commissioned. But a few days later Michael telephoned saying he thought it was absolutely imperative that the headstone should be laid. Artangel fund their projects from a variety of public and private sources, which includes a group of patrons known as 'the company of angels'. One of these 'angels' is Harry Handlesman, a millionaire who made his fortune in property. Michael thought he would be the right person to approach to sponsor the headstone. We met once, briefly, in a West End club. He told me he was from an Orthodox Jewish background which he had since left behind. I felt some regret in Harry's voice as he was talking and I understood all too well the agony of leaving the orthodox world. He said at the end of our conversation: 'It will be a great *mitzvah* to pay for the tombstone of this lonely *tzaddick*.'

With the funds in place I went directly to Elfes to choose a memorial. I spoke with Carol Wayne first to see if she had anything in mind, but she was happy to let me choose the stone. I visited the showroom many times before deciding on a plain marble base and headstone bearing the simple inscription 'May his soul rest in peace'. The one addition to the memorial was a hand carved, closed marble book resting on the base.

The day for the consecration arrived, which coincided with the ninth of *Av*, the first day of the festival of *Tisha B'av*, one of the most solemn days in the Jewish calendar. It is traditionally a day of fasting and mourning to commemorate the destruction of the first and second temples. In more recent history it has also been the day chosen by many enemies of the Jewish people to start pogroms and expel Jews from their homes. It was a fitting day to mourn, to remember – a day which Jewish people all over the world set aside for thinking of those they have lost.

I was wearing the same dress I had worn over two years ago to visit the cabbalistic rabbi in Jerusalem. His words – 'through your search you will find the right path' – were ringing in my ears as I made my way to the grounds, hand-in-hand with my husband, Adam. I marvelled at the role I now found myself performing. Instead of living an orthodox life, through the rabbi's prompting I had spent these years tracking down a man who had lived in a room I had stumbled across while searching my own family's roots. His story had interwoven with mine, and in the process of finding his grave I had met my husband and had a son, who we decided to call David. As the facts of David Rodinsky's life and death unravelled themselves my own life began to take a different direction. The day had come for David Rodinsky and I to free each other.

I invited a number of people to the consecration who had known David Rodinsky or been touched by his story enough to come and pay their respects. Adam and I arrived early; I wanted to see the stone in place before the service. The caretaker of the cemetery was standing outside his office, dressed in black with a large Homburg on his head which cast a dark shadow over his beard. I asked if I could go and visit the grave before the service. When I said the name Rodinsky his mouth broke into a wide smile and he became very animated. 'I read about you in the *JC*, I think that it's wonderful what you are doing, come with me, I'll take you straight over there.' We walked together to row WA25. What a joy to see the shining white marble memorial in the place of the former gravel plot. I was delighted to see there were already some stones placed on the tomb, signs that others who had possibly read the book or heard about the story had come to visit. As I was admiring Rodinsky's new resting place the caretaker's foot hit metal. He bent down and picked up a small tin plate on a rusty stake. It was the plaque with David Rodinsky's name and date of death etched on it that had marked his pauper's grave. The caretaker passed it to me, brushing off the mud with his sleeve, saying 'I think you should have this.'

Slowly but steadily the other mourners arrived. My parents were there with Bill Fishman, who was soon talking animatedly with Anthony Rudolf and Alan Dein. There were two men of similar age standing in the corner who I had not seen before. They introduced themselves as Ivan Reback and Michael Jimmack. I wondered what David Rodinsky would think about their unlikely meeting at his consecration thirty years after his death. Deep in conversation with the man from the grounds I spotted Monty Richardson, who seemed to know everyone else there. The noise levels in the prayer house grew as more people arrived and we waited and waited for the rabbi who was supposed to be taking the memorial service.

I began to pace anxiously up and down the gravel path outside. The caretaker joined me and as time went by he looked worried too. 'I'm going to phone to see what's going on,' he said. A few minutes later I could see him running from his office back towards the prayer house, motioning for me to follow, telling me between gasps that the rabbi had fallen ill and was being taken to hospital as we spoke. 'Don't worry', he said, 'I'm sure Monty will be happy to officiate instead, he has done so many times before here.' So that is exactly what happened. In wonder I walked over to Rodinsky's new headstone, and around his grave my grandfather's friend Monty conducted a moving service and led us in reading together the Kaddish for David Rodinsky. Just as the story was ending it folded back on itself to the very beginning. I had come to Whitechapel over ten years before to learn more about my grandfather and his life, and as David Rodinsky was finally being laid to rest I had met the one person who could unlock those stories for me. As Monty finished reading the prayers he asked me if I wanted to speak, but there was only one thing I really wanted to say: 'May his soul truly now rest in peace.'

Just before we left the grounds Monty invited us all to wash our hands. He explained the significance of this to those who did not know: 'The ritual act of cleansing our hands symbolizes our resolve to improve ourselves and our lives, and to put thoughts of death and decay behind us.' Then he said to me: 'You have set him free, now it is time to move on.'

ACKNOWLEDGEMENTS

First, I wish to thank my friends and family for their loving support, particularly Adam, without whom I could not have completed this project. Also, a special thanks to my mother and mother-in-law, for looking after baby David. I shall be permanently indebted to my agent, John Parker, for his ability to recognize that I was capable of writing this book and also to Granta for believing in the project. I feel privileged and grateful to have received constant guidance and editorial advice from Iain Sinclair and my editor at Granta, Neil Belton. Many thanks to the photographer Danny Gralton for the permission to use his haunting image of Rodinsky's room (page 33) and to the photographer Marc Atkins, whose photographs appear on pages 51 and 72. Throughout my time in East London countless individuals have shared their memories with me, allowing me a window into the world of the Jewish East End. I would like to thank the following people whose interviews appear in this book: Bella Lipman, Carol and Alvin Wayne, Sidney Lynn, Mr Rossi, Mr Katz, Michael Jimack, Viki White, Michael Scheider and Lorna Shames. I owe much to Professor Bill Fishman, Samuel Melnick, David Jacobs and Alan Dein for their historical expertise and advice on Jewish history. I would also like to thank the various chairpersons of the Princelet Street Heritage Centre, who have supported my work in the building and given me access to the Rodinsky archive: thanks first to the late Donald Chesworth, and also to the late Rabbi Hugo Gryn and to Susie Symes. I would also like to express my thanks to Dominic Dyson, former co-ordinator of the Heritage Centre, who helped me set up my original residency in the building, and to Andrew Byrne of the Spitalfields Historic Buildings Trust for his constant help and support during my time spent in East London. Many individuals and institutions have helped me with research during my quest. I would like to thank the following: Zevick Shafir and Nili Oz of the Arad Arts project, Israel, Ricky Burman of the Museum of the Jewish East End, Rosemary Weinstein at the Museum of London, David Webb of the Bishopsgate library, Saul Issroff of the Jewish Genealogy Society of Great Britain, Nitza Spiro of the Spiro Institute, Evelyn Friedlander of the Hidden Legacy Foundation, Elanor Bergman of the Jewish Institute in Warsaw, Dina Abramowitz of the Yivo Institute in New York, Dr Robert Rodensky, the Bancroft Road Local History Library, the United Synagogues Burial Society, the Federation of Synagogues Burial Society, and Jewish Care. Much of the research for the book was conducted in Poland, and I would never have got there without the help of Rafael Felek Scharf whom I am very grateful to and will be forever inspired by. I owe a special thanks to the Archie Sherman Charitable Trust for their continued support in my endeavours. Thanks also to Dr Hannah Mausch, of the Polish Cultural Institute and the Ministry of Polish Culture, for arranging my scholarship for my official visit to Poland. Thanks are also due to Dr Joachim Russek for allowing me to attend the conference at the Judaica Institute in Kraków and to Professor Antony Polonsky and Professor Jan Gross for their inspirational lectures I heard there. I would also like to thank the other individuals I met in Poland and wrote about: Mr Muller, Ignancy Bielecki, Gabriel Finder, Fern Hauck, Rachel Nuremberg, Lili Cole, Robert Gadek, Irena Karszniewicz, Jacob Balter, Ran Karni and Tomasz Kuncewicz. In Israel I met many others whose stories have enriched this book, thanks to: Nili and Amos Oz, Liz Blazer, Johnny Kamiel, Jeremy Portnoi, and Jen Meyers, and I owe special thanks to Rabbi Aubrey Isaacs for opening my eyes to Judaism and for being such a wonderful and patient teacher. Finally, I would like to add that all the information in this book is only as true as the memories of those I have met and interviewed.

For this paperback edition, I would like to thank all the people who wrote to me with their thoughts about the book and their additions to the story, all of which were gratefully received and much appreciated. Special thanks to those whose letters have been included in the afterword; Martin Genis, Judith Dell, Binnie Yeates and Francis Milat. Much thanks to Mike Pattison, Nicholas and Kate Johnson, and Anthony Rudolf for providing the extra photographs published in this edition. I would also like to take this opportunity to publicly apologize to John Freeman for including his image of Rodinsky's room in the hardback edition of the book (page 95) without crediting him.

Thanks to everyone who came along to the readings and contributed to the lively debates that followed each one. Many thanks to Iain Sinclair for getting me through every reading and for being such a generous collaborator. Thanks to everyone at Granta for all their help and support, particularly to Gail Lynch who worked so hard both during and after publication. Many thanks to everyone at Artangel for all the work they put into the Rodinsky project; to the designer, Mark Diaper, to Mel Smith, Geri van Noord, Sally Lycett, James Lingwood, and a huge thank you to Michael Morris. Special thanks is due to Rodinsky's angel, Harry Handlesman, and my new friend Monty Richardson. Thanks to Michael Joseph for his help and for showing 'Kirsch Family'. Thanks to Nicholas Johnson for his contributions. I would like to thank again Professor Bill Fishman and Rafael Felek Scharf for being such a constant support to me and for bestowing the honour of reading with me. Thank you to David

Rodinsky's family for their help and support and appreciation of my endeavours, and a special thank you to the rabbi in Jerusalem who helped me on my path to happiness.

Rachel Lichtenstein

ACKNOWLEDGEMENTS

With thanks to my agent, John Richard Parker, whose inspiration it was to approach Rachel Lichtenstein and invite her to write an account of the quest for Rodinsky. To my editor, Neil Belton. And all those who gave interviews, dropped hints, or accompanied me on some part of the journey: Kathy Acker, Marc Atkins, Saskia Baron, Bob Bentley, Andrew Byrne, Brian Catling, Hilary Gerrard, Gerry and Pat Goldstein, Pip Goldstein, John Harle, Sandy Lieberson, Michael Moorcock, Alan Moore, Chris Petit, Nicholas Pounder, Steve Radmall, Dennis Severs, Paul Smith, Susan Stenger, Susie Symes, Paul Tickell, Jah Wobble, Patrick Wright.

Iain Sinclair

GLOSSARY

Alav ha-shalom, may his soul rest in peace.

Bensch, grace after meals.

Besheret, deemed by God.

Bet midrash, house of study or prayer.

Bimah, the raised platform in the synagogue from which the reader leads the service.

Cheder, Hebrew school for young children.

Chevra, society/association/congregation.

Chometz, bread, leaven.

Davven, to pray.

Dybbuk, term used for the soul of a dead sinful person that attaches itself to a living body and refuses to leave until exorcized.

Ellul, the sixth ecclesiastical month. It is Jewish practice to sound the *shofar* during the weekdays of this month, heralding the arrival of the New Year.

Erev Pesach, the evening before Passover.

Eruv, wire perimeter drawn around an area that allows orthodox people to carry on the Sabbath.

Frum, religious.

Halacha, Jewish law.

Hashem, another word for God. Literally, the name.

Havrusa, study partner.

Kiddush, the prayer recited over wine in the synagogue and at home, on festivals and the Sabbath.

Kippa, skull cap worn by religious Jews.

Krank, sick.

L'Chaim, a toast made at celebrations. Literally, 'to life'.

Mea Shearim, ultra-orthodox area of Jerusalem.

Melamed, teacher.

Mensch, Yiddish term, meaning important/excellent/person of worth.

Meshuganer, an idiot or fool.

Mezuzah, small container of verses from Deuteronomy fixed to doorpost.

Mikve, a cystern or bath of natural spring or rain water, used by orthodox Jews for ritual purposes.

Milluim, yearly national service duty of one month required of Israeli males aged eighteen to fifty.

Mimuke, aunt.

Minyan, quorum of ten adult males needed for prayers and services.

Mitzvah, good deed.

Mohel, a man qualified to perform circumcisions.

Nebish, pitiful person.

Nefesh, soul or essence.

Neshama, soul.

Olam hasod, secrets of the world.

Pesach, Passover.

Rachmones, untranslatable Hebrew term meaning a combination of charity, sympathy and mercy.

Rosh Hashanah, the Jewish New Year, falling on the first of Tishri. Traditionally thought to be the first day of creation. It is also known as the Day of Judgement and the Day of Sounding the *Shofar*.

Seder, the meal and ceremony on Passover eve.

Shabbos, Yiddish term for the Sabbath.

Shames, from the root of the word meaning 'to minister' or 'to serve'. The beadle of the synagogue, often known as the caretaker. His function is to attend to the needs of the synagogue and congregation. (Derivatives include *shammas, shamash, shammes.*)

Shavuot, the Feast of the Weeks, celebrated seven weeks after Passover. It celebrates the giving of the Torah on Mount Sinai and in Israel marks the beginning of the summer harvest. It is customary to decorate synagogues with flowers during this festival.

Shaytels, wigs worn by orthodox Jewish women.

Shema, the oldest Jewish prayer, said twice a day by observant Jews.

Shmatter, Yiddish term for old rags, rubbish.

Shofar, ram's horn.

Shul, synagogue.

Stiebel, Hasidic house of prayer. Literally, a small room.

Tallit, an outer prayer shawl, with thread in four corners and blue stripes.

Tefillin, small leather cases containing parchment with paragraphs from the Bible, to be attached to the left hand and head by orthodox men during prayer.

Tishri, the seventh ecclesiastical month and the most important period in the Jewish calendar, including Rosh Hashanah, the fast of Gedaliah, Yom Kippur and Sukkot.

Treyf, unkosher food.

Tzaddick, a righteous/holy person.

Tzadokam, acts of charitable kindness.

Tzitzit, a four-cornered undergarment worn throughout the day.

Yad Vashem, Holocaust museum in Jerusalem.

Yahrzeit candle, memoral candle for the dead.

Yeshiva, school for rabbinical and Talmudic studies.

Zaida, grandfather.

Zohar, the most important literary work of Cabbala, written in the form of a mystic and allegorical commentary on the Pentateuch, in Hebrew and Aramaic.

SELECT BIBLIOGRAPHY

Peter ACKROYD. *Hawksmoor*. Hamish Hamilton. London, 1985.

Rodney ARCHER, Powell JONES. *The Harlot's Curse*. Preston Editions. London, 1990.

Cecile de BANKE. *Hand over Hand*. Hutchinson, London, 1957.

Michael BILLINGTON. *The Life and Work of Harold Pinter*. Faber and Faber. London, 1996.

Chayim BLOCH. *The Golem (Legends of the Ghetto of Prague)*. Self-published. Vienna, 1920.

Simon BLUMENFELD. *Jew Boy*. Jonathan Cape. London, 1935.

Brian CATLING. *The Stumbling Block its INDEX*. Book Works. London, 1990.

Brian CATLING. 'Written Rooms and Pencilled Crimes'. From: *Future Exiles*. Paladin. London, 1992.

Paul CELAN. *Poems of Paul Celan*. (Translated by Michael Hamburger). Anvil. London, 1968.

Paul CELAN. *Breathturn*. (Translated by Pierre Joris). Sun and Moon Press. Los Angeles, 1995.

Margaret COX. *Life and Death in Spitalfields, 1700–1850*. Council for British Archaeology. London, 1996.

Aleister CROWLEY. *Jack the Ripper*. Privately printed. Cambridge, 1988.

Dan CRUICKSHANK, Peter WYLD. *London: The Art of Georgian Building*. Architectural Press. London, 1975.

Salvador DALI. *Le Mythe tragique de L'Angélus de Millet.* Jean-Jacques Pauvert. Paris, 1963.

Kerry DOWNES. *Hawksmoor.* Thames and Hudson. London, 1969.

Pierre de la Ruffiniere DU PREY. *Hawksmoor's 'Basilica after the Primitive Christians': Architecture and Theology.* Offprint from *Journal of the Society of Architectural Historians.* Vol. XLVIII, No. 1, March 1989.

William J. FISHMAN. *The Streets of East London.* Gerald Duckworth. London, 1979.

Geoffrey FLETCHER. *Down Among the Meths Men.* Hutchinson. London, 1966.

John FREEMAN. *London Revealed.* Little, Brown. London, 1989.

Albert II. FRIEDLANDER. *Riders Towards the Dawn.* Constable. London, 1993.

Sylvie GERMAIN. *The Weeping Woman on the Streets of Prague.* Dedalus. Cambridgeshire, 1993.

Mark GIROUARD, Dan CRUICKSHANK, Raphael SAMUEL etc. *The Saving of Spitalfields.* The Spitalfields Historic Buildings Trust. London, 1989.

Gina GLASMAN. *East End Synagogues.* Museum of the Jewish East End. London, 1987.

Willy GOLDMAN. *East End My Cradle.* Revised edition. Robson Brooks. London, 1988.

Robert GRAVES, Raphael PATAI. *Hebrew Myths.* Cassell. London, 1964.

Z'ev ben Shimon HALEVI. *Adam and the Kabbalistic Tree.* Rider. London, 1974.

David HARTNETT. *Black Milk.* Jonathan Cape. London, 1994.

Joseph C. LANDIS (ed.) *The Dybbuk and Other Great Yiddish Plays.* Bantam Books. New York, 1966.

Barnet LITVINOFF. *The Burning Bush (Antisemitism and World History).* Collins. London, 1988.

Emanuel LITVINOFF. *Journey Through a Small Planet.* Michael Joseph. London, 1972.

Jack LONDON. *The People of the Abyss.* Isbister. London, 1903.

Colin MACCABE. *Performance.* BFI Film Classics. London, 1998.

Peter MARCAN. *Artists and the East End.* Self-published. London, 1986.

Jonathan MEADES. *Peter Knows What Dick Likes.* Paladin. London, 1989.

Samuel C. MELNICK. *A Giant Among Giants.* Pentland Press. Durham, 1994.

Gustav MEYRINK. *The Golem.* Dedalus. Cambridgeshire, 1985.

Gustav MEYRINK. *The Angel of the West Window.* Dedalus. Cambridgeshire, 1991.

Michael MOORCOCK. *Michael Moorcock's Multiverse*. Serial composition in 12 parts. Helix, DC Comics. New York, November 1997–October 1998.

Alan MOORE. *Voice of the Fire*. Gollancz. London, 1996.

Leo PERUTZ. *By Night under the Stone Bridge*. Harvill Press. London, 1989.

Harold PINTER. *The Caretaker*. Methuen. London, 1960.

Harold PINTER. *The Birthday Party and Other Plays*. Methuen. London, 1960.

Harold PINTER. T*he Dwarfs*. Faber and Faber. London, 1990.

Thomas PYNCHON. *Mason & Dixon*. Jonathan Cape. London, 1997.

Winston G. RAMSEY. *The East End, Then and Now*. After the Battle. London, 1997.

Angelo Maria RIPELLINO. *Magic Prague*. Picador. London, 1994.

Raphael SAMUEL. *East End Underworld (Chapters in the Life of Arthur Harding)*. Routledge and Kegan Paul. London, 1981.

Raphael SAMUEL. *Island Stories* (Vol. 2 of *Theatres of Memory*). Verso. London, 1998.

Rafael Felek SCHARF. *Poland What Have I To Do With Thee?* © Rafael Felek Scharf and Judaica Foundation. Kraków, 1996.

Iain SINCLAIR. *White Chappell Scarlet Tracings*. Goldmark. London, 1987.

Iain SINCLAIR. *Downriver (or, The Vessels of Wrath)*. Paladin. London, 1991.

A.E. WAITE. *The Quest for Bloods (A Study of the Victorian Penny Dreadful)*. Edited by Ayresome Johns. Privately printed. London, 1997.

Arnold WESKER, John ALLIN. *Say Goodbye: You May Never See Them Again*. Jonathan Cape. London, 1974.

David WIDGERY, Mark HOLBORN (and others). *Markéta Luskačova (Photographs of Spitalfields)*. Whitechapel Gallery. London, 1991.

Patrick WRIGHT. 'Rodinsky's Place'. *London Review of Books*. 24 October 1987.

Patrick WRIGHT. *A Journey through Ruins (The Last Days of London)*. Radius. London, 1991.

Patrick WRIGHT. 'Ghetto Blaster' (on Emanuel Litvinoff). *Guardian* Weekend. 27 March 1993.

Israel ZANGWILL. *Children of the Ghetto*. Reissue. Leicester University Press. Leicester, 1977.

Israel ZANGWILL. *Ghetto Tragedies*. McClure and Co. London, 1893.

Israel ZANGWILL. *The King of Schnorrers*. Reissue. Heinemann. London, 1931.

Israel ZANGWILL. *Dreamers of the Ghetto*. Heinemann. London, 1898

INDEX

THE SPITALFIELDS CENTRE
a permanent celebration of immigrant life

19 Princelet Street, once home to David Rodinsky, is today a mysterious and magical place. This unrestored Huguenot silk merchant's home has survived through centuries of poverty and neglect, and the beautiful Victorian East European synagogue built over the rear garden is now the last surviving example of its kind in London. Spitalfields, on the eastern fringe of the City of London, has been shaped by succesive waves of immigration as the late seventeenth century Huguenot settlers arriving from France were followed by Irish, Jews and today's predominantly Bangladeshi community.

The Spitalfields Centre is working to save this special building, to preserve its extraordinary poetic spirit, and to give it renewed purpose as a place of stories, a celebration of rich diversity, that will explore the lives and cultures of the successive groups of incomers who sought refuge and freedom in this area before moving on into the wider British community.

The Spitalfields Centre is a registered charity, number 287279, which depends upon donations to repair and preserve this precious Grade II* listed building. If you would like to help save the house and synagogue, and help the trustees to be able to open Rodinsky's room to the public, then please send your contribution to the Spitalfields Centre, 19 Princelet Street, London E1 6QH. Covenants, however small or large, are especially beneficial to the charity, which will be happy to send forms or discuss other tax-efficient ways of giving.

Please help the Spitalfields Centre to preserve 19 Princelet Street and to give it a fine new purpose as a place to build tolerance and understanding in our multicultural society.